Growing ORCHIDS

Cattleyas and other epiphytes

Growing
ORCHIDS

Book Two
Cattleyas and other epiphytes

J. N. Rentoul

Lothian Publishing Company Pty. Ltd.
Melbourne Sydney Auckland

First published 1982
by Lothian Publishing Company Pty Ltd
11 Munro Street, Port Melbourne, 3207

© J. N. Rentoul 1982
Reprinted 1982, 1985, 1987, 1989

National Library of Australia
Cataloguing-in-Publication Data:

  Rentoul, J. N. (James Noel), 1909–
    Growing orchids-cattleyas and other epiphytes.

  Bibliography.
  Includes index.
  ISBN 0 85091 147 8

  1. Orchid culture.   I. Title.
  635.9'3415

Printed in Singapore

Contents

The Epiphytes

Brasso cattleya — Mrs J Leeman

Introduction

Unlike the first volume, in which only two orchids were described, this second book contains so many different types that they cannot all be grouped in one glass-house even when at times they belong to the same genus.

Where the cymbidiums and paphiopedilums are both single-genus diversities, the orchids of this book are capable of being combined in units which contain as many as five and six different genera. At times these combinations were preceded by natural cross-pollinations, the proving of which was mostly a matter of flowering man-made cross-pollinations which verified suspected combinations or yielded the pleasant surprise of a flower which was a replica of something collected as a species and regarded as such.

In the period when these plants first became known or even early in their accession to a place in horticulture they enslaved the European races with the beauty of their flowers, the extraordinary way in which they grew and the sheer magnitude of their diversity and numbers. Men who have perpetuated their memories by the greatness of their contributions to science and an understanding of the world we live in have exercised their talents in pursuit of knowledge about orchids.

Among these men were Charles Darwin and Alfred Russell Wallace, who both speculated on why orchid plants should have such intimate relationships with their pollinators, Darwin particularly in southern America and Wallace in the Asian area. The often imagined mimicry of the insect world by flowers, or perhaps vice versa, intrigued both these men, and neither could supply a definite answer.

But Dr Wallace, mentioned in other parts of these books, had this to say: 'There is a tendency in nature to the continued progression of certain classes of varieties further and further from the original type — a progression to which there appears no reason to assign any definite limits . . . This progression, by minute steps, in various directions, but always checked and balanced by the necessary conditions, subject to which alone existence can be preserved, may, it is believed, be followed out so as to agree with all the phenomena presented by organised beings, their extinction and succession in past ages, and all the extraordinary modifications of form, instinct and habits which they exhibit.'

Naturally, so far as orchids are concerned, this transition from one form to another, however gradual, has been hotly disputed by botanists and others. But from all the evidence to hand it appears to be a reasonable supposition which has all but ended before it has begun so far as orchid cultivation by the European races is concerned.

The orchid species, indiscriminately plundered, have been reduced to such low numbers that the modifying hand of nature has so little to work on and the phenomenon cannot be observed by botanists in the years to come with sufficient data to make the whole thing credible.

Mr Donald Beaton, a contributor to *The Cottage Gardener*, which was published in the 1850 decade and contained orchid information and notes, also expressed a thought on the matter which ran parallel: 'There is not the slightest doubt about Oncidiums, Dendrobiums, Epidendrums and all the great families sporting like the Calceolarias; nor that nine-tenths of the pride of botanists — the species — are mere seedling varieties which get fixed in time by local influences. There is not such a thing in nature as a species as meant by the botanists.'

While Mr Beaton may not have realised the time scale involved, his insight into orchid growing and their botany in what we consider the infancy of the cult is an example also of the philosophy of twentieth century growers who stop to think about the plants they cultivate. For those who are sceptical or consider the subject a bit too deep for them, they have only to consider the Australian dendrobiums to appreciate the point.

In the natural order of things the cross-pollination of two distinct or even related genera is less frequent than the cross-pollination of two species of the same genus. But it does occur. It is triggered by changing climatic conditions, the evolution of associated ecological components and even by the appearance of a new pollinating agent, be it a bird or an insect. The principal requirement is that there shall be a similarity of the two proposed parents. This similarity could even be the realignment of two genera which had separated from a single origin in the distant past.

When all things are considered, the hybridist is not always as clever as he appears, because he copies all the time; he does not create. In looking at the achievements of the hybridist over the last 100 years one is apt, perhaps, to be a bit conceited about it all.

Although some of the original cultivators of orchids as a pastime rather rigidly set their faces against cross-pollination and the production of hybrids, to the point at times where they would bar such plants from their collections, the stage was set by the 1890 decade for possibly the mightiest piece of artificial horticultural innovation ever seen in the history of man. Not only was it by far the largest achievement in production of hybrids from original genera, but within the fallibility of humanity it was also the best documented and still is.

Many puzzling aspects of hybridism have come to light and it is impossible to detail even minute parts of them. A tangible instance is that of the Australian dendrobium hybrids. We know possibly all of these which occur naturally and it is in their duplication by artificial means that the hand of nature is so clearly displayed. It does not need acceptance of the theories of Charles Darwin to understand that when we produce artificial hybrids we thwart the laws of natural selection and frequently this is displayed clearly in the flowers. Reference to the graph in another part of the book explains this better. We produce something quite unlike the article nature produces and there must be a real but nevertheless almost unbelievable reason for it: *Does nature seek to change things all the time? Is our world changing so much that something must be done to rescue the passengers, even the floral section, and 'something' is constantly doing this by producing 'something' which copes with the changes?* All those 'somethings' must be capable of conversion into tangible entities, but we do not know how to do it.

The loathsome way humanity handles its environment on Earth causes deep pain to some, to others no emotion at all. The prevailing thought that everything should be sold at a profit, even our naturally growing orchids, is so abhorrent yet so hard to change. Allied to it is the proposition that it is up to the next generation to take care of all the iniquities of the present one. But this time, instead of a message, all we have left is a question: *Is it already too late?*

The Nurseries and Distributors

There was a considerable number of nurseries and distributorships operating in Britain, Europe and America from 1850 onward, some remaining in business for many years. At times consignments of plants were sold at auction in the rooms of various sales people and the prices paid for plants ranged from pence to guineas, the old term for one pound and a shilling, with occasional specialties bringing figures in the hundreds of pounds. Only a few of the nurseries are noted in this book and possibly they were the most important in the world in their time. Some may wonder why this section is included in the book, but it is always better to understand a pastime completely, from its origins to active participation.

A most disgraceful episode in the history of horticulture was the unrestricted and reprehensible stripping of the orchid habitats. It may not have appeared so bad when the acts were perpetrated, but the lack of foresight and common greed shown alike by collectors, nurserymen and dealers and the wealthy growers cannot be excused or minimised. Although growers perhaps were less to blame than the other groups, nevertheless they contributed by extending their facilities until it was common for one of them to buy upward of 5000 plants of one genus, flower as many as survived, keeping selected varieties and discarding the remainder.

Many of the botanists whose memories today are enshrined among the great of past centuries were equally guilty. It seemed that the collecting of orchids and other exotic plants became a contagious disease and once infected there was no remission. The sins of the collectors are well documented but those of the other classes engaged in the pastime are not so well known. Frequently some of them had little part in the senseless aftermath of the great expansionary period between 1860 and the end of the century because their collections outlived them and were sold off under the terms of their wills.

There were some redeeming features in it all. The collection and cultivation of orchids led to an understanding of their place in the plant world and almost certainly assisted the cause of botanists and scientists who accepted the theory of evolution in further propounding and almost proving the truths they insisted on. The occurrence of so many natural hybrids among the Central and South American orchids still gives cause for believing that opposition to their theories has little to help it. Several other factors less important to the everyday orchid grower also add to the evidence.

In the years of tranquillity between 1890 and 1916 great speculation on the theory of Gregor Mendel entered into orchid growing and while it did not seem to add very much to his cause through the medium of orchids because of the incidence of known cross-pollinations in naturally collected plants, it did exercise the minds of hybridists about the future of popular genera of the time.

But the collectors were the people who, while they did not have all the fun, did have the honor of discovering new and more beautiful flowers, the habitats and origin of which some went to great pains to conceal. It was big business. But it was the sort of big business which brought them little fortune because most of this was shared out among the dealers or nurserymen and the wealthy growers.

Of all things to practically put an end to the collection and despatch of species to the markets in Britain, Europe and America, it was the orchids themselves. After the initial success of James Dominy it took quite some time for cross-pollination and hybridising to begin in earnest, but once it started the attention was diverted away from the species and they had a chance to recover a little.

James Veitch and Sons

The great nursery of James Veitch and Sons could perhaps be taken as an example of the participants in a trade as lucrative as the slave trade of an earlier period and in retrospect just as reprehensible. The name Veitch is, like the name Sander, almost synonymous for orchids. The strange part is that it was all established for so few men and for such huge amounts of money.

James Veitch and Sons' nursery was commenced about 1800 by John Veitch in Devon and his son James started what was known as the Exeter Nursery about 1832. His son, also called James, started the orchid section about 1834, inaugurating a business which employed a large number of men and overseas staff as collectors in the ensuing years. James the younger was 'orchidised' by serving a couple of years at the nursery of Rollison in London. In 1853 the Veitch nursery was moved to London and then began what is a fairy-tale story of plunder and riches and wonder and competition.

It was Harry J. Veitch, who must have lived and slept and dreamed orchids, who became the heart of an enterprise of some fifty years standing. He produced Veitch's *Manual of Orchidaceous Plants*, in which much of the history of the cult is to be found. He also formed the Orchid Committee of the Royal Horticultural Society and in his late years was knighted for his services to horticulture.

It is difficult to allocate merit in order to any one of the Veitch collectors because they mostly worked in different fields and contributed to the overall strength of the firm. The number of orchids they collected, as to genus, species or natural hybrids, is impossible to estimate. But it must be in the order of many millions considering the number of years they were operating.

The brothers William and Thomas Lobb covered all the known orchid habitats in Asia and America, both beginning their careers in the Veitch nursery. William was assigned to Brazil in 1840 and in his period there sent back, among other novelties, *Phragmipedium caudatum* and *Cycnoches pentadactylon*.

About 1843 Thomas was sent to Singapore and worked his way steadily through Indo-Asia collecting and despatching to Veitch's nursery such orchids as *Vanda tricolor*, *Vanda coerulea*, *Paphiopedilum villosum*, various cymbidiums and many other species. One of these, a bulbophyllum, was subsequently named *lobbii* in his honor.

Lewis Castle, of the Royal Gardens, Kew, England, writing of Thomas Lobb in 1887, had this to say: 'Like most successful men, he was quite modest ... the tradition even yet lingers at Chelsea that if Tom Lobb ever went so far as to say a plant of his own finding was "nice" or "pretty" then everybody from Mr James Veitch himself downwards, all were on the tiptoe of expectation, for they felt convinced it must be an extra fine thing'.

John Gould Veitch also collected in Japan, the area which was then known as the South Sea Islands and Australia. However, his promising career was very short and he died at the age of thirty-one years in 1870.

William Lobb spent seventeen years in South America and Mexico collecting for the Veitch nursery and died in San Francisco in 1863. But his brother Thomas lived a very full life. After collecting for the Veitch nursery for about twenty years he returned to England and died in Cornwall aged well over seventy years.

Bowman, another Veitch collector, went to Brazil in 1866 and after a period there went to Colombia, where he died some two years later. He also fell victim to one of the various diseases so easily picked up by Europeans. He is credited with the discovery or rediscovery of *Miltonia vexillaria*, so eagerly and for so long sought by the British nurseries.

George Downton was sent to Costa Rica by the nursery and collected for them from about 1870. It was here that he also met Endres. Downton, unlike others of the fraternity, eventually settled in Central America, where he died in 1895. He was an unsuccessful exporter, as most of his consignments died.

Endres had worked with Skinner in collecting orchids for James Bateman and he was successful in locating *Odontoglossum warscewiczii*, among other orchids, which had been unsuccessfully sought for many years. Endres was a halfcast Indian and worked for Veitch for a long time. His name is perpetuated in *Miltonia endresii* and other orchids.

He remained with the Veitch group until about 1873, finding during this period considerable areas of *Cattleya dowiana* var. *aurea*, a plant which found a ready market in Europe and Britain. Endres apparently knew the correct season in which to gather and prepare the plants for their debilitating sea voyage, which was possibly one of the reasons for the failures of Downton and others.

J. H. Chesterton was among the most remarkable men employed by Veitch because he entered the trade only by chance. While employed as a valet to a wealthy traveller he consulted the firm about packing and preparation of plants. He subsequently brought home what Veitch said was the best consignment of plants he had ever seen. Chesterton was offered employment and from 1870 to 1878 he collected in Colombia, Peru and other places, sending to the Veitch nursery a large consignment of *Masdevallia coccinea* variety *Harryana*, a genus most difficult to acclimatise, dehydrate, pack and consign overseas. He also sent a large consignment of *Miltonia vexillaria*. Chesterton later went into business on his own account as a collector and exporter and died in South America in 1883.

Gustav Wallis was born in Hanover, Germany, in 1830 and travelled to Brazil for a German nursery about 1856. He apparently left their employ while there and was subsequently employed by Veitch as well as Linden. He made the journey right across the South American continent from the source of the Amazon River to its mouth. He also went to the Philippine Islands on a search for phalaenopsis, which proved unsuccessful. Returning to South and Central America, he died there from fever about 1878, adding his name to the list of victims of a precarious occupation.

Walter Davis worked with the hybridist James Dominy at the Veitch nursery for some years before they sent him to South America in 1873, most particularly for *Masdevallia veitchiana* but also for other orchids. One of the most adventurous of collectors, he worked over the mountains of Peru and Bolivia for some years, climbing to altitudes of 5000 metres searching for plants. In his brief career there he covered much more territory than most of the collectors.

In the Asian region F. W. Burbidge and Charles Curtis worked for James Veitch and Sons in the 1870-90 period, Burbidge returning to Britain to take up an appointment at the Botanical Gardens of a Dublin university after collecting and despatching plants to the nursery. Charles Curtis was joined by David Burke, another Veitch employee. Curtis worked in the islands and the mainland area of Asia for some six years, bringing in many new orchids and having his name perpetuated by attachment to some of them.

5

David Burke was born in 1854 and his journeys as a collector took him to South America as well as Indo-Asia and it was in Amboina in 1897 that he died a lonely death at the age of forty-three years. Burke knew quite well the area where he took his last assignment.

His last words to Charles Curtis before leaving for the Moluccas were: 'I'm off again and if I make a good meal for someone I hope I shall give full satisfaction.' Such were the possibilities facing orchid collectors in the late years of the nineteenth century. He was one of the last of the notable collectors employed by James Veitch and Sons.

The health of most of the Veitch collectors was impaired by their arduous lives, travelling mostly on foot, horseback or on mules, few living to the age of Sir Harry Veitch, who died in 1924 aged eighty-four years.

Charles Curtis died in 1928 after holding the appointment of superintendent of the Penang Botanic Gardens from 1884 to 1903. Both he and his son, Charles, were most knowledgeable on orchids, the younger Curtis editing *The Orchid Review* (England) from 1932 to 1958.

The nursery business of James Veitch and Sons was broken up some years after the death of James Veitch in 1907 and the orchid component passed to Black and Flory. This ended the reign of a remarkable dynasty in the distribution of orchids collected in almost every country of the world.

Sanders

H. F. C. Sander was undoubtedly the most outstanding figure in the orchid world of the years 1860 to 1910, with perhaps a few years on either side of the period for good measure. He was born in 1847 and from boyhood knew what he wanted for a career. Simply, it was to work with plants and trees.

He commenced work at a nursery at the age of twenty and soon formed an attachment to orchids that was to last his whole life, in the golden years of which he was known as the 'Orchid King'. This rather theatrical title meant quite a lot more than the words indicated.

Henry Sander started his own business after a few years with his original employers, at whose nursery he made the acquaintance of Benedict Roezl, a famous plant collector and explorer. They also formed a business arrangement and Roezl started sending Sander consignments of orchids and other plants from South America, to the advantage of both. The business grew rapidly at St. Albans (England) and soon expanded, becoming the clearing house for millions of plants over the following years. That figure is scarcely an exaggeration. Sander believed in advertising and soon was staging plants at all the great horticultural exhibitions which were a feature of the period.

His aim was to obtain all the best plants he possibly could, never hesitating to pay very high prices for species which he wanted. The aim was to create the finest hybrid orchids possible and in the 1980 period we are looking at the end result of that aim.

History records that a plant of *Cattleya skinneri* found by one of Henry Sander's collectors was so huge that when he was at last able to purchase it and send it to St. Albans the end of a glass-house had to be removed to get it in. *The Orchid World*, a publication of the pre-1914-18 war, states that a special glasshouse section was created for it. The plant measured over 2 metres in diameter, almost the same height and weighed well over half a tonne. When Roezl, who bought the plant, saw it first it had upward of 1500 opened flowers and some buds yet to break.

A list of the outstanding novelties brought to cultivation by Sander is almost impossible to compile, but among them is *Paphiopedilum insigne* var. *sanderae*, the effect of which on the hybrid Slippers is immense. There were few exotic plants which the Sander establishment did not import, from begonias and anthuriums to the diminutive plants of *Sophronitis coccinea*, which, if he had a favorite orchid at all, was his fancy.

Sanders seemed to have no fewer than twenty-odd collectors working for them at any one time and while it may be difficult to select one as outstanding, Micholitz would probably head the list. Roezl, Sanders' first big collector and exporter, following the extraordinary growth of the trade, was able to retire in a short period to his home in Prague, but Micholitz continued with Sanders for a much longer period.

The expansion of Sanders to Europe and America brought management problems. *The European establishment comprised some 250 glass-houses, fifty of which were devoted to orchids*. The American operation was disposed of, but St. Albans and the European sections continued with the help of his three sons, Fearnley, Fred and Louis, whose names are perpetuated in hybrid orchids.

Veitch was not the only orchid 'wholesaler' to produce a book, as Henry Sander's beautiful volumes of *Reichenbachia*, with their color plates and plant history, are among the masterpieces of orchid literature. The period was studded with magnificent publications, possibly none better than this.

The Sander nursery in Belgium was greatly affected by the war of 1914-18 and in failing health Henry Sander visited it at the end of the conflict. He died in 1920 after a whole life seething with activity surrounded by all sorts of plants and flowers. In his lifetime his reputation was that his patience never failed him, courtesy never deserted him. With his death something vital was lost, because he was always too busy to write a biography. He was aged seventy-four.

Henry Sander's son Frederick will be remembered possibly long after his father is forgotten because of his unflinching attack on the horrible mess of names bestowed on hybrid orchids by various breeders. The publication of his lists was one of the best features of a century of orchid growing and we can in 1980 look to it in confidence to trace most of the pedigrees of our hybrids. Unfortunately there are some gaps, but without *Sanders' List of Orchid Hybrids* it would be an impossible task to keep track of the hundreds of thousands of cross-pollinations.

The hybrid list was published monthly in the English *Orchid Review* first in 1922. This magazine is the journal of the Orchid Committee of the RHS and was commenced under the editorship of R. A. Rolfe, who died in the same year as Henry Sander. The committee suffered such a loss that the magazine was not published for six months and orchid growing lost one of the most estimable of men. Publication of *The Orchid Review* was recommenced and has not missed an issue since then after starting its career in 1893.

The collectors

Of the number of collectors, possibly hundreds, who operated in all the areas in which orchids could be profitably exploited only a few are recorded in this section and then only briefly. Much of the literature associated with this activity is long out of print, some has disappeared for ever and a great amount varies from book to book. But generally this summary was applicable to the craft as a whole; a craft in which the word could be used in its dual sense. There was little communication between the men so engaged and all kinds of strategems used to throw opposition off the scent of a new find. One of the most abominable of all the operations was in the collection of a particular paphiopedilum where the collector, having taken all the plants worth while, fired the area to destroy the smaller and worthless remnants so that no one else could get even these. Not all collectors, however, were so bad.

Wilhelm Micholitz, a German from Saxony, seemed to have the personality which suited Henry Sander and was apparently the ideal type to be explorer-collector in what at that time was almost unknown territory. He was a little younger than Sander and must have joined the firm some time following the departure of Roezl.

There was scarcely one country containing orchids left unvisited by Micholitz, even Australia being on his itinerary. A snippet from this period of his travels is enlightening. He corresponded freely with Henry Sander and this extract is from one of his letters; written in 1912:

'I arrived at Thursday Island with a good number of *D. superbiens*, mostly fine plants. I have also some *D. bigibbum* and *D. johannis*. The latter seems to be a most floriferous thing and well worth cultivating.' After remarking on the extraordinary number of adventitious growths on *Dendrobium superbiens* and scarcity of seed pods, he continues: 'Here it is no picnic, the south-east wind howling through the rigging, the dinghy in which one lands is a mere nutshell and at ebb-tide one has a quarter of a mile or more of coral reef to wade and clamber over. The beach is mostly strewn with rocks and huge boulders. But worst of all is the continual tossing and rolling of the craft when at anchor.'

Anyone who has ever spent time on a small boat will appreciate the last part of his letter for the horrible experience it was.

However, Micholitz seemed to be at home in any part of the world, whether collecting masdevallias in Peru or phalaenopsis in the Philippine Islands. On completion of an assignment he would visit the nursery first, looking through all the collection, possibly for plants he had collected unflowered, spending some time with the cultivators explaining the conditions under which many of them grew. After a few weeks' holiday he would be off again. He was mixed up in revolutions, travel hazards and all the attendant ills which beset Europeans in the tropics. His collecting was more in the Asian region than the American and he apparently got on quite well with the natives and knew how to handle them.

Micholitz is mentioned in other parts of this book as well as in the book on cymbidiums and paphiopedilums. He was unfortunate in later life, because despite the enormous value of the plants which passed through his hands he died almost penniless, his savings invested in the wrong sort of bonds, probably German as well as other countries, and eked out his final years collecting botanical specimens and teaching English. The latter may be well understood considering the beautiful construction of the sentences in his letters. He had a flair for making the invisible lifelike in description. He died in December, 1932.

William Boxall was born in England in 1834 and apparently was interested in horticulture from his earliest years. He obtained a position in the nursery of Hugh Low and Co. and in that time must have been associated with the section devoted to orchids and their cultivation, possibly seeing the development of the pastime from its earliest days.

With the establishment of vast orchid collections, principally in the wealthy industrial area of the Midlands, Hugh Low and Co. decided to have their own collectors in the field and sent Boxall to Burma. Some of the pre-history of collecting in that country was supplied by the plants sent back to England by the Reverend Parish and an army officer named Benson, both of whom were most interested in the subject.

Among Boxall's discoveries in Burma was *Dendrobium wardianum* and he collected and shipped thousands of plants of that beautiful dendrobium back to England. One of the features of this orchid is its habit of casting all the leaves from the pseudo-bulbs almost as soon as the bulbs are mature and when they are consigned to another country the plants upon acclimatising in the first year flower most profusely and perhaps for the last time.

Cymbidium lowianum was another of his triumphs, flowering in Low's nursery about 1879, as outlined in the book on cymbidiums.

His assignment in the Philippines resulted in many thousands of plants of phalaenopsis being sent to England. In this genus he was most successful and studied the method of partially dehydrating the plants after they had been tied to flat pieces of wood. They were packed thus in crates and the loss rate was comparatively light.

His journeys and searches in the south-west and south-east Asian areas took him as far south as Australia and adjacent islands, where he collected *Dendrobium bigibbum* (known then as *Dendrobium phalaenopsis*), *Dendrobium superbiens* and other orchids.

His forays were not confined to the Indian Ocean and Pacific regions and he was assigned to Central and South America by Low and Co., with whom he appeared to have spent almost his whole active life. Unlike some of the other collectors, he never bothered much with dried specimens for the botanists, of either the better known genera or the smaller botanical interest species.

All told, Boxall must have collected and shipped hundreds of thousands of plants in his career in what at that time was considered a most exemplary occupation. He was a recipient of one of the first Victoria Medals for Horticulture in 1897 and although not in good health over the latter part of his life, he was a member of the Orchid Committee and attended most of the meetings after his election.

One of the more fortunate of the collectors, he died in his sixty-sixth year in 1910, possibly in his later years looking back with a great deal of satisfaction on a most unusual life of travel and working at what he most liked doing.

Louis Forget was a Frenchman who, although one of Sanders' collectors in the twilight period of bulk consignments from the Central and South American provinces, had a very nebulous history before his first assignment to Pernambuco, Brazil, by that firm to collect *Cattleya labiata* soon after its rediscovery in areas other than those originally stripped. He sent thousands of plants of this orchid to his employers.

Forget also discovered *Cattleya victoria regina* growing in association with *Cattleya leopoldii* in an area not previously visited by him. He returned to the area the following year with the intention of taking a consignment in the same way as he had with *Cattleya labiata*, but in his words: '... I had a terrible time over it, but could not get one.' He did not realise at the time that it was a natural hybrid between *Cattleya leopoldii* and *Cattleya labiata*, consequently somewhat scarce. No doubt he would have liked a large consignment of it. Subsequently identified, it was accepted as a naturally occurring species or hybrid, depending on how it was viewed.

He also rediscovered *Laelia jongheana*, about which little was known, in the Minas Gerais region of Brazil, where he found it growing in the same habitat as *Cattleyas bicolor*, *walkerana* and *loddigesii*, all of which were considered cool-growing orchids. Only one, *Cattleya loddigesii*, is found amenable to cool culture in artificial conditions, indicating how easy it is to make mistakes in this way.

The large number of cattleya species had no terrors for Louis Forget, and his knowledge of the Brazilian section of the genus was extensive and intelligently visionary when it came to the natural hybrids, even when they occurred with laelias. His observations of the two genera in the one habitat led him to believe that cross-pollination was not only possible but almost inevitable, and having roamed over most of Brazil, he was one of the few collectors who documented his finds and knew a great deal about the habitats and their climates. In this way he was able to identify positively both the species and the numerous hybrids stemming from both inter-generic and natural pollinations.

In addition to the Brazilian orchids, Forget had a close knowledge of the odontoglossums of Colombia and Peru, particularly the habitat and identification of the varieties of *Odontoglossum crispum*. He frequently said his favorite area was along the eastern slopes of the Peruvian Andes Mountains and it is a matter for regret that he did not leave a record of his travels and more information to counteract the popular glamorous 'orchid collector' image brought to the public by less experienced and unreliable plant sleuths. Perhaps he had visions of doing so in his older years, but unfortunately he never reached them.

On one occasion he collected a large consignment of *Cattleya rex* in Peru, only to see it totally lost in a shipwreck. His preparation of the plants for the long voyage to Sanders' nursery probably took many weeks and he had to return and do the job all over again. His description of the large plants growing in the forest was most lucid as '... flowering profusely on bulbs as large as *Laelia purpurata* and constituting one of the finest sights I ever saw'.

Louis Forget discovered, among many other orchids, *Anguloa uniflora*, which had been described by the observers Ruiz and Pavon as far back as 1794 and not noted since.

Sanders referred to him as '... a remarkable man. He appeared to have an iron constitution and scarcely ever complained of his health in all the 23 years throughout which he was collecting and exploring.'

His name is commemorated in *Masdevallia forgetiana*, *Brassia forgetiana* and also in the multi-generic hybrids forgetara, between brassias, aspasias and miltonias.

Sanders' collectors did not all live long or healthy lives, for Arnold died in the Orinoco region of Venezuela, Falkenberg (Panama), Klaboch (Mexico), Endres (Rio Hacha), Wallis (Ecuador), and Schroder (Sierra Leone), and these were only a few of the men who lost their lives in pursuit of a commodity to satisfy a relatively small number of orchid growers in Britain, Europe, and America.

Louis Forget, having apparently worn out his 'iron constitution', died in a hospital at Rennes, France, in August 1915.

Hugh Low, born in 1824, was a member of a family long established in horticulture, but during his life he occupied a position in another sphere which enabled him to travel as well as enjoy a horticultural pastime.

Originally going to Borneo with James Brooke after being persuaded to abandon an appointment with the East India Company in the Far East, he had ample opportunity to make contact with the native races and the rich orchid population of northern Borneo. James Brooke was a colonial administrator, later knighted and becoming known as the Rajah of Sarawak. Hugh Low also later gained the distinction of knighthood in the Rajah's service, first as a colonial secretary and later as Sir James Brooke's treasurer.

He wrote a book in Sarawak in which he recalled his first contacts and remarked: 'My object (the collection of plants and seeds) led me more into the country and amongst the tribes of aborigines than any other Englishman who has yet visited the shores of this island'.

It should be remembered that in 1840, when he took up the appointment, the 'aborigines' were more interested in collecting heads, particularly white ones, than in noting the plants and flowers growing so richly beside them.

Hugh Low developed a packing system for his plants and sent many consignments back to his brother in England. Possibly his most outstanding discovery was the plant originally named *Vanda lowii*, which he sent to Lindley, with the request that it be named *Vanda lindleyana*.

It was a most peculiar orchid, rampant in growth and producing two totally different colored flowers on the one raceme. The racemes of flower also reached great length. The dimorphic flowers consisted of a group of tawny yellow flowers dotted with red-brown, the remainder on the spike being deep reddish brown with yellow reticulations and yellow-colored patches and occasionally producing flowers midway between the two. Dr Lindley preferred to call the orchid *Vanda lowii* and declined the honor in his own name.

Subsequently the botanist Bentham allocated the orchid to the aracnanthe family, Schlechter classed it as *Vandopsis lowii* and finally Rolfe classified it in a new genus of two members, with the name *Dimorphorcis lowii*.

Hugh Low was the first known European to have ascended Mount Kinabalu, on which journey he found many new orchids and a large number of other plants new to horticulture. Several genera include orchids named in his honor as the discoverer, including *Paphiopedilum lowii* (Lindley).

Hugh Low's brother Stuart visited him at least once and probably more frequently and as he was active in the family business no doubt took the opportunity to see and also collect orchids. But at the same time it is possible that the interests of the firm were more toward the other exotic plants which grew so luxuriantly in northern Borneo.

While initially being disappointed at finding the orchids so hard to see and collect, Hugh Low soon developed the collector's perception and was able to sort out the orchids from all the other epiphytes which at times resembled them. His descriptions are complete to the point where identification is quite easy.

Unlike collectors, as previously remarked, in addition to his book he also kept a complete record of his activities in a diary, which is still in the possession of his family. It was of considerable assistance to botanists as well as collectors and biographers.

His descriptions of packing and despatch of plants by the sailing ships of those days may sound a little primitive in the days of air transport, but they were modelled on trial and error and remained exemplary for as long as the slow transport of the times prevailed.

Sir Hugh Low survived in a country full of hazards for Europeans, not always in the best of health, and his knowledge of orchids in the Borneo area was passed on to others together with the botanical information about other plants. He died in England at the age of eighty-one.

John Rager, an American collector of the 1900 era, operated mostly in Central and South America, particularly in the search for cattleya species. By that time most of the accessible sources had been all but cleared and it was necessary to get into new areas, sometimes over very difficult country.

Colombia was one of his principal gathering points and he sent consignments of cattleyas, particularly *Cattleya warscewiczii* (*gigas*), *Cattleya chocoensis*, *Cattleya trianae*, *Cattleya mendelii* and *Cattleya schroderae* to American importers. He is quoted, in reference to *Cattleya gigas*, as having found plants in great quantities 'climbing up the mountains until actually dwarfed by the cold and ultimately stopped, but refusing to die and producing small new growths each year with a new leaf to keep the plant going'.

Rager also collected in Venezuela and Brazil, but the central Cordilleras of Colombia amazed him with the profusion of orchids which grew there. One of the masdevallias he discovered and described has never been rediscovered and in both instances where he managed to collect a few plants they died in transit. It was probably a hybrid form and from the description of color and size could have been one of the outstanding members of the genus.

In the later stages of his collecting career Rager was one of the few men engaged in the trade who expressed concern at the inroads both European and native collectors were having on the orchid genera, more particularly the natives, whose consignments, at times numbering hundreds of cases, on being opened at their destinations revealed nothing but the rotting remnants of once beautiful plants.

It was not only the orchids which were so rapaciously stripped. E. H. Wilson, working in the expansive years of the late 1800 period, sent back to England in five years no fewer than 25 000 dried specimens of plants, including orchids, seeds of 1800 different species and 30 000 lilium bulbs from Tibet and southern China.

Australians were no less guilty in the treatment of their native orchids. Reg Leaney, who did much for Australian orchid growing and encouraging the cultivation of our own epiphytes, writing to the English *Orchid Review* in 1934, had this to say:

'Just recently while on the first of my 1934 series of orchid hunting expeditions, I had an excellent opportunity of studying *Dendrobium falcorostrum* in its native haunts. I discovered quite a new patch and the reader will obtain some idea of its abundance in this area when I mention the fact that I took 142 really large plants (and what I call large plants are big specimens) from one tree. Of course, this is rather phenomenal. But as I had to cut down a tree approximately 5 feet in diameter and the timber as hard as iron, I chose a tree with the maximum number of plants and the minimum girth.'

Reg Leaney possibly did not realise the implications of his actions or that in the future there would be both government and private 'Reg Leaneys' operating to the extent that *Dendrobium falcorostrum* is in danger of being at risk as a botanical specimen or a member of the Australian native flora.

Several of the collectors wrote colorful books of their travels and adventures, but in many instances they portrayed a totally different world from that experienced by such men as Micholitz or Forget and much of their color was invented rather than physically experienced. Apart from these books, the literature associated with the period — and it is most beautiful as well as informative — indicates to the world of a century later what was unfortunately a never-to-return era of man's appreciation as well as his destructiveness. Unfortunately it still goes on, but with a much diminished source of plants on which to work.

The pressures on governments by private individuals, corporations and statutory bodies said to be entrusted with the preservation of the world's resources are constant and unremitting, with profit the primary motive. If profit is to be taken regardless of the future then there is little prospect that any of the orchids of the world may survive.

At their destinations, mostly in the glass-houses of wealthy fanciers in Britain, Europe and America it is regrettable that the plants did not evoke by sheer weight of numbers some realisation of what was happening. Small voices were heard, but they were disregarded. Instead it was left to the greatly enlarged number of growers two generations later to come to grips with the problem in their native countries and object to the consignment of their beautiful and rare orchids to other countries.

In concluding this brief review of nurseries selected from a large number engaged in the orchid trade and but a few of the number of collectors who found the supplies for them, it may add credibility to an incredible story to note that in Brazil alone 148 botanists and part-time collectors for herbariums and such, without mentioning the army of commercial operators, took plants for identification and cataloguing. In Peru it all commenced much earlier with the Spanish botanists Ruiz and Pavon about 1778, with the following years ones of continuous exploitation and decimation.

Considerable credit should be given to the botanists such as Schlechter, who for almost their whole lives moved from country to country making a catalogue of orchids, researching to the depths their known history and adding to the pool of knowledge shared by interested people all over the world. He had many similar minded contemporaries and they will be forgotten, unfortunately, before the nurserymen and collectors.

Laeliocattleya canhamiana (C. mossiae x *L. purpurata),* raised by Veitch's Nursery, 1885.

Epiphytes —
The way they
grow

Most of the orchids in this book are from the catalogue of epiphytes and all from Mexico, Central and South America. The word epiphyte is applicable to a host of plants inhabiting the environment between ground level and the tops of trees, some occurring on the basement and a large number on the topmost strata. Some, indeed, grow on rock surfaces almost exclusively, others on trees as well as rocks, like the Australian Dendrobium speciosum. The derivation of the word is from the Greek word *phuton*, a plant — usually indicating plants which grow on other plants or trees yet are not parasitic or living on the sap of their host.

Living in this state, many orchids are dependent on what is called an ecosystem or close association of other growing things sharing a common environment. This environment is made up of all the things which affect their lives — the sun, the air, the rain — and the insects and other things which pollinate their flowers and finally providing for the germination and growth of their seeds. So life goes on!

When orchids are taken into cultivation the first thing to do is give them some semblance of the things which govern their lives when they existed naturally. Although it is practically impossible to duplicate these conditions, steps can be taken to model their cultivation on the necessities of life and cleverly at times to dupe them into conforming to a new way of life.

It is necessary to appreciate the type of root system which orchids grow. Some have a far-reaching system which clings to the host tree like those of phalaenopsis, some dendrobiums and cattleyas or laelias. This root system is also just as much at home on a rock habitat where plants such as laelias grow. Instead of the word epiphyte, they are referred to as lithophytes or rupicolous plants.

The second type of root system is one which, in addition to providing anchorage for the plants, such as that of the clinging system, is aerial and quite free of contact with the host tree. It is common on some oncidiums and dendrobiums, its purpose probably as much to catch and hold decay material as to absorb moisture from the air.

The third system is entirely aerial, like that of rodriguezias and other similar orchids, some vandas, aerides and even monopodial plants like angraecums, with a certain amount of the root system seeking out food and moisture wherever they can find it and it is part of the marvel of orchids and their cultivation to note how instinctively clever the roots are at finding them.

In cultivation all three types of root systems must be tamed to a degree and either induced or forced to enter pots or containers and preferably remain there. In addition, other forms of cultivation such as growing orchid plants on fern or cork or wood mounts are giving them a little of their natural way of growth while still restraining and confining them in what could be termed an unnatural way.

The differences between genera must be understood at some period in orchid growers' lives and the sooner this knowledge is gained the better. This applies particularly to such orchids as odontoglossums, lycastes and similar orchids which must have humus and decay material on which to work and in which to grow. Their roots would be completely lost in the search for food on surfaces or in coarse aerated mixes such as used for cattleyas, to mention only one genus.

Although most of the world's population of orchids occurs in a tropical zone each side of the equator, they grow at different altitudes and this gives a great amount of difference in the temperatures at which they should be grown. While it is easy to state that a certain orchid growing, say, in the Philippine Islands has a certain temperature in its growing period and another at its dormant period and yet another in its flowering phase, a balance must be struck between it and all the other genera cultivated, finally to come up with a recommended lowest temperature and a rather flexible upper range. It is quite certain that unless a total growing area is devoted to a single genus, rigid temperature recommendations and control are meaningless. If the genus is composed of hybrid units generated from several species the odds are that no such temperature control to suit them all could be worked out.

In the final analysis the best way to approach orchid growing is to decide, according to the climate in which one lives, what type of orchids will be grown and the degree to which their growing conditions can be stabilised. To give some semblance of planning, three sets of growing conditions emerge — cool, warm and hot.

The temperatures associated with these three conditions are a minimum of 50 degrees with a possible lapse of a few degrees over a season for cool-growing orchids; 55 degrees minimum with a lesser scope for lapses for warm-growing orchids and 65 degrees with no scope at all for a lapse for the heat-loving genera. Although these temperatures are in the superseded Fahrenheit system, it is by far a more satisfactory system than the conversion, which gives 10 degrees Celsius for the cool-growing genera, 12.75 degrees for warm-growing genera and 18.2 degrees for the hotter-growing genera.

The fractional breakdown for Celsius is almost critical, but it can be reduced to the three figures of 10, 13 and 18 with a fair margin of safety.

Construction and orientation of a glass-house or growing area can have an appreciable effect on both heating and maintenance of warmth. This should be part of the planning when alternatives exist. The type of heating should be suitable to the demands placed on it and before selecting a genus or multiple genera to be grown a little thought should be given to the expense of maintaining the best conditions for them.

Ferns and Mosses

Ferns and mosses are natural associates of epiphytic orchids and each assists the other in forming an ecosystem from which all benefit. While that is all very well in natural habitats, once it enters the cultivation area the system breaks down.

Considering the ferns first, it is unwise to allow the small ferns that develop from spores introduced into potting materials to grow and mature. The root system of ferns is intense and while it poses no threat in natural conditions, once it proliferates in a pot it strangles the orchid roots and starves them by absorbing all the moisture and preventing the aeration of the potting material. They should be removed as soon as they commence to grow on the surface, potting them and growing them separately if they are worth while.

In general, pots of ferns and other plants which thrive in glass-house conditions add to the atmosphere the same features which they contribute to natural environments. They form part of an ecosystem which promotes growth without direct plant contact.

Mosses fall into two groups — those which assist growth and those which by the surface nature of their growth prevent aeration of potting materials and turn them sour. There is a third moss used in orchid growing. It is the decayed form of sphagnum moss, usually termed peat-moss, and it has a place in orchid culture almost impossible to duplicate with other materials.

Starting with the living mosses, those dense felt-like finer mosses which thrive in glass-house conditions should be discouraged as they start. There is no chemical way of doing this and they must be scraped from the surface of the potting material and discarded outside the glass-house. These mosses also form part of the ecosystem in natural conditions but lose their value completely once they enter cultivation areas.

It should be noted, however, that there is usually a reason for their germination from spores or their propagation from tiny introductions. The potting material is usually at fault because of its nature or because of the type of pot in which it is used. It begins with drainage. If the potting material is well constituted, surface conditions are almost unsuitable for development of mosses to the extent that they dominate the surface. The constitution of the potting mix should be reviewed so that the coarse drainage part of the mix is as conspicuous on the surface as any other part of the mix.

Sphagnum moss is usually the only living moss which has a part to play in orchid growing and it has two uses. As a propagating medium it is most useful, with the ability to promote root growth from epiphytic orchid rhizomes faster and cleaner than other mediums. It also has another use, as illustrated in the photographic section, in retaining the surface of potting material if it is liable to wash out when watered. In this it can be used too lavishly and may do the same thing as the closely growing velvety mosses recommended for elimination. If used as a topping it should be stranded on the surface to act like a breakwater and a good test for the suitability of the compost or potting material is that the moss will grow. If it does not show signs of growth from either the small tufty heads or from the strands the mix may be either too acid, which is unlikely, or it may be alkaline. See illustration page 101.

Sphagnum moss is also a good means of finding out if the water supply is good or bad, because if the supply is alkaline the moss goes pale and will not grow. If, however, the moss turns dark green it is possible that the mix is too acid or the drainage and aeration insufficient to promote growth. This will also be reflected in lack of virility in the orchid plants.

The decayed form of sphagnum moss is widely used for retaining water or moisture in what otherwise could be a barren and useless mix. There are many types of sphagnum moss and the areas from which they originate can produce a peat-moss which is too acid at times for use as an orchid-growing medium. It is a cause which too frequently may be put down to other things and there is no real way of testing peat-moss to be sure that it is correct.

Too much peat-moss in a mix is just as bad as too little and if other decay material is used, such as peanut shells or leaf, broken down or fresh dropped, it should be weighed in with the peat-moss and allowance made in the drainage content.

One test for a potting mix for most orchids, not thoroughly reliable for general use but good enough to provide confidence in a mix, is to fill a pot with it, water it thoroughly and then sprinkle a teaspoonful of bird seed on the surface and scratch it in. If it grows strongly, which will take about a fortnight to occur, the material can be taken as reasonably good and the orchid plants put into it.

To some degree climate indicates what is needed as an additive to mixes for epiphytes and some growers prefer to use only bark and drainage material. But odontoglossums, to consider only one genus, are epiphytic orchids and need a state of almost constant moisture in the potting material. To get them to this state and continue it the potting mix must have some absorptive material. Neither bark nor cork is very absorptive.

All the other epiphytes such as dendrobiums, cattleyas, lycastes and hundreds of other genera need moisture maintenance at some period of their cycle, mostly in the growing or flowering periods, during which a dry period, however short, may halt the root system. This halt may take a day or two to pick up or it may take a week or more. Peat-moss fulfils this moisture retaining role, but its use should be moderated by the realisation that it is easily possible to overdo it.

Live sphagnum moss as an entire growing medium is not satisfactory for the ordinary grower, although it is frequently recommended for such orchids as dendrobiums, to mention only one genus. While it is ideal as a medium for starting a small plant on its way, whether a seedling, meristem or propagation, once a root system is developed it should be put into a compound growing mix as already described. The reaction of sphagnum moss in bulk in pot sizes up to 10 and 15 centimetres is to compact under watering and fertilising into a sodden mass which is most unwholesome for roots. Orchids need food to grow and there is none at all in sphagnum moss or tap water.

For rejuvenating a damaged root system sphagnum moss is ideal even in such pot sizes as mentioned, but as a constant medium there is far too much scope for error in fertilising and watering epiphytic orchids.

The Three
Essentials

The three prime necessities of life for orchid plants, of course, are air, light and water. There must be a balance of these features. Too much light means too much evaporation and although epiphytic orchids inhabit three different sectors of the environment, in cultivation it is quite possible to find a reverse system more applicable, with a plant enjoying much brighter light than in its original habitat.

The light should be adjusted for epiphytes exactly the same as for cymbidiums and Slippers by shading with shade-cloth or painting the roof or by using a fibreglass or plastic tint to give all-year protection. A recommendation of a certain grade of shade-cloth is not possible, because for one genus it will be totally different as distance from the equator increases or decreases. The climate can be affected considerably, too, by the distance from the sea. Frequently quotes of so many foot-candles of light for different seasons are given, but these have very little to do with any other grower than the one who went to the trouble of measuring his or her own light intensities at such times of the year. Each grower must realise that his or her system is very much an individual thing modelled on a general set of rules and modified to suit.

Most glass-houses need a system of forced ventilation instead of relying on the opening and shutting of ventilators to create an air flow. Of all plants orchids are most demanding. Air flow is vital to them and it should be built into the growing area. For those fortunate people who grow their plants entirely outdoors there are no problems except in moist, humid, hot and still days, when the fungus infections permeating the air in the form of spores get a chance to settle and grow and set up decay problems in leaves and growths.

The best system is to build in one which allows the circulation sytem to take air from outside the growing area if enclosed in a glass-house or to have the capability to recirculate the air inside the growing area without admitting more. It can be done with either two fans or one, depending on the design. This is also illustrated in the photographs.

In closed cultivation like glass-houses, ventilators are essential and both lower and roof ventilators should be *open fractionally all the time*, more in warm weather than cold, even where forced air-flow systems are used such as fans or air conditioners.

Watering orchids is simplicity itself. Imagine the plants growing in the forests where they originated. Even if they are hybrids they possess the same characteristics. In the rainy season they all commence to grow. It usually occurs in the warmest part of the year, although there is no real difference in seasonal temperatures of some of the tropical countries. However, it is seasonal and spurs the orchids into growth.

This wet season may last as long as three months or more, or it may be divided into two distinct periods. As the rains diminish the plants are both maturing and in many instances commencing to flower. The flowers, if they are fertilised, set their seed pods and go into a dormant period. Each orchid genus has a different ripening period for the seed pods, but it coincides with the weather pattern and the seed pods burst and scatter their seed in the preliminaries to the wet season again. In the intervening period between the wet seasons the plants may become completely dry and dormant for months at times and suffer no harm because they are morphologically designed over millions of years to conform to the pattern.

In artificial cultivation all we can do is imitate to the best of our abilities the cycles nature imposes on the plants; and when it is realised that we tend to cram into our cultivation scheme so many different genera with so many different seasonal requirements, the complexities of orchid growing are apparent.

This may be overcome only by working at it and not trying to treat all the plants as though they all came from one strata in the forest, one altitude and one seasonal cycle. This can be done in a rather easy way provided we group only the plants accustomed to the temperature ranges of cool, warm and heat loving in their correct climates.

Going back to the root systems, the epiphytes should be given copious water in their growing period and then staged through what should be their semi-dormant or dormant period. This is where the closed bench with a 5 centimetre bed of absorbent material such as a 50/50 mix of sand and scoria or sand and other coarse aggregate shows its advantages. Throughout the period of dormancy the bench should be kept moist to wet all the time and the plants stood on it but not watered. The plants which need water during this period should be isolated out and given what they need. But regardless of the fact that the dormant plants are not watered for up to six months or more, they will stay plump and come to no harm.

The type of pots used in this system is immaterial, but if they are plastic they should have holes in the bottom of the pot as well as in the sides. If none are there when purchased they should be bored or burnt out with a hot iron. For some genera clay pots may be preferred, but a collection grown in the one glass-house or growing area should all be in the same type of pot.

In general watering principles, there is always a little indecision even with experienced growers and mistakes may be made. But it is advisable to water thoroughly each time and to let the plants almost dry out before again watering. Pot size has a great deal to do with the proper application of the process and they should be sorted out so that there is no confusion.

A great deal of consideration has been given to the merits or otherwise of what is known as overhead spraying or watering, which consists of turning a fine spray of water over the plants in their growing season. Generally it is sufficient to water the benches and the floor of a glass-house and leave the foliage of the plants dry. The natural evaporation of this moisture is sufficient to give the leaves all the humidity they need without actually spraying them. In some instances it is more beneficial to leave the foliage dry at all times but not to worry unduly if odd plants become accidentally 'drowned'.

The type of water is important and domestic supplies should pass as fit or unfit for orchids. In areas where chlorinated water is the only supply available a tank should be installed and rain-water used. It is almost certain that the orchids will do better if they are given water with a neutral or slightly acid reading on test. Alkalinity might suit a few genera, but a general collection would show poor results in growth and flowering and frequently a grower blames the potting material when the water is at fault.

Preparation of Potting Materials

'The symbiotic relationship between the roots of different orchids and the bark of trees in which they grow forms a most interesting study and the effort to collect from the forest and establish plants in our garden trees becomes at times a problem. On certain trees the plants languish for no apparent reason, in others the results are most gratifying.'

Those words were written by James Clay Harvey in Mexico in 1906 and they stemmed from a wealth of experience in growing orchids, first under glass in California and until his death in later years growing them under entirely natural conditions in his Mexican garden. Harvey was a tropical agricultural consultant and his method of growing orchids as garden plants attached to trees has encouraged many others to do likewise.

Growing epiphytes has changed over the period of their artificial culture from the original moss and peat-turf mixtures to fern fibres from the roots of osmunda and similar ferns in a full circle to a material on which they grew naturally.

It was not the words of Harvey which led me to try growing orchids naturally, nor was it from any knowledge of the bark of the casuarina or she-oak. It was, if anything, growing two or three plants on an apricot tree in a Melbourne suburb that led to my collection of some 400 to 500 plants of twenty-five-odd genera growing on casuarina trees near the sea on Westernport Bay, southern Victoria. It is a frost-free zone and it is impossible to convey even remotely the feeling one has on a spring morning walking about among the trees and looking at the flowering plants. It almost sounds and seems like an attack of romanticism in what is a very average and absorbing hobby.

The bark of various trees has become an almost universal orchid potting medium. At times used on its own, at others combined with other materials, it is one of the most durable cultural aids ever devised. Not perfectly absorbent, it does not become waterlogged. The preparation of the material, however, is just as important as in the days of fibrous mixes and the grades used for various genera should be chosen with care.

Although sometimes available in graded sizes, it is mostly stocked in rough mixed sizes. A series of sieves should be made or bought to grade it, starting off with flywire to get rid of the dust. The other meshes should be 4 millimetres, 7 or 8 millimetres and finally 10 millimetres, using the residue for larger plants and pots.

The grade of sieved bark used should be related to the size of the pots. For very small plants in tubes and pots the No. 1 size of 4 millimetres should be blended with dust-free particles from the flywire sievings which will pass through a 2 millimetres mesh commonly used in kitchenware, but not flywire.

For pots between 6 and 8 millimetres the next grade should be used and so on through the range of pot sizes. Rather than lay down a set of recommendations to govern the size of bark used, the grades should be related to the plants and pots which are being processed in what should be an obvious suitability.

The additives for a potting mix which are of the breakdown type should not be blended with the bark and drainage portion of the mix as the medium is made up. The bark and drainage material should be thoroughly mixed in proportions which will give good water clearance without appearing too arid soon after watering. Some growers use the bark unadulterated, but a little coarse sand, lacking other things such as charcoal or gravel, has a lot to recommend it.

The bark and gravel should be thoroughly hosed until quite wet then shovelled into a plastic bag, the neck tied and left to sweat for a couple of days. This should be done as a preliminary to repotting or potting new plants. When the potting mix is needed the bag should be emptied on to the path or wherever it is mixed and the peat-moss or peanut shells or leaf content added. The heap should be thoroughly mixed again and then bagged for another day or two before being used. As peanut shells are an unreliable inclusion because of mouldiness sometimes developing, it may be good procedure to wet them thoroughly and leave them for a few days to exhaust that trend.

If peat-moss is used it should be thoroughly broken down to almost powder form so that no lumps are left to form wet spots. Peanut shells are mostly dry when bought and they should be moistened as outlined in the previous paragraph. Leaf content should preferably include some twiggy material, particularly if oak leaves are used. While not the only leaves possible for a good mix, they are as good as may be had. The debate over using leaf 'mould' for orchids began about the year 1900 and it still goes on. But, depending on the style of culture applied and the 'intuition' of the user, it can be very good, particularly for things like odontoglossums and dendrobiums.

Whatever genus is grown, repotting into dry material has little to recommend it other than perhaps the easy way the material flows into the pots. But if the material is damp without being wet it flows nearly as well and the roots do not have to surrender up some of their moisture to the dry potting medium.

The preparation of mounts to which plants may be tied is much simpler, because this type of culture is applied only to plants from which it is desired that excess water flows away immediately. They do not have to be pre-damped or soaked, but may be used as needed. However, most growers will find it fitting to use a small pad of sphagnum moss and perhaps a little fibre if it is obtainable under the base of the attached plant to retain a little moisture and give the roots something through which to penetrate before attaching to their host slab.

Although some growers use wire and plastic ties and even string to attach plants in this way, nylon fishing line is considered by many growers to be best, as it may be undone when no longer needed and used over and over again, with none of the ill effects from some of the wires used.

It should be realised when using bark that it is sometimes unsuitable if artificial fertilisers are used; and if plants show the tendency for the roots to discolor or decay as they contact the bark, an immediate change should be made, the bark put out again to weather and a fresh start made. It is seldom possible for the character of such potting materials to alter in time for the plant to become vital again.

There are as many potting mixtures as there are orchid growers. Most growers are also inconsistent and vary their mixes from one plant to another as well as from one year to another. However, stability should be aimed at, with direct reference to any one of the three types of root systems outlined in the first section.

A very good starting point is to compound the type of mix which will shed

21

all the water poured through it, retaining just enough to leave the material moist to wet. Such a mix could be modelled on having one part of bark of a size consistent with the plant to be potted, half of one part of moisture-retaining and slow decay nature such as peanut shells or leaf content such as oak with some twig included and one part of purely drainage material such as gravel charcoal or scoria, again considering the type of orchid and the size pot into which it is proposed to put it.

It would be foolish to pot a fine-rooted orchid such as an odontoglossum, for instance, in a 10 centimetre pot using coarse potting materials. The material as well as the pot should be matched to both the root system and the nature of the orchid concerned. Most growers, beginners or experienced, can see at a glance what is needed.

The variation in mixes should be part of experience, so that if a mix appears unsuitable even after only a few weeks, a replacement should be made with a modified mix to take care of the undesirable features of the first one.

Charcoal should be tested for suitability rather than used without knowing anything about it. Stocks of potting materials should be built up some time before they are needed and a plant which is not too highly regarded used as the guinea pig. Mostly either gravel or red scoria is quite safe to use, but pine bark should be weathered or boiled before use.

For the second type of root system pot culture is not recommended. The plants should be mounted on small sections of branches of suitable trees, avoiding those such as pines, which exude aromatic resins. Oak, casuarina, even fruit tree prunings from apricots, plums or pears are also suitable. Weathered sections of hardwood are useful and less expensive than cork or tree-fern mounts.

These sections may be drilled and hung with a wire hook or they may be planted in pots with a base filling of 2 centimetre aggregate such as shown in the photographs. If a plant such as an oncidium or a Brazilian miltonia hybrid is cultivated, a thin section of tree-fern is perhaps more suitable than a wooden mount to allow portion of the fine roots to penetrate into the fern as well as allowing for the profuse aerial root system to choose the free air as the plant decides.

For the last group of aerial rooting plants such as vandas the coarsest of potting material is sufficient. It must serve two purposes — support for the plant by holding the base of the growth firm in the pot, even if a stake must also be inserted to assist, and also a source of plant food from absorption of water and nutrients and perhaps as a shelter for roots.

But again the material should be graded to suit the size of the pot and the type of plant growing in it. Some growers may prefer to use only chunks of bark and broken pot for filling, others use only coarse lumps of charcoal, and others again a mixture of decaying wood and charcoal or coarse bark. Decaying wood has an attraction for the coarser roots associated with completely aerial systems and its use may prevent the usual habit of such plants of sending out great lengths of exploratory roots searching out food sources. This is a habit particularly of vandas.

If these types of orchids are grown entirely outdoors, as they fequently are in climates which suit them, they should be given the benefit of immediate supplies of food in the rockeries or beds in which they are grown. In such natural conditions they also can withstand overwatering and overfeeding much better.

As much as possible these accommodations for plant root systems are illustrated.

In warmer areas, with high seasonal rainfall, on plants which may be exposed to it, or even under protecting roofing with open side ventilation through woven shade-cloths, most bark potting mediums may prove failures and harder material such as scoria should be blended with proved suitable additives. The grey scoria is inferior to the red type for this purpose as it has been found to develop undesirable mossy growth on the surface. The growth of this moss should be inhibited with weak solutions of sprays containing iron or the surface inch of the potting mix replaced with limestone chips or other rocky aggregate which does not encourage this mossy growth.

All soft additives should be eliminated from potting mediums in tropical climates and replaced with durable materials. The shells of Queensland nuts have been noted in the mixes favored by tropical and semi-tropical growers in some instances and the hardness and durability of these shells is well known. Charcoal has favor with most orchid growers, but it should be regarded as a blend material and not a base to which additives may or may not be made. While growers in cooler climates seek to retain humidity and moistness in potting mixes, the reverse should be adopted for tropical climates and all excess moisture given the chance to drain and evaporate away fairly quickly.

Fertilisers

Where weak solutions of liquid nutrients are mentioned they may be understood as comprising either organic derivatives as from animal or bird manures or seaweed derivatives; or they may be liquified, inorganic solutions of chemical compounds containing nitrogen, phosphorus, et cetera, which may be bought at most nurseries and garden supply shops. The chemical composition is usually given on the outside of the pack and generally speaking there is little or no difference between most of them. After a time experience and individual preferences may be worked out, but there is no necessity to keep to the one brand. A weak solution would be in the order of about one heaped teaspoon to about 20 litres of water. If liquid fertilisers such as Maxicrop or fish emulsion are used the water should be slightly discolored and no more. *Both these liquid fertilisers may be added to organic or inorganic nutrient liquids.*

Broken down further by another 10 litres of water, these liquid nutrients may be used constantly provided the plant is active in the growth stage, with no ill effects to either the plants or the potting material. Dormant plants or those in flower do not derive any benefit from applications of liquid or solid fertilisers, as in neither stage can any good effect be obtained by added fertilisers.

While some nurserymen recommend changing from one fertiliser to another to suit the plants in growing or maturing and flowering stages, such advice is best disregarded until sufficient growing experience lends confidence and judgment. All nutrient systems should be chosen to suit the climate and the style of growing of each individual and what suits one may not necessarily suit another.

Nutrient solutions derived from organic materials such as bird or animal manures should also be in weak forms and should not be used to take the place of correct growing procedures or flowering of plants. Forcing maximum efforts from plants by the use of fertilisers instead of good culture leaves a price to pay and it is usually the loss or severe retarding of plants.

Solid fertilisers are usually organic and are better suited to semi-terrestrial orchids such as cymbidiums and paphiopedilums. However, applications of blood and bone or hoof and horn fertiliser to epiphytes when they are in full growth may assist the plants, but should only be given if the liquid fertilisers are discontinued.

Some growers may work out systems based on slow-release fertilisers such as Mag-amp, Osmocote and other formulations, but a certain amount of care is needed if they are applied to orchids which go through periods of dormancy in their annual cycle. This is particularly applicable to epiphytes and an overloading of the potting material with a continuance of fertiliser release will quickly kill the dormant root system as well as souring the potting material as watering is tapered off.

A great amount of importance is attached to various minerals and elements by well-meaning scientific people who expect ordinary growers to follow some type of laboratory technique in their plant growing. Some of the 1950-80 literature is saturated with meaningless information on foot-candles of light and trace elements and things that never enter — and never could enter — the growing processes of those ordinary growers.

The basic information they seek is how to make the plants grow, how to make them flower and how to keep them growing and flowering. This is all bound up with simple formulations and the fertilisers needed to carry out all those functions are all available so easily. Blood and bone fertiliser is rich in phosphorus, iron and many other necessary elements, but most ordinary growers are apt to use it without noting in writing what they are doing or even marking the pots so treated. One of the easiest ways of doing this is to buy a packet of plastic toothpicks in three or more colors and stick them in the pots as they are top-dressed — red for one month, green or yellow for the next application and so on, putting down in a small notebook, without fail, what has been done or not done.

If nutrient fertilisers are used, they, too, should be noted. Most of them are rich in nitrogen and will balance blood and bone. Any other important element like magnesium may be added by buying a packet of Epsom salts and adding as much as will cover a one cent piece to a 12 litre bucket of half or quarter strength Aquasol or Garden Gold or whatever fertiliser is used. For the plants in cymbidium-type mix the best fertiliser is a large teaspoon of hoof and horn fertiliser applied and worked into the top of the potting material in October and again in early March.

The primary lesson to be learned in potting methods as well as fertilising is that if a plant is forced to do more than it normally is able to cope with in ordinary seasons and ordinary methods there is a price to pay in possible disease and eventual plant loss.

Pests and Diseases

Generally a clean glass-house means a clean orchid collection, although there is no point in going to extremes and trying to sterilise it like an operating theatre. All rubbish should be kept off the floor, particularly dead leaves and plant offcuts and empty pots. Leaves which drop from plants should be gathered and put into a bucket or tin in the glass-house and cleared out every few weeks. Unnatural mosses should be cleared from places where they should not be growing, as they add to the cover for pests.

Pests which infest glass-houses are sometimes hard to control because they are seasonal and frequently damage plants or flowers before they are noticed. Anywhere there is moisture and decay, a natural state of things in most glass-houses, woodlice, or slaters as they are generally known, usually manage to find their way into what to them is a congenial climate and a source of food. Their diet includes root tips if they are available and this frequently halts plant development while the plant seals off the affected area and commences a root point from the remnants of the old one. It seems that unless roots of most epiphytes are a certain length it is impossible for plants to do this and a new start has to be made from the rhizome.

Slaters do eat roots, despite what some people imagine. The best way to control them is to exclude them if possible by flywiring ventilators and all low openings in the walls of glass-houses and sealing all those cracks that develop or were part of the building operation.

Moving into the glass-house, the benches should be kept clear of the walls and plants arranged so that the leaves do not touch the walls. The benches should be based on single pillars set into the earth after the style of the illustration in the section on glass-houses. Alternatively, brick pillars may be built to take the cross-members supporting the benching. These posts or pillars should be painted with a lasting contact poison such as DDT, which will quite effectively stop the woodlice from reaching plant level. At the very least it will minimise the possibility of the pests becoming as numerous as they sometimes seem to be. There are few baits which are fully effective against them, but if any are available they should occasionally be scattered around the floor to make sure the slaters are fed on the right diet.

Other mobile pests like ants, cockroaches and various beetles also infest glass-houses if given the opportunity. Ants are among the worst because they bring in 'outsiders' like scale and possibly aphids and implant them on sappy stems and foliage. Although there is a great deal of prejudice about using various poisons in the open, where their effect is sometimes drastic, there should be no compunction about using them in enclosed spaces like glass-houses. Dieldrin should be used to control ants in the glass-house and also outside if their nests can be found. It should be mixed at the recommended strength and poured down the holes leading into the nests.

Ants use glass-houses as hatcheries for their young and it is common to see long lines of them carrying embryos or eggs in their mandibles. This is just as bad a habit to let go as the transference of pests from outside. With adoption of bark as potting material instead of the old fibrous filling the problem is partly solved. But they still get into pots through drainage slits. The transfer line of ants should be stopped with sprays outside and inside and if pots are infested they should be immersed to their full depth in a bucket of weak Dieldrin solution for at least ten minutes. The ants which surface should be sprayed with an insecticide. Slat baskets or other containers suspended in the glass-house should be watched over the summer months for ants. They work very quickly and in a couple of hours by sheer numbers they will transport some thousands of eggs and embryos into a hatching area.

The pests which ants bring into the glass-house are usually scale insects, which they place on the sappiest parts of the plant when they are quite young. Scale insects are also mobile at a certain stage of their lives and may enter on their own. As scale of all kinds sucks the sap from the leaves and perhaps the flower stems of orchids they digest it and exude a sweet substance on which the ants feed. If this substance settles on leaves of orchids and other plants it eventually develops moulds of various kinds which may be as damaging to the plants as scale.

The best way is to keep the ants and scale outside, but once noticed every plant should be examined, particularly underneath the leaves and protected spots like the interior of growth sheaths, to find the infestations. Infested plants may be dipped or sprayed with preparations available at all nurseries and plant distributors. Names do not mean much as regards proprietary lines, but if a vendor or shopkeeper is asked for a spray to deal with scale it will be supplied.

Some growers have a regular spraying program which is carried out seasonally, whether pests are present or not, but one important point is to follow up the first application with another about a fortnight later.

Aphids usually appear in the early to late spring and may enter a glass-house unnoticed because they are so small. They also make for the sappiest parts of plants such as flower stems, flower buds and new growths. They will also lodge in spots where they are not sprayed with a hose and develop rapidly by budding and division rather than by the usual process of egg to young. When they infest flower stems or buds the usual insecticides cannot be used because they distort the flower parts and cause other damage. A solution of 50/50 methylated spirit and water should be used as a fine spray with a hand sprayer, or it may be painted on with a small brush. Again it should be a habit to go over the plants again a week later to make sure the stems and buds or growths are clean. A cheap hand sprayer charged with this methylated spirit mix should be kept handy all through the year because it is effective with all sorts of pests, particularly mealy bug. Most growers manage to keep this pest out of their glass-houses, but once it enters some months may be necessary to get rid of it completely. Where orthodox sprays are useless because of the outer coating of the insect, methylated spirit penetrates this armor quite well.

Proper care of glass-house plants, including things like anthuriums and ferns as well as orchids, should include a regular spray program at least twice a year in spring and summer rather than winter or autumn. The type of spray should be systemic — that is, one which is absorbed by the plant itself. These sprays have the reputation, if not complete ability, to render the sap poisonous to such things as scale.

Most sprays are dangerous, but not necessarily the vehicles for a lot of the panic statements so frequently put out about them. They should be used with care, in the same way as other poisons are used, with a good deal of care used to see that skin surfaces are not contacted and thoroughly washing the hands and face when the job is done, regardless of contact or not.

The flow through the glass-house of a stream of air is one of the necessities for plant health and this stream, whether induced by a fan, which is the best, or simply the natural flow through a low ventilator, may be used with good effect to keep the glass-house relatively free of all insect pests. Shellguard pest strips fixed where the air flows past them do a very quiet and efficient job of keeping the pests under control. They should be fixed where they will not become wet when hosing or damping down, such as under the benches near a ventilator; or if a fan is used, fastened in the air stream. A glass-house of 4 to 5 metres long by 3 metres wide should have three pest strips fixed in various positions and larger glass-houses will take more than that number. Most pests come in through the ventilators and these should be flywired where possible in areas where pests are a problem.

Most diseases which affect epiphytic plants are virus or fungus induced. For the first there is little chance of curing it and there is no use getting emotional about it if a plant is noticed in someone else's collection. The probabilities are that everyone has plants which they know or do not know have virus. It is sometimes there but invisible.

Recognition of virus in epiphytic orchids is not easy and it is frequently visible more in the flowers than the foliage. Streaky color in the leaves of plants such as cattleyas may be noted, but if the flowers are also streaky or have odd colored areas in the petals and sepals it could be almost certainly caused by virus. Occasionally the leaves also show black necrotic patches and if it occurs regularly in new growths the verdict is the same, and plants which become virus carriers should be put in the incinerator and not allowed to infect the rest of the collection or sold off cheaply, as so frequently happens.

Brown rot is not nearly so prevalent in epiphytic orchids as in cymbidiums and it is usually the result of poor ventilation and high humidity. Even in cold conditions where brown rot symptoms are frequently noted good air circulation will prevent it starting. If it appears in a glass-house two things should be done. The ventilation should be improved and the interior of the roof sprayed with an anti-fungus preparation, of which several are available. It is usually the same infection which attacks stone fruit and this occurs in high humidity and still air.

Slugs and snails are always likely to infest glass-houses and orchid collections because they are mobile like the ants and can be controlled only with baits. These should be frequently scattered about the floor of the glass-house and one or two left on the surface of potting material where they will be the first food contacted by slugs or snails. Protection should start outside the glass-house, however, and all rubbish and objects which will give them daytime shelter should be kept cleared away. With use of plastic pots the storage problem is much easier than for clay pots. Stacks of pots should be baited for the odd snails which may find a place there. Ants also find their way into pot stacks to use the shelter as incubators for their eggs.

It is remarkable how easy it is to control all the pests which threaten glass-house plants if something regular is done about it. An hour once a week should cover the usual sized collection and it is always best to prevent rather than cure. For some a year is a long time to wait for a plant to flower again and for many orchid growers it may also be a chance of flowering a well-grown plant that may take up to four or five years to reproduce. It is too bad that so much work should go to feed some insects or an odd slug or snail.

*Cattleya intermedia
alba*

Odontioda margia

The Glass-house

After building six glass-houses and growing orchids in five of them for thirty-five years, they were left behind in a retirement move to a coastal home.

Sooner or later all orchid growers come to the conclusion that they need a glass-house. 'I' is not a word I like using, but in relation to orchids it has become a necessity in this short resume on glass-houses. After eight years of growing orchids entirely outdoors in southern Victoria eventually a glass-house became a necessity for me, too. Although much of the collection of some 500 plants growing on the trees and in natural forks and bases comprised Australian orchids, included in the miscellancy were zygopetalums, cattleyas, laeliocattleyas, laelias, sophronitis and hybrids from that genus, masdevallias, bulbophyllums, odontoglossums, epidendrums, lycastes, altogether numbering some twenty-six genera, all of which flowered in those conditions. The need for a glass-house became apparent as the flowers opened and became weather spotted or battered by the sometimes high winds. It was all a lot of fun and proved that orchids can be grown without all the protection that is commonly thought to be necessary.

I took the easy way out and bought a prefabricated, packaged unit 3.17 metres long, 2.55 metres wide and 2.27 metres high at the ridge. In the old measurements it is 8 feet by 10 feet. As a 'starter' for any orchid grower it is about right because it can accommodate enough plants to keep him or her busy and happy. These prefabricated glass-houses are made by several manufacturers and no preference can be expected one over another.

Although such prefabricated glass-houses are very suitable for cooler and temperate climates, it is possible that they would be a little too much of enclosures for tropical or semi-tropical climates without some modification. The style of glass-houses should change for those climates into roofed protection and almost open sides that give good air flow through and over the plants in periods of high humidity. This means that in northern parts of Australia a design along those lines would be better than prefabricated units and this allows for different, easy construction and different roofing material.

Experience of outdoor growing, in whatever climate, soon shows the advantages of roofed, protective structures into or under which plants may be moved as the flowers open. Fading is controlled and provided humidity is kept low there is little marking of flowers. Where possible slightly lower temperatures than the plant goes through in developing its buds should be provided for fully opened flowers.

Before ordering or buying or building a glass-house a grower should have some idea about the main genus which will occupy it, the area available for it and, most important, the aspect. Epiphytic orchids need fairly bright light, even if it must be stifled by painting or shade-cloth in the brighter periods of the year. If, say, cattleyas are the intended plants, they should preferably get morning sun if it is not possible to trap sunlight for them all day. Their leaves should thus be light green instead of dark green, the growths stout and not long or spindley.

As illustrated in the first book, glass-houses can be built to take advantage of natural outlook. The erection of a prefabricated unit is not beyond the capabilities of either male or female growers, as they are delivered with comprehensive instructions; and although two hands can do it quite well, four are much better. The photographs and explanations tell the story much more clearly than words can.

Before looking at the advantages of a prefabricated glass-house consideration of alternatives for warmer climates should be thought about. Treated pine in these structures will cut the cost of galvanised piping, which may have an advantage in durability. Treated pine posts and timbers may be used for roofing and fastening fibreglass or corrugated plastic sheeting is simpler with wood. Its use need not be restricted to warm climates, as a very good glass-house may be built using double walls of fibro-cement sheet and either plastic or fibreglass for the light section. If cost is a consideration, put it on paper and possibly this type of plant shelter will be found cheaper than a prefabricated unit of the same size. In the warm areas shade-cloth may be used for some or all of the sides because it is only necessary to break the force of the wind and a good draught of air will flow under the roof.

The prefabricated glass-house photographed and described is an Eden, but there are several makes available, mostly advertised in gardening magazines and orchid publications. They are on an almost equal footing as far as price is concerned, but let us look at the good points of an Eden structure.

It is fabricated from corrosion-resistant aluminium, but there is no life period which may be put on it. It is possible to buy sections which may be fitted to the original and within reason there is no limit to the length which may be constructed. The end wall may be moved out or left intact with a doorway between the sections. The sliding door will not fit into the addition and must be removed and the extended structure closed off between sections with plastic drops if this is needed.

The glass is fitted into the framing on a plastic strip seal and held in place with spring clips, which make it very simple to put in or replace if broken. It is also pre-cut to size and the clips holding the overlap of the sheets are stainless steel.

The ridge is slotted to take aluminium framing to hold a tubular section over which shade-cloth may be drawn. The guttering, although small, takes clips to hold similar tubular sections over which the shade-cloth is tied down to clips which fit under the base of the structure. The shade-cloth may be taken off in seasons when not wanted and rolled up and stored.

Insulation may be bought with the assembly to tape into the interior. It is air bubble type and the sheets will not be very easy to put up and take off once the glass-house is filled. However, if fitted correctly it may cut the heating bill considerably.

Various extras may be bought with the unit, including misting equipment, automatic watering devices and heating units.

The shelving or benching which may be purchased is optional, but it may be better to follow a similar system to that photographed. If it is decided to purchase the shelving it may be modified to suit orchids; and for anyone not able to fabricate benches or do heavy jobs, the total kit provides a solution to what otherwise may be a problem so great that orchid growing is almost ruled out. The total installation in 1980 prices for an 8 × 10 would be somewhere in the vicinity of $1000. It is not competitive with a home-built brick structure.

There is a ventilator in each side of the roof and in all sizes including and above the 8 × 10 a louvre is provided for fitting into one side. The ventilators may also be fitted with automatic opening and closing devices, but for general orchid growing it is better to manipulate these by hand — open always a certain amount and more in summer than in winter.

As the glass is pre-cut and packed, fitting it into the frames does not pose a problem. But as usual with all prefabricated units, no matter what they are, certain frustrating moments crop up, particularly when there are not enough fingers on a hand or when there are not enough hands on one body. It is useless quoting prices, but there is little doubt that it would be far cheaper to design and build a glass-house than to buy and erect a prefabricated unit. However, once a foundation is in, an Eden glass-house of the size quoted could be easily erected in a day. It is just as easily dismantled and removed.

Let us get on with it.

A good foundation is necessary. Some prefabricated glass-houses are advertised with wooden bases and the Eden is no exception. It offers treated pine bases cut to size for all its modules, made up from 15 × 5 centimetre timber. However, a concrete base is far more permanent. The one illustrated is 25 centimetres deep and 10 centimetres wide, capped by 5 × 5 centimetre treated pine, which is fixed to the concrete by bolts inserted when it was just poured. The better the base the less likelihood of pests like slugs or slaters getting inside to work their way through the plants. It will be noted, also, that water has been brought inside the base before it was poured, the pipe standing just inside where the door will open.

Instead of being confronted with a mass of metal when the ties about the packing case are removed, the framing is bundled in separate sections. Despite this, it could be expected that in many instances a sense of bewilderment is the first thing that overtakes the builder. A flat area where the pieces may be laid out is most welcome and in this way they will soon fall into place and be bolted up like this end wall. The bolts slide into slots in the sections and a good fitting spanner should be bought or borrowed to tighten the nuts, both of them also aluminium. In the door end, also on the rafters in the roof, I found it a good idea to slide one or two extra bolts into the slots. They later became most useful and as there are plenty provided they do not run short. The instruction sheets are clear and carry illustrations of the respective sections.

33

Once the plates to hold the walls and ends are installed the sections may be lifted about freely. The wall section is the first and if an extra pair of hands are not available a prop will hold it erect or nearly so while one side of the end wall is attached to it and this is repeated with the other side. A certain amount of unbolting and bolting up again seems to occur, however well the erection is planned. It may also be an advantage if a light tie of twine is used to hold the sections in place until they can be bolted together instead of bolting them in the first instance. Do not tighten the nuts all the way on to the bolts, so that a certain amount of flexibility is retained to move the sections a little to pick up the alignment of connecting bolts. Once the two wall sections and the two end walls are joined the structure should be checked for squareness, which can be found by measuring from corner to corner diagonally. If the structure is out of square a great amount of difficulty will be found in fitting the glass. The diagonal measurements should be accurate to less than 2 millimetres. It may be necessary to adjust the wooden bearers on the concrete or the base plates if they are put in.

Once the frame is squared up the rest of the roof is assembled and the diagonal braces put in. The whole thing is so accurately drilled that everything fits perfectly if the rules and instructions are followed. Once everything is checked the spanner should be put on every nut, and see that they are tight without applying too much pressure. Being aluminium it is possible to strip the threads easily if they are forced. At this stage of erection it is best to decide on the height and size of the benches and put at least the start of uprights and bearers in place as shown in the photograph. The glass-house having only a 2.27 metre height (just over 7 feet), the benches should be reasonably low so that taller plants are not too close to the glass. No matter what type of house is put up, as much of the interior work as possible should be done before the glass is put in place.

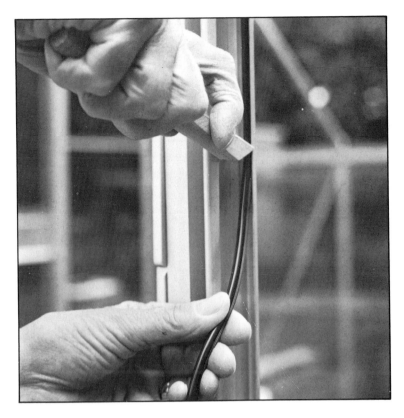

The next stage is getting ready for the glass. The sealing strips are inserted in the slots provided in the uprights and roof sections. This plastic strip, if inserted in warm weather is inclined to stretch as it is inserted and should not be cut into lengths which do not go completely from end to end of the slot without stretching. If gaps are left at the bottom pests may find their way easily through the thin slots between the glass and the bearers. A small wooden tool is included with the assembly to make insertion easy. Make a final check to see that the insert is right to the bottom, even if it may be a little short at the top.

The glass is packed into cases which are quite heavy to handle and difficult to move about. After delivery they should be kept dry and not allowed to stand out in the weather. Once wet the sheets tend to stick together and become even more difficult to separate. The lower sheet of each section should be stood in position against its bearers with their plastic strips and wire clips inserted each side to hold it in place. It may be found that the wire clips need a little adjustment or bend to make them fit firmer in their grooves. Once in, clips are placed on the top edge of the sheet and the second sheet stood in these clips and again wired into place. From then on it is progressive and easy; if the structure has been properly squared the roof glass fits in easily, but if it is out of square the strut and rafter screws may have to be slackened to align the rafters correctly. It may be best to do the roof first. In Eden packaging a dozen or so more wires would have improved final fixing of the glass.

Complete with door and shade-cloth in place, the glass-house is ready for occupation. The second problem with the Eden may be found in fitting the door and it is almost certain that some help would be needed with it. But again it is all accurate and bolts together easily. On a normal glass-house a hinged door would be fitted, but this sliding door is fitted with weather and draught strips and is airtight when closed. The bench on each side is an island type, with no connection to the walls so that pests cannot crawl up and on to the plants. Only three uprights are used, but they are heavy to take the type of bench. The trees which shade this glass-house are deciduous, so that in winter full sunlight enters it. In positioning a glass-house, surrounding trees should be considered and if they throw dense or permanent shade throughout the year some other place should be sought.

This is what is known as a closed bench. It is built up with 5 × 5 centimetre treated pine on the large bearers shown in the preceding photograph and the top is fibro-cement sheet, the edging is fibro-cement corner strapping and the depth of bedding 4 centimetres. The bedding is made up of equal parts of scoria and sand. It is rough and holds a lot of moisture. The bench runs the full length of the glass-house and the path between it and the bench on the other side is about 45 centimetres (about 18 inches) wide. The path may be solid or screenings retained between two treated pine edgings put down on the floor and held in place with treated pine or red-gum pegs.

For some orchids an open slat type bench like that in the foreground is better than a closed bench. The construction is the same as for a closed bench as indicated here but on this side there is no scoria and sand covering on the closed section. At each end of this bench an upright of 4 centimetre pipe is dug into the ground and a length clipped to them just underneath the glass and level with the front of the bench, from which plants may be hung. The roof would not stand this hanging treatment. The floor on each side of the path has been covered with a 5 centimetre deep layer of buzzer chips from treated pine, which is as durable as the material from which it came. Ordinary wood chips decay quickly, but bark chips may be used as substitute for the treated buzzer chips, the general idea being to keep down weed or other unwanted growth under the benches.

The glass-house complete with heater and air system. In the upper right-hand corner of the glass-house a fan has been installed which throws a draught of air diagonally across the roof toward the far corner. The unit attached to the lower left-hand corner contains an air conditioner which has had the heater side isolated and put through a thermostat which cuts it in at 10 degrees Celsius and cuts out when the glass-house reaches 12 degrees. The air unit of the conditioner is operating continuously and forces air into the glass-house through the large plastic pipe visible through the glass. This pipe has air vents in the opposite side which throw a constant stream of air across the floor of the glass-house and so across the slat bench, which is set only 30 centimetres above the floor. The unit is one of the smallest made, usually supplied for caravans, but it is adequate for the job to which it has been adapted. It has been boxed for protection and also so that the outside entry for air may be blocked off and air taken from a duct entry from the glass-house. It is very efficient.

Automation

Within reason automation is a very handy system for looking after glass-house plants when the grower is unable to give them daytime care. The system is not altogether satisfactory for orchids because several genera prefer that the leaves remain dry most of the time, day and night. For most epiphytes like cattleyas and dendeobiums, laelias and many other genera it is an ideal way to provide humidity and thorough watering at set intervals. Only at one stage does the system break down — it is unable to cope with weather changes and the need to cut out overhead misting or watering of plants. Even this may be allowed for by inserting an overrider switch to operate when the temperature drops below a set figure.

As a substitute for the personal touch all automation is found wanting when growing a mixed collection of orchids. A great deal of individual care is needed with plants which do not all grow and flower at the same time. However, even this can be controlled in a fashion, as will be seen in an analysis of the system. The type illustrated and all similar systems were designed primarily for use in propagating houses where all types of plants are raised and has not been specifically designed for growing orchids. It does have some advantages, however, which will be explained in the illustrations.

But before turning to them, there are some other things to consider. A certain amount of automation is used in other stages of orchid culture which are not illustrated in this section.

It seems obvious that in some ways we must turn back the clock to the old-fashioned construction techniques which integrated more closely the living areas and the glass-house, with a domestic section once known as a conservatory which was sometimes warmed by hot-water pipes distinct from the real domestic arrangement. Based on a similar style, this could be developed as an integrated unit utilising the same heating equipment.

Rising costs of energy sources, particularly for heating, leave little comparative difference in cost between oil, gas and electricity. The most important feature associated with their use is the amount of wasted energy which is exhausted through vents or flues when using gas or oil and the amount of energy wasted with electric heating from a basic cold stage.

Propane gas, that is bottled gas, offers an inducement over the use of other heat sources because it may be burnt inside the glass-house without producing toxic fumes. The by-product is largely carbon dioxide, which is a basic plant food source. This system has been freely used in orchid growing over many years and burners were developed for this type of heating. It has the real advantage that there is very little heat loss in a properly constructed growing system, particularly in the small to medium range. There are distinct advantages in using such a system as a ground-level heater to warm a closed bench for growing genera which need higher than normal temperatures. Automation may not be as easily applied to this form of heater for obvious reasons, but a low-consumption setting for a controlled ignition from a pilot jet could probably be arranged through a thermostat. A certain amount of individuality would emerge in such a system.

Natural gas or coal gas cannot be burnt in glass-houses because of the toxic fumes generated in the process. This means that some form of heat exchange such as heating circulating water would be needed or dry-heat ducting installed with the waste gases exhausted at some point through the sides or roof. Both systems are predesigned to waste a large proportion of the heat generated and thus become most uneconomical. In addition to this, dry-heat systems need a humidifier to maintain the correct atmosphere and this would be an added cost. Automation of such a system, however, would be no more difficult than for any other type. Such a dry-heat system was illustrated in *Growing Orchids, Book One.*

Oil heating annually becomes more expensive and the only way in which this may be counteracted on economy grounds is to make the initial planning part of the domestic establishment and installation. It is far easier in a new design than trying to modify existing domestic heating appliances to include a glass-house as an afterthought. There are several American designs for such a plan and they have been illustrated at times in orchid publications.

Most oil heaters work on forced draught principles, whether heating water or air and the heat loss in the flue is one of the bugbears that has not been realistically tackled. It seems inconceivable that some effort has not been made to include a copper coil heat transfer system in flue construction to use this enormous wastage.

Electricity is without doubt the cleanest and most effective heating medium in at least one respect — it is the most easily automated. There are two ways in which it may be used, first as directly applied interior units and second as a prewarmer for circulated air. It is impossible to say which is best because one form or another may be suited to different glass-houses. For small glass-houses, however, the air circulation form would appear to be best, with enough flexibility to grow all genera. Another form of electrical heating is to feed power into heating cables immersed in a gravel or sand bed on a closed bench, but probably this would be a little more expensive than air heating.

It should be noted that while gas and oil are more suitable for cooler climates, electric installations are more economical in climates where the need is occasional when temperatures lapse below recommended minimums. Such systems are easily controlled with sensors and thermostats.

Automation of light control is occasionally discussed as though it is one of the necessities for good growing, but unless orchid growing is to be a scientific project there is little use for it in the changing weather patterns to which normal plants become accustomed.

Air flow, on the contrary, is one of the necessities frequently overlooked. It is best installed as a permanent fixture independent of ventilators, which may be controlled to close down to a fractional opening but never tightly shut.

There is no end to the amount of automation and conversion which may be introduced into orchid growing, with the limiting horizon, of course, the cost factor weighed against the economies achieved in energy costs. An estimate, to quote a rough-and-ready figure, of $1000 to electrically automate and integrate a glass-house system should be offset against a fuel or energy cost escalation over a reasonable period. The initial cost may be high, but if the sum can be offset against production or savings in running the glass-house it should be adopted. The alternative seems to be to abdicate from orchid growing or commence growing less demanding genera and to expect less than first quality flowers.

The following system is designed for only one medium in cultivation, that of watering. If the others are thought about, the various relevant authorities should be consulted. It may be best, at that, to slightly discount their claims for performance in the various equipment.

The first picture shows the control panel, which covers several functions. Beginning at the left-hand side, the large control disc with its pins is almost self-explanatory. By using the small knob at the lower edge of the disc the system may be operated manually at any time. If the disc is used, it is divided into four periods of the 24-hour day. If the pins are left in the disc the system will operate and water the plants every two hours; if the pins are taken out the system will still move around the clock but will miss the period for which the pin is missing. A setting mark is almost obscured by the shadow of the small disc pins.

The small disc indicates a period of fourteen days and there is a small setting mark at the lower edge which allows the day to be set for commencement. If a pin is removed the system will be inoperative on that day. If it is to operate every second day then alternate pins will be left in or removed.

The four levers at the top of the instrument control the duration of the spray operation. The levers may be set to operate for prearranged periods of 30 seconds, 60 seconds or full on, which will mean a continuous spray for the period determined on the larger disc and for the days set on the smaller disc. Any of the levers may be positioned in the off setting and that section of the line does not receive any water. In this instance line 1 is set for 30 seconds, line 2 is off, line 3 is for 15 seconds and line 4 is off.

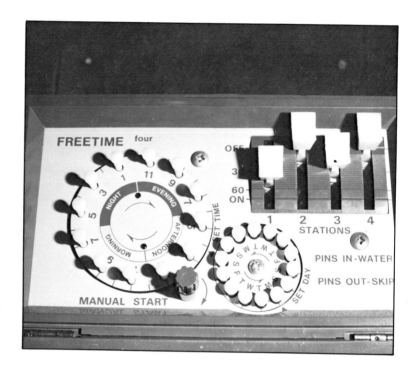

The second picture illustrates the operative part of the system as distinct from the electrically set controls. The system has four electrically operated valves to which wires run from the control panel. The water is supplied to four distinct prearranged lines which may contain any number of outlets within the capacity of the supply. There are three control gate valves. One allows flow direct to the outlets, the other two control the passing of the supply through a tank containing a nutrient mixture which is proportioned into the outlets operating. There is no way of closing off any section of the outlets so that one or more does not get nutrient, except by using the levers on the control panel and cutting out lines.

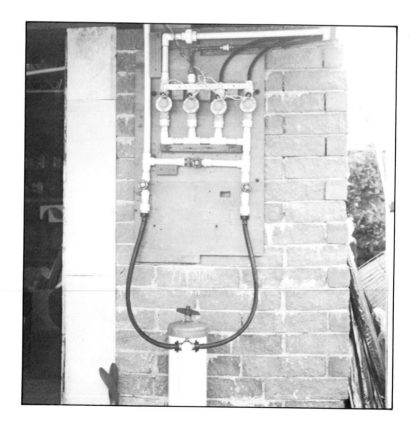

The use of plastic water piping has made the job a lot easier for ordinary people and provided a water outlet is available the job may be done by a handy man or woman. The black plastic tubing also simplifies the job and makes installation flexible and easy. The parts spread out on the two hands comprise nearly all that are necessary. The 'T' junction allows a change in direction while allowing a flow to continue on to another section. The large threaded piece is an adaptor which fits common 1.27 centimetres (½ inch) pipe threads from the main supply. The bend also allows a change of direction without kinking the tubing. The two nipples are a common small misting jet and a nipple set on a boomerang-shaped base which may be fastened in a certain position to direct the spray where it is wanted. The small plain nipple, if the pipe happens to get a twist, may send the spray to a point that is useless. In picture no. 4 the various pieces are shown inserted into the tubing. It may be necessary to heat the tubing and the part in hot water to get a joint and it may also be necessary to put a clip around the pipe to prevent it from being forced out by water pressure.

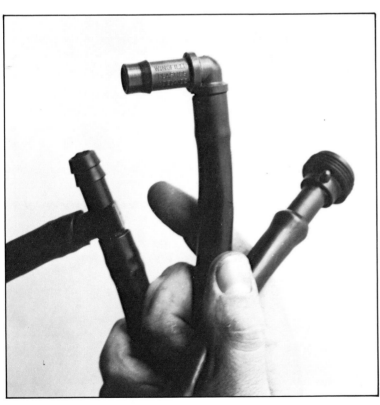

Pictures nos. 5 and 6 show the use to which the boomerang-shaped nipple is put. The point on the 'V' is used to penetrate the plastic tubing with a hole of the correct diameter to take the thread moulded on the end of the nipple. Either a plain nipple may be used at any point or a boomerang-shaped fitting to use as a fixing point. Plastic tubing is usually recommended by the unit manufacturers and the whole thing may be bought fairly readily from suppliers of irrigation and humidifying equipment.

The heart and soul of the unit, of course, is the electrical timing device. While it has its uses, such a system should be carefully considered. It is not by any means the whole answer to watering orchids and is simply ancillary equipment to do some of the work normally undertaken during the day which, for various reasons, it is not possible to do manually. It also is better used on a single genus of orchids. It could be invaluable for cymbidium culture, cattleya growing or the propagation and growing of small seedlings, particularly if they are grown in large numbers.

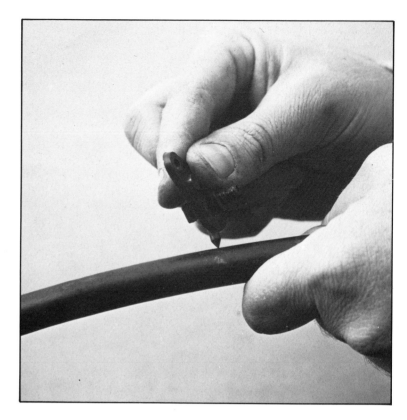

For small batches the simpler system shown in the pictures nos. 7 and 8 are much more satisfactory. The seedlings are picked out from flasks or other containers into small ice-cream trays full of sphagnum moss, preferably growing moss, enclosed in plastic bags and left to their own devices for four or five weeks. After that time they should be given fresh air by opening the bag during the day and closing it at night. The internal moisture in the bag should be maintained and after about two months the seedlings should have developed new roots and be ready for handling and benching in a group on their own. At this stage, if they have been handled in the correct season, they should be capable of absorbing all the moisture that spray systems can give them at appropriate intervals.

Some seedlings will not take this treatment and must be hand reared right to flowering stage, as the foliage, however durable and clean on the original species such as odontoglossums and miltonias, to mention only two, is not able to stand excessive moisture or even damping down in some glass-houses.

Cultivation
Methods

Some epiphytic orchids are unsuitable as pot plants and over the course of time several methods of cultivating them have been thought up. In the literature of the days of the 1820 to 1900 period many growers, as distinct from the owners of glass-houses, took the trouble to find out how epiphytic orchids grew and went to some further trouble devising ways of containing the plants while giving the root systems fairly free running to enter the potting material or to become completely aerial.

Little has changed from those first early methods, which used slat basket-like containers, sections of suitable trees, clay pots with holes in the sides as well as the base, and even woven willow baskets with few canes or withes in the sides. As long as the receptacle was capable of holding some form of growing material it was used. In addition, it was found that some epiphytic orchids grew and flowered much better when they were suspended in the air rather than grown on a bench.

In all the time elapsed since those first efforts at improving on original destructive orchid growing, only two outstanding changes occurred. First was introduction of plastic pots, second the abandonment of fibre as a growing medium and adoption of various barks for the purpose. The shape of pots has not changed, but the production costs for clay pots have soared so high that few growers now use them. Most in use are very old, some which survived being at least 100 years old and well cared for in consequence. It is always a debatable point among growers of various genera whether the plastic pot or the clay pot has advantages from the point of view of culture. It can be settled easily if the view is adopted that it is the grower who makes a success or not of either form of pot.

While some orchids seem to like a potting or mounting system which gives the roots a great amount of freedom, others seem to prefer the confined space of a pot and not too large at that. Many dendrobiums, if put into too large a receptacle, seem to either remain static or decline and it is the root system development which dictates this. All epiphytes grow a proportion of their roots with a propensity to cling to surfaces, which must be attractive to the roots in the first place. If such a satisfactory contact is made the root immediately develops an underside adapted to clinging while the upper or exposed surface of the root remains natural. A phalaenopsis root or a cattleya root illustrates this very well.

If the receptacle is too large or the potting medium uncongenial the roots do not find a satisfactory surface on which the underside can form and cling or the potting medium is such that the tips die off and do not grow out far enough to reach the side of the receptacle to fulfil their function. The result is an unsatisfactory growth pattern and a similar flowering pattern. If anything could be said in favor of clay pots as against plastic pots it is on this point. The underside clinging surface of roots forms much more readily on clay pots than on the smooth non-porous plastic pots.

Classifying plants according to their habits should not confine a whole genus to a certain way of potting or mounting. Some laelias are quite at home in pots, an instance being *Laelia gouldiana*, which may also be grown attached to a slab of cork or section of a tree branch. The orchid in illustration no. 1 is *Laelia rubescens* and although mounted on a slab of tree-fern, which some orchids find compatible, very little of the root system has been attracted to it and remains aerial. No reason for this was apparent except that the fern was unsuitable for this particular plant; perhaps too acid but hardly too alkaline. It takes little variation to turn the roots away from a host.

Experience with a certain type of mount is not always a good guide for its future use because what may suit one genus may not suit another. As mentioned earlier in the book, each orchid has its own particular host tree or rock surface in a particular environment. Having proved that laelias like the casuarina as a host, it was decided to use this medium and to divide the plant as it was growing away from each side. Instead of pruning the root system, as it was not being put into a pot to deteriorate further, it was left intact and bedded in the small pieces of osmunda fibre which had been used as backing for the plant base. No roots, having once proliferated in the air, will grow or survive if put into a container such as a pot.

The two sections of the laelia attached to pieces of casuarina, which has a rough bark. While the division on the left has the most root, it is not indicative of the root system of this laelia grown in this fashion. After a year or two the root system will grow only as long and as dense as fulfils the needs to feed and anchor the plant. The roots had to be more numerous on the fern mount as they depended more on absorption from the atmosphere than on contact with a host which the plant disliked. Sections of wood or cork on which similar plants are mounted may be suspended if there is a strong enough overhead support for them or they may be potted and benched like this. The pot around the base of the stick is filled with small screenings and as this sort of filling could prove a shelter for pests it should be sprayed periodically and a few slug pellets left on the surface.

There is a great difference in virility of plants grown on live trees and those mounted on sections of branches, whether grown in a glass-house or the open air. After some years watching plants treated both ways it appears that a live tree must have some food source in or on the bark which is not present on a mount. However, this source seems to become exhausted after some years and plants must be relocated. Where possible plants should be grown as freely outdoors as in the glass-house and this is when an interchange from indoors to outdoors comes into the picture. They should be selected for tolerance and a number of the laelias have this factor. But plants put outdoors, either permanently or staged through the summer, should be well-established divisions and not small, weak or untidy pieces which fail to get potted. Correct time for attachment is when new roots appear, which in many epiphytes is the prelude to growth, nylon fishing line being used to tie the plants firmly to trees or mounts. Do not pull the line too tight or it may cut into growths or the rhizome.

46

Many oncidiums find tree-fern compatible, as the greater part of their root system is aerial. This picture illustrates the climbing nature of the oncidiums, with the subject at the top of its tree-fern mount and still going. The next move is to attach another piece of tree-fern to the top of the mount and let the plant carry on if that is possible, until it has come to the stage where the rhizome may be severed and the mounts separated. The *Brazilian miltonia* in the other picture is more suited to tree-fern than casuarina stick mounts because the root system is also partly aerial. There is a slight difference in handling miltonias as they throw out a dense mass of roots, many of which appear vertically from the enclosing bracts about the base of the pseudo-bulbs. Some are attracted to a potting mix while others remain totally aerial. However, unlike oncidiums, the tree-fern sticks should be placed in pots for miltonias and some other genera. Oncidiums may be treated either way, with the mounts suspended or potted as there is room for them in the glass-house.

What looks like a jumble of pots and plants is really a tidy collection of oncidiums and small epiphytes like sophronitis and miniature cattleya hybrids hanging on a space-saving rack of wire mesh. Some of the plants are mounted on cork slabs and pieces, others on tree-fern blocks. Most have some type of backing for the rhizome-based plants to sit on. The backing has a dual purpose, first to hold moisture on an otherwise barren cork surface and second to give the roots a natural medium in which to proliferate. Some cork slabs are manufactured from cork granules of various sizes compressed with an adhesive to form a block which is fairly open and porous, others are natural bark sections stripped from trees. Both have proved ideal mounts for orchid plants, but with the granulated type it is possible to buy sections which have been spoiled by a glue which is repellent to orchid roots.

This is the type of pot developed some eighty or more years ago for epiphytes, not necessarily orchids. It was manufactured for Sanders and patented. No one was allowed to copy it unless under licence and Sanders sold thousands of these pots, most of which have disappeared. There is a great amount of difference in clay pots so far as quality is concerned. A light colored and lightly baked pot is not nearly as good for growing orchids as a well-baked red. Even in the reds, however, certain clays give a better pot than others, some having better capillary action in transmitting water from the inside of the pot to the outside and vice versa. None has the open-air effect of fern or cork mounts, but a collection must be sorted out into the different classes of orchids which prefer alternative growing or cultivation methods. It would be unlikely that an odontoglossum would grow on a cork or fern mount as well as in a pot and the reverse is possible with similar epiphytes like the oncidiums.

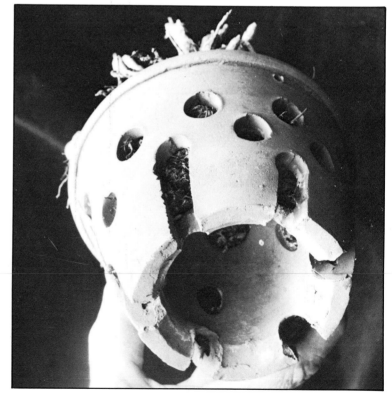

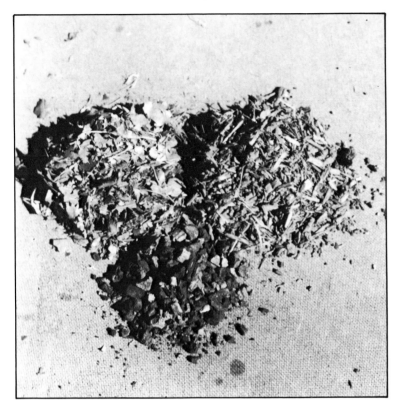

The basic materials for a good potting mix for epiphytes. On the left is one part by measure of rubbed oak leaf, on the right one part of bark and in front half of one part of charcoal. The charcoal has been passed through a 5 millimetre sieve, which gives some idea of its size, and it is sieved dust free like the bark. The bulk of the mix is bark, as the leaf is not compressed in the measure. This type of mix is suitable for pots up to about 8 centimetres, but above that it should be coarsened with larger bark, but retaining the smaller grade in proportion, so that the mix is still solid enough to anchor the plant. Variations may be thought up by including peanut shells instead of the leaf content or by using coarse gravel or scoria instead of charcoal. Once having good root development and growth, a mix should be standardised and used permanently, although it may be found that some orchids like different mixes and do not grow as well in what is used as the standard mix. Marketing of bark in Australia is not very well thought out and some scope exists for a good supplier as long as orchids are grown.

Propagation

The aim in growing epiphytes should be to promote regular growth not only from the lead portion of the plant but from the older pseudo-bulbs or growths so that a pot or receptacle or mount is covered with virile growths and few leafless pseudo-bulbs. This may be encouraged by severing the plant into sections as it grows, making the older parts produce shoots if they are unwilling to do so when attached to the main portion. Once this is done it soon becomes necessary to take the plant apart and start it off again in one or more propagations from the original. As each growing effort is usually an annual process it is fairly easy to estimate how long a plant will stay in a pot or receptacle. Once allowed to outgrow the pot the vigor of the plant declines and the pseudo-bulbs begin to appear smaller. These smaller growths are no less vigorous but they have no real base to which they may attach and no food source to build them up. There is another way of tackling this problem and it will be featured in the next book. The following pictures give a resume of the process involved and the best way to go about dividing an overgrown plant which is still within its original pot and not overhanging the rim.

Most epiphytic orchids develop into sizes suitable for each genus. As denoted in the book section on cattleyas, some reach proportions unknown in cultivated plants. This bifoliate cattleya has reached the size usually considered maximum development in glass-house growing and it should be repotted. As will be noted, the last pseudo-bulbs are almost overhanging the side of the pot and new roots have nowhere to go. Another thing to be noted is the enclosing sheaths on the pseudo-bulbs, which some growers prefer to strip off rather than let scale or other pests shelter beneath them. In a clean glass-house scale would not get a chance to commence, let alone be in a position to take over plants as suggested.

The exposed root system shows clearly that it is healthy and a grower would be faced with alternatives. Either the plant could be potted on into a larger pot or it could be divided into sections to again start growing to its former size. If potted on, a similar grade of pine-bark should be used and it should be worked well down into the root system so that no air spaces are left. Where it has fallen away from the base of the root system it should be replaced by inverting the plant on one hand and filling the gap as well as possible before putting it into a pot. The plant should go no deeper than it was originally, so some filling will be put in to keep the base of the pseudo-bulbs level with the rim of the pot. Once the pot is considered to be full of bark it should be dumped on a firm bench or the ground to further consolidate the potting mix, but not allowing the base of the plant to go down into the pot.

51

Unlike cutting into a cymbidium, when it was decided to divide this cattleya the rhizome or jointing parts of the plant between the pseudo-bulbs was the point at which it was attacked. After severing the rhizome in a simple division of the plant into two as near as possible equal parts the root system was carefully separated. As the root system of most epiphytes is brittle, where it travels horizontally around the interior of the pot it must be unravelled and kept as intact as possible. The potting material is probably exhausted and will fall away fairly easily. What does not fall out should be poked out with the secateurs or a pointed stick until all that is left are the roots.

Some idea of the mess is obvious from this picture and it will be noted that most of the root system inside the root ball is dark and possibly useless once the divisions are taken clear. Long roots are very hard to put back into pots once they are unravelled and no plants should be handled like this until the growing season, which in ordinary conditions would be about the end of October through to the end of March and into April. If the root system on any part of the plant is doubtful it is better to make a decision about fully repotting it or temporarily potting the plant or divisions until a new root system is developing, which may take some weeks. In the meantime the plant should be put into a loosely wrapped ball of sphagnum moss.

This division is ungainly because of its excessive width, which will need a large pot to contain it, equally as large as that from which it was withdrawn. Another feature is obvious; several of the pseudo-bulbs are below the potting level owing to the climbing habit of the rhizome. The difference between the bases of the lowest and the highest pseudo-bulbs is about 5 centimetres, so the propagation would be better divided into two, the useless pseudo-bulbs in the centre removed because they will drop their leaves anyway. The two parts may then be folded in on one another and centred in a new pot, with the prospect that not only will the growths break into shoots in one place on each part, they may also double, so giving the start to a very nice specimen plant in another two years.

This is the best part of the plant. It has the youngest and best growths of the propagations and the best root system. It should go back into the pot from which the whole plant was taken. All the dead or doubtful roots should be removed and it is possible that it will lose one or two of the leaves from the tops of the older pseudo-bulbs. If handled at the correct time the root system will take about three or four weeks to produce buds on the older roots or perhaps one or two new roots on the latest made pseudo-bulbs. In many ways plants like the original whole specimen indicate by new root growth that they may be repotted and it is good cultivation practice to watch for this indicator before starting the job. It may not happen until near Christmas, but is worth waiting for.

This is what the operation amounted to — one very good plant, a doubled-up pair of propagations in a smaller pot and a smaller propagation again which will eventually fill the pot. It is a good propagation to use as an exchange or to sell in or out of flower to someone who may want it. This propagating series was based on a bifoliate cattleya which may have a neater and shorter rhizome habit than the single-leafed group, but the process would be similar in each instance. One point at which they may differ is that in a single-leafed cattleya a division of the rhizome a year before potting is to take place will usually produce a well-started propagation by the time that comes around. In other epiphytes there are differences in all genera and they must be studied to find out which is the best time to handle and which is the best method.

There are usually some 'leftovers' in a potting process. These remnants are leafless and as such are not good prospects for growth. However, if put into a plastic bag with a handful of moistened sphagnum moss they may produce shoots. If the orchid concerned is worth this wait it is a good way to set them up. If growth shoots develop, the offcuts should be planted in small pots with a little moss until they have the second root, upon which they may be potted into bark or whichever growing medium is used and benched in the normal way with the other plants.

Orchid breeding and hybridising

This chart proposes a system of cross-pollinations which could well exist under the Darwinian system of natural selection. In all species which have become stabilised in a habitat a wide variation usually exists in the type of flowers produced from the hundreds of clones which can be supposed to be flowering in their season. All these clones have what is known as a gene pool and it is in the continual recombination of these genes that a species survives and eliminates the weak links in the chain of survival. It is a natural process which defies any logical explanation other than survival.

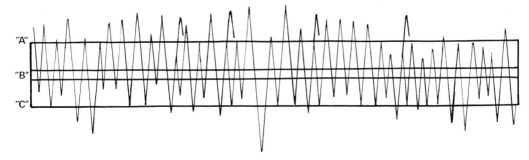

"A" — Recessives — outstanding shape or color. Broken lines — tetraploids & mutations.

"B" — Typical general forms which self-pollinate easily but are selective with "A" and "C", which are compatible with each other as seed-bearing or pollinating clones. "B" is a dominant line, with the greatest plant population.

"C" — Recessives — poor quality or color.

In natural selection the exchange of genes in cross-pollinations would run between the two "B" lines for the normal type forms of any particular orchids except those in transition from one form to another, such as emergence of natural hybrid forms stabilising to form another species, in which case there would be an exchange between the two species concerned as well as their hybrids and no true pattern could emerge to give a type form for some considerable time.

Nature being what it is, despite the transfer of pollen from one flower to another by pollinators in natural conditions, it is not by any means certain that the seed capsule will produce viable seed or that it will even be initially receptive to pollen from particular types of the species which are incompatible with it. In the breeding pattern some clones are certain to be found which will act only as pollinators or in the reverse role as seed producers, a factor which is probably reversible year by year. In this way a species stabilises and while it never comes to the stage where the total species is identical in morphological terms, it is obvious when looked at in total that it has a similarity which is simple and understandable, yet the differences are probably marked in color and shape of the flowers. *Dendrobium speciosum* is a prime example.

In contrast to natural selection, human cross-pollinations are effected only along the "A" line, with the result that the gene pool, which dictates not only the character of the species concerned but its life, is reduced by the entire content of the "B" line and the "C" line, which are equally important to survival. Unfortunately, in hybridising, this factor is completely lost and if occasional resort to the "B" and "C" lines is made, the desired characteristics of the "A" line would not be so frequently lost. It is a pattern and nature is very keen on patterns.

The terms dominant and recessive indicate the way various things like color and shape appear in generations of plants. They refer just as effectively to human beings. With some people fair hair and blue eyes are a constant feature in families. But it is possible for two fair-haired, blue-eyed people to have a dark-haired, brown-eyed child. That would be an instance of a recessive feature becoming a dominant in that individual, who in turn could see a reversal of the feature again to have a fair-haired, blue-eyed child.

In the species *Sophronitis coccinea* the dominant color is red in the flowers, but some clones have paler flowers and these are the recessive features. Over the course of several generations the ratio of red to paler flowers never changes and the species is stabilised. If for some reason, such as a climatic change, it became necessary for the plants to have paler flowers to survive, the recessive features would become dominant and *Sophronitis coccinea* would be mainly yellow to cream flowered. The adaptability of all forms of life to their environment is necessary for survival and once that adaptability is lost the species or genus concerned ceases to exist.

Left to their own devices, any of the hybrids produced by man in the orchid families, in their own genus or into other genera, would soon revert to a pattern of uniformity based on the plants which could adapt. The sort-out would be fairly rapid and by the end of a century possibly 75 per cent or even more of the orchids would have passed into oblivion, mainly because of the selective breeding of dominant features rather than dominant features picked out in ratio by natural selection.

In theory this graph is applicable to hybrid cross-pollinations as well as species and while there may be conflicting factors such as the involvement of several species or even other genera, natural selection would still follow the pattern while human cross-pollinations would still select the "A" line and above. The broken lines above the "A" line represent clones which develop more than the normal number of chromosomes and are eliminated in the natural breeding program unless by an extraordinary chance they cross-pollinate with another similar clone.

Two pedigrees are appended and both are almost self-explanatory. While that of the odontoglossum complex is involved, it is not complicated because the odontoglossum species *O. crispum* appears 20 times through it, surfacing finally in the beautiful wilsonara which is illustrated in the color pictures. It owes a lot to its immediate progenitor *Odontioda* Florence Stirling. Through the pedigree *Cochlioda noezliana* appeared only twice, *Odontoglossum pescatorei* (syn. *O. nobile*) 6 times and *Odontoglossum triumphans* only once. To all outward signs the oncidium contributed nothing except perhaps the intricate patterns on the petals and sepals. On balanced judgment it could not be termed an "A" line breeding table, but the odds are that all the way through very few "C" line hybrids would have been used. The size of *Wilsonara* Salgrin is not even average for a good odontoglossum, a characteristic which most probably could be attributed to the oncidium intrusion. The spike also was short, which is not at all what most hybridists seek. (See page 107.)

The brassolaeliocattleya pedigree could be taken as an example of "A" line breeding, with the finer varieties of the cattleya species, which number seven in all, probably chosen as the medium for cross-pollinations. In the hybrids it is doubtful if a "C" line flower was chosen for any one of them, thus putting the recessives a long way in the background. Both *Laeliocattleya* Bonanza and *Brassolaeliocattleya* Norman's Bay were award-winning material, with the poorer types discarded. *Laelia purpurata* entered the pedigree only twice and at that through the same primary hybrid *Laeliocattleya* Callistoglossa, raised and named in 1882 by Veitch, and *Brassavola digbyana* came in only once. Although it came in at the fourth generation back from *B/c.* Memoria Crispin Rosales, the effect is still noticeable. (See page 86.)

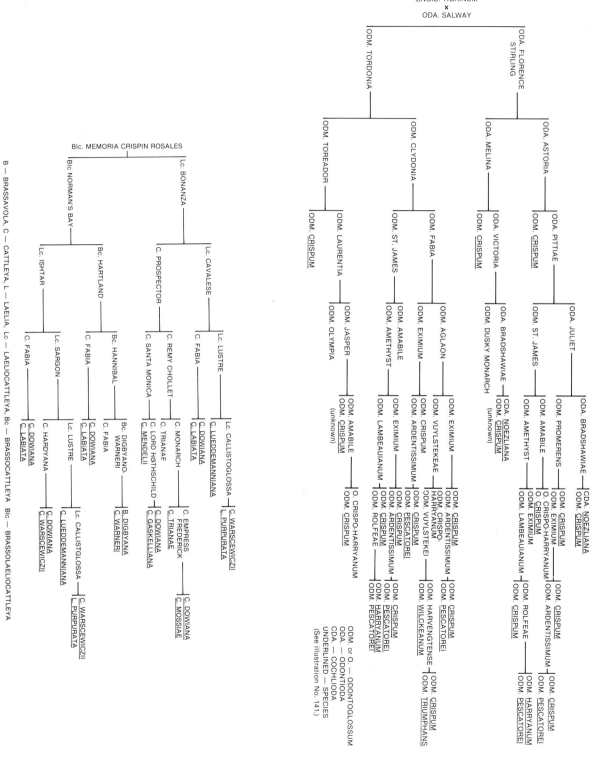

WILSONARA SALGRIN

ONCID. TIGRINUM
×
ODA. SALWAY

ODM. TORDONIA

ODA. FLORENCE STIRLING

ODM. TOREADOR

ODM. CLYDONIA

ODA. MELINA

ODA. ASTORIA

ODM. CRISPUM

ODM. LAURENTIA

ODM. ST. JAMES

ODM. FABIA

ODA. VICTORIA

ODA. PITTIAE

ODM. CRISPUM

ODA. JULIET

ODM. OLYMPIA

ODM. JASPER

ODM. AMABILE

ODM. AMETHYST

ODM. EXIMIUM

ODM. AGLAON

ODM. EXIMIUM

ODA. DUSKY MONARCH
(unknown)

ODA. BRADSHAWIAE

ODM. ST. JAMES

ODM. AMABILE

ODM. PROMERENS

ODA. BRADSHAWIAE

(unknown)

ODM. AMABILE
ODM. CRISPUM

ODM. LAMBEAUJIANUM

ODM. EXIMIUM
ODM. ARDENTISSIMUM

ODM. CRISPUM
ODM. VUYLSTEKEAE

ODM. EXIMIUM
ODM. HARRYANUM

CDA. NOEZLIANA
ODM. CRISPUM

ODM. EXIMIUM
ODM. AMETHYST

ODM. CRISPO-HARRYANUM
O. CRISPUM

CDA. NOEZLIANA
ODM. CRISPUM

O. CRISPO-HARRYANUM
ODM. CRISPUM

ODM. CRISPUM
ODM. ROLFEAE

ODM. CRISPUM
ODM. ARDENTISSIMUM

ODM. CRISPUM
ODM. PESCATOREI

ODM. ARDENTISSIMUM
ODM. VUYLSTEKEI

ODM. CRISPO-
HARRYANUM

ODM. CRISPUM
ODM. PESCATOREI

ODM. CRISPUM
ODM. ARDENTISSIMUM

ODM. CRISPUM
ODM. HARRYANUM

ODM. CRISPUM
ODM. PESCATOREI

ODM. CRISPUM
ODM. PESCATOREI

ODM. HARVENGTENSE
ODM. WILCKEANUM

ODM. HARRYANUM
ODM. PESCATOREI

ODM. CRISPUM
ODM. TRIUMPHANS

ODM. CRISPUM
ODM. HARRYANUM

ODM. PESCATOREI

ODM. or O. — ODONTOGLOSSUM
ODA. — ODONTIODA
CDA. — COCHLIODA
UNDERLINED — SPECIES
(See illustration No. 141.)

Blc. MEMORIA CRISPIN ROSALES

Blc NORMAN'S BAY

Lc. BONANZA

Bc. HARTLAND

Lc. CAVALESE

C. PROSPECTOR

Lc. ISHTAR

Bc. HANNIBAL

C. FABIA

Lc. LUSTRE

C. SANTA MONICA

C. REMY CHOLLET

C. FABIA

Lc. SARGON

C. FABIA

Bc. DIGBYANO-
WARNERI

C. FABIA

C. LORD ROTHSCHILD

C. TRIANAE

C. MONARCH

Lc. CALLISTOGLOSSA

Lc. LUSTRE

C. HARDYANA

C. DOWIANA
C. LABIATA

C. DOWIANA
C. LABIATA

Bc. DIGBYANA-
WARNERI

C. DOWIANA
C. MENDELII

C. DOWIANA
C. TRIANAE

C. EMPRESS
FREDERICK

C. DOWIANA
C. LABIATA

C. LUEDDEMANNIANA

C. WARSCEWICZII
L. PURPURATA

Lc. CALLISTGLOSSA

C. LUEDDEMANNIANA

C. DOWIANA
C. WARSCEWICZII

B. DIGBYANA
C. WARNERI

C. DOWIANA
C. GASKELLIANA

C. DOWIANA
C. MOSSIAE

C. WARSCEWICZII
L. PURPURATA

O. CRISPO-HARRYANUM
ODM. CRISPUM

B — BRASSAVOLA, C — CATTLEYA, L — LAELIA, Lc — LAELIOCATTLEYA, Bc — BRASSOCATTLEYA, Blc — BRASSOLAELIOCATTLEYA

57

Habitat Location Maps

These maps of Mexico and Central and South America are not strictly accurate, nor is the list of species the total number of cattleyas and laelias which grow in these regions. They are solely to indicate the concentrations of the genera and convey some idea of at least one of the habitats they occupy. Most orchid growers have a very vague idea of the countries in which their orchids originated and it is the aim of this book to give a little information about them. A great amount of literature has been poured out in reference to orchids, some of it accurate, some inaccurate. The list of reference books from which much of the information was drawn is at the back of this volume, some of it now unobtainable outside libraries, but all of it worth pursuing and buying if available.

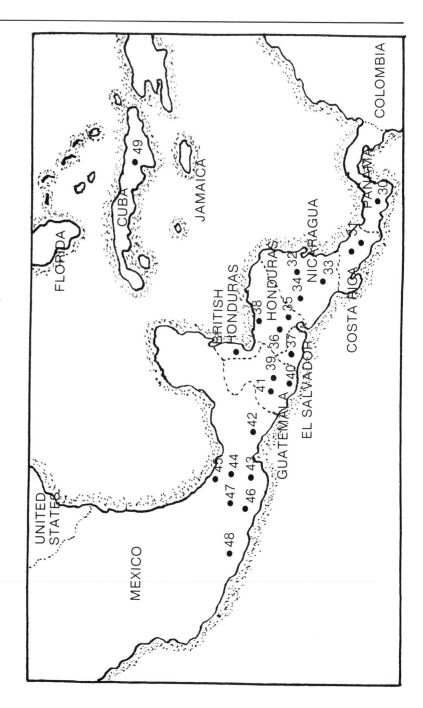

Maps of origin — Laelias & Cattleyas

LAELIAS:

albida 43
anceps 43, 44, 46, 47
autumnalis 46, 47
cinnabarina 7, 8, 10
crispa 8, 10, 11
flava 10
furfuracea 43, 46
gouldiana 43, 44, 46, 47
grandis 4
harpophylla 10, 11
lobata 8
perrinii 8, 9, 11
pumila 8, 10, 11
purpurata 3, 4, 5
rubescens 35, 39, 40, 41
speciosa 43, 44
superbiens 36, 39, 42
tenebrosa 11, 13
thompsoniana 43, 44, 46, 47
xanthina 13

RHYNCOLAELIAS:

digbyana 38
glauca 45

CATTLEYAS:

aclandiae 13
aurantiaca 36, 37, 39, 42
bicolor 8, 9, 10, 11
bowringiana 38A
dowiana var. aurea 22; dowiana 31, 31A
eldorado 14
forbesii 3, 4, 7, 8
gaskelliana 26, 27
guatemalensis 30, 39, 41
guttata 3, 10
harrisoniana 4, 8, 11
intermedia 3, 5, 7, 9
labiata 5, 7
lawrenceana 28
loddigesii 1, 2, 8, 9, 11
lueddemanniana 26
luteola 19
maxima 20
mendelii 23
mossiae 25
percivaliana 24
schillerana 12
skinneri 23, 24, 31, 32, 33, 34, 39, 40
superba 15, 16, 28, 30
trianae 21
walkerana 7, 10
warneri 5, 11
warscewiczii 22

Climatic areas of South America

The continent of South America is rich in orchid species, but the greatest areas of concentration are surprisingly small when compared to the overall area. The green areas contain 75 per cent of the genera and possibly the same percentage of species, while the whole of the rest of the continent contains only 25 per cent of the genera. The significance of the colored areas is, however, climatic and not really a reference point to the orchid population.

The green areas are those with temperate climates, regardless of their position relative to the equator. They include the lower mountains, foothills and some of the high mountain plateaus, where there are few dry periods through the year, the humidity is relatively high and there is a constant air flow in all seasons of the year. The air flow seems to be the most important feature, but again there is relationship between air, light and water. Most of the orchids of the world grow in this environment.

The red areas are those of higher temperatures and higher humidity at lower altitudes. They are mostly coastal areas, but the whole of the Amazon River basin has this pattern. The temperatures are usually in the high 30 degree Celsius range for most of the year, but in some seasons there is relatively little rain while in other periods the country is deluged and large swamp areas form. The orchid population of the red area is rather small considering its size.

The yellow area is savannah or plains country at an altitude of about 500 to 1000 metres, rather dry although traversed by rivers, along which most of the orchid population occurs. Temperatures range from 35 to 40 degrees in the daytime to almost zero at night, the rainfall intermittent and not seasonal in the true meaning of the term. Some of this country is swamp region and such orchids as catasetums are found in it, where for some months of the year they are growing in a wet area which later dries up and they go into dormancy after casting their leaves.

The blue areas are cold high country and low country at southerly latitudes, where the orchids are mostly terrestrial, growing and flowering in the warmer periods of the year then casting their leaves and going into dormancy. Terrestrial orchids which form tubers such as those of the pterostylis of Australia would be prominent in the orchid population.

The white area comprising the residue of the land mass is almost wholly uncongenial country so far as orchids are concerned, with seasonal and ecological components suited to it. While these areas have definite boundaries on the map, no such state occurs, because in each instance fringe areas exist and the borderline is very shadowy, with rivers carrying at all times some orchid populations where the climate is conducive to growth.

The rivers, according to the source of this map, Orchidaceae Brasilienses, are the migration routes by which orchids spread over the country, the wind carrying the seed in stages so that in time, perhaps in the order of thousands of years, a species could traverse a great distance and in the course of its travels change considerably to conform to a new climate or environment. Wind is the means of travel and the seed designed by evolution so that it floats on the wind.

The great Andean mountain chain stretching down the continent is responsible for most of the blue area and it is this mountain bastion which limits the numbers of orchids on the western flanks because of wind and water vapor deflection. The greatest concentrations of orchids occur in the region of Colombia in the north and Rio de Janeiro area in the south, both extremely rich at one time and so devastated by collectors.

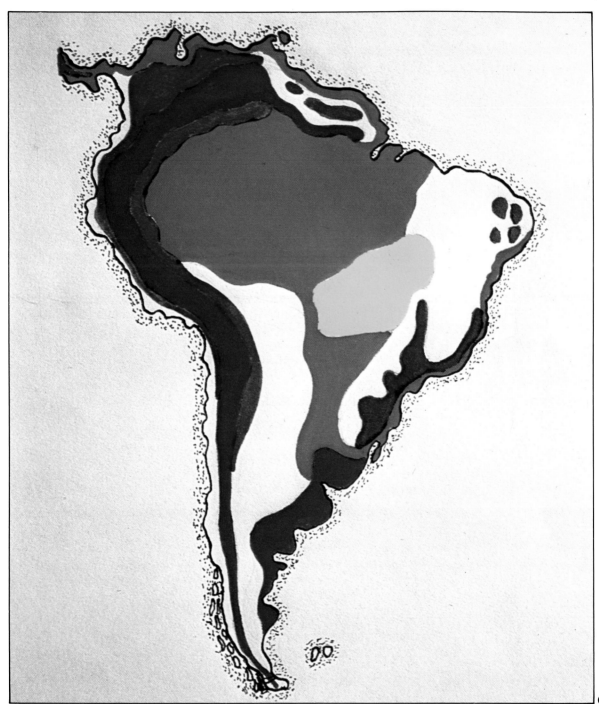

CATTLEYA LODDIGESII (Lindley). So far as known, this was the first cattleya grown and flowered in Britain, if not Europe. This cattleya, grown on a casuarina tree (she-oak) in southern Victoria flowers every year, which indicates the adaptability of the orchid. Grown in this way, orchids need a little more attention than glass-house plants and fertilising and watering are part of a regular summer program.

Glass-house plants of the same orchid do not seem to develop the intensity of color of outdoor plants. This is a division of the same clone. *C. loddigesii* belongs to the bifoliate cattleyas, which have more than the one leaf of the labiata-type plants. The pseudo-bulbs are pencil-like and grow to about 40 centimetres tall. *C. loddigesii* flowers in early to late autumn and then is dormant over the winter.

A cattleya plant growing on a live casuarina tree. Where possible in suitable climates some orchids should be grown as garden plants as distinct from glass-house plants and trees planted if necessary for this purpose. There are orchids which are almost frost resistant and a considerable amount of added enjoyment from the cult follows successful flowering of outdoor grown plants. Such plants, I feel, do at last 'wear out' the position they occupy and must be replanted. (Right)

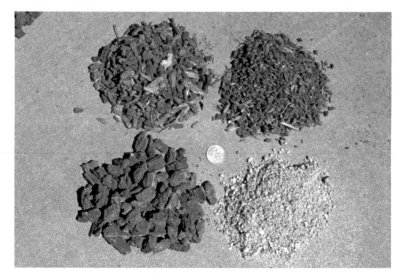

Grading bark for potting mixes is a necessary part of good cultivation. This picture illustrates the three grades mentioned in the text and they can be sieved still further to get finer grades. Once separated the various grades may be blended to suit all types and sizes of plants from tiny seedlings to cattleyas in large pots. The gravel is river washing and it should be a mixture of all sizes from sand to coarse grains, but if charcoal is used it should be put through the sieve process and blended so that the potting material is not too airy yet not solid as it could be with fine inclusions. The coin is a 5 cent piece, 19 millimetres in diameter.

CATTLEYA INTERMEDIA (R. Graham). It might well be mistaken for *C. loddigesii* when not in flower, the leaves of both being more or less ovoid or lance shaped. Most of the bifoliate cattleyas, South American as well as Central American, are morphologically similar. *C. intermedia* flowers in the spring from sheaths which may have been made months before, and it may put on two growths in the year if an early summer start is made with the first. It is one of the easiest cattleyas to grow in the warmer climate group.

The white form of *C. intermedia*, but not a pure albino form, as the tinges of color in the labellums show. White forms are not as common in the bifoliate cattleyas as in the labiata section. In both groups the whites with colored or color-tinged lips are the result of cross-pollinations between the albinos and colored forms, a percentage of which would be white.

CATTLEYA INTERMEDIA var. *AQUINII*. The flower has what are known as 'splash' petals, a mutation which is uncommon and beautiful. It is also a dominant characteristic in a lot of hybrids when this form is used. For some reason a 'set' seems to have formed about these flowers and they are not as popular as their beauty seems to deserve.

CATTLEYA GUTTATA (Lindley) is a Brazilian cattleya with many forms and colors, some of them very beautifully speckled and blotched. The original plants were collected from the Organ Mountains near Rio de Janeiro, the source of so many orchids in the early days of their cultivation.

CATTLEYA SKINNERI (Bateman) is a spring-flowering orchid which may be cultivated into a specimen type plant fairly readily because in suitable conditions it has the good habit of making multiple new leads. C. skinneri is variable in color and includes white as well as pure albino forms. It is a Mexican bifoliate.

CATTLEYA BOWRINGIANA (Veitch) is one of the first cattleyas to flower in the autumn and the strongest grower of the bifoliate type. The pseudo-bulbs on well-grown plants may measure up to 50 or 60 centimetres and the racemes carry fourteen or more flowers. Most of the bifoliate cattleyas have thin sections where the pseudo-bulb meets the rhizome, but C. bowringiana growths have a bulbous base.

CATTLEYA PORTIATA 'Mel' is a hybrid between C. Portia and C. labiata, the cross-pollination being between the orthodox cattleyas and the bifoliates. C. Portia made by Veitch in 1892 and flowered in 1897. The modern term for these cattleya hybrids is cluster type, C. Portia ranking among the best. The original clone on which the name was based was exhibited in a silver medal group of orchids at a Royal Horticultural Society meeting in November 1897.

Some of the clones of C. Portia have a slight blue tinge and it is not surprising that hybridists chased the fantasy of a blue cattleya over many years, so far in the year 1981 with little success. The illustrated variety is the clone C. Portia 'Coerulea' and depending on culture is at times quite bluish.

CATTLEYA LABIATA (Lindley). This is a lithograph of the supposed type form of this orchid. Several authorities consider this title applies to a group of South American orchids, but as they are spread far and wide through the continent there is very little to sustain its application to so many different flowers. There is so much variation within each member group that it is almost impossible to establish a type form in so great a lapse of time since the original discovery, let alone relate one species to another. C. labiata originally was supposed to have been discovered in Brazil. The section on cattleyas offers some information on this point but no solution to the puzzle of its first discovery.

65

CATTLEYA TRIANAE (Linden and Reichenbach f.) is among the prized flowers of Colombia, a South American country which has more than its fair share of beautiful orchids. This is the variety *delicata* and it was known in collections in 1861, when it was noted by Warner in one of his orchid publications. It is something of a tribute to culture as well as the orchid to have survived for over 120 years at the time this was printed. It was earlier known as *C. rollisonii*, and was probably first collected and sent to Europe, not England.

There is a great amount of variation in all species, but never more apparent than in this comparative picture of another clone of *C. trianae*. This would be the more common type and if reference is made to the graph illustrating hybridising an idea may be formed of how nature uses these different types to maintain stability in each genus. It would be almost beyond an ordinary grower to identify and name such variations, despite a knowledge of the finer clones like the variety *delicata*, or the equally beautiful variety *the premier*. Both these flowers would be above the 'A' line of the graph and the flower to which this title refers below the 'B' line. (See page 56.)

CATTLEYA SCHRODERAE (Reichenbach f.) known as a variety of *C. trianae* and also a species in its own right. It is variable in shape and color and is one of the most delightfully scented of the cattleyas. It was more widely known and grown by American fanciers, some of whom had large collections of *C. schroderae*. Little of its influence appears in modern hybrid cattleyas, but some of the hybrids like *Laeliocattleya* G. S. Ball (the combination with *Laelia cinnabarina*) were beautiful cluster-type, slender-stemmed brilliant flowers.

CATTLEYA MENDELII (Backhouse) is another native of Colombia, known at the time of the great period of the collectors as New Granada. This cattleya is described by Veitch as 'often growing on exposed precipices and on bare rocks.' While not as variable as *C. trianae*, it has white varieties as well as pure albino forms with the golden-yellow splash on the inside of the tube formed by the lip. This cattleya was used extensively in hybridising with, however, only half the number of early cross-pollinations that *C. trianae* has to its credit. This is a pastel drawing by Joan Skilbeck.

CATTLEYA MOSSIAE (Hooker) is the national flower of Venezuela, which is on the northern coastline of South America. Venezuela is a country of extraordinary mountain formations and *C. mossiae* is usually found on the coastal sections of the mountains at about 1000 to 1200 metres. It is most variable, with some of the white forms having deep purple lips. The variety *wageneri* is a pure albino and its use is illustrated in the hybrid cattleyas, in which it appeared to induce genetic variations of great benefit to further cross-pollinations.

CATTLEYA PERCIVALIANA is also a Venezuelan orchid, found almost exclusively growing as a lithophyte. It was originally sent to Sanders by the collector Arnold, the history of whose brief life is covered in relation to masdevallias. The labellum of *C. percivaliana* is very different from that of other members of the labiata group, to which it belongs. This is a reproduction of a lithograph by J. Nugent Fitch, an artist noted for his beautiful work in the late 1800 period.

CATTLEYA GASKELLIANA
(Reichenbach f.) is another
Venezuelan orchid with a fairly wide
distribution and great variation. Like
the other members of the so-called
labiata complex, it also has albino
and white varieties. *C. gaskelliana*
grows at similar altitudes to *C.
mossiae* and flowers in much the
same period.

CATTLEYA DOWIANA var. AUREA
had a far more glamorous image
than many of the other South
American cattleyas because of its
color, which varied from pale
creamy yellow all the way through
to deep gold lined with purple-
crimson on the petals. It is intensely
colored and most variable. The real
C. dowiana, however, is nondescript
by comparison and the variety *aurea*
was always more keenly sought.
This is a pastel drawing by Joan
Skilbeck from an old lithograph.
Bateman and Reichenbach shared
its naming.

CATTLEYA BICOLOR (Lindley) is
native to the Minas Geraes region of
Brazil and other minor sources. It is
a bifoliate, infrequently used in
hybridising, but there are at least
six natural hybrids common in its
habitats. A variety with a blue-
tinged labellum instead of the usual
brilliant purple-red was known at
one time but is possibly now rare. *C.
bicolor* grows at about 700 metres in
a warm climate and has a most
distinctively shaped and colored
labellum for a small cattleya.

CATTLEYA VIOLACEA (Humboldt, Bonpland and Kunth) was a very early discovery among the South American cattleyas, originally found by the explorer Humboldt, its synonym *C. superba*. At the time Humboldt found this orchid it grew prolifically along the Orinoco River and its tributaries in Venezuela and was also subsequently found in various other locations. It was introduced to the British fanciers by Sir Robert Schomburgk, who found it in what was then known as British Guiana, now Guyana. While not rare, it is nevertheless difficult enough to find in any numbers where it once grew in thousands. This is a photograph of an old lithograph.

CATTLEYA LUTEOLA (Lindley) grows in Colombia, Ecuador and Venezuela and until the search for yellow to gold cattleya hybrids it was neglected. It is mostly found at elevations of some 1000 metres, has up to eight flowers to a stem and in warm, bright conditions is constantly in growth and flower. The color of the flowers again indicates the amount of light the plant will tolerate.

CATTLEYA GUATEMALENSIS (T. Moore), a natural hybrid between *C. aurantiaca* and *C. skinneri*. Its early history is obscure, but it was recognised as a natural hybrid possibly as far back as early specimens collected by Skinner, has remained comparatively rare and is seldom noted in orchid collections. Like many primary hybrids, *C. guatemalensis* is a sturdy grower and flowers easily and prolifically.

CATTLEYA WALKERANA (Gardner) was found by Gardner, who rediscovered *C. labiata. C. walkerana* was also found in several other localities by other people, one of whom noted that it was 'growing high up on the smooth and hard bark of a species of jacaranda, scattered over an arid plain and exposed to the hot currents of air that frequently blew over it.' It was named after a travelling associate of Gardner named Walker. No doubt at times that hot and arid region was just as much at the other weather extreme and flooded, humid and wet for months on end.

CATTLEYA BONANZA 'Bold Adventurer' is a pure-bred hybrid cattleya so far as its history is known. It has two infusions of *C. mossiae*, two of *C. trianae*, one of *C. mendelii* and one of *C. dowiana*. It also has one unknown parent and it could be supposed, on account of the labellum, that it was a brassocattleya. None of the antecedents of this cattleya were, so far as known, albino or white forms of the species.

CATTLEYA BOW BELLS (*C.* Edithiae × *C.* Suzanne Hye) was the amalgamation of fine albino forms of the species, as outlined in the text. This was a key to the excellent shape of not only white cattleyas and various other inter-generic hybrids, but also to many fine colored forms. It was originally raised by Black and Flory, the successors to the Veitch orchid connection.

CATTLEYA BOB BETTS (*C.* Bow Bells × *C. mossiae* var. *wageneri*) was raised by the American hybridisers McDade. It was perhaps intuition which led them to return to the species again and although it was inbreeding, the result exceeded expectations and *C.* Bob Betts also had its share of success. These white cattleyas have great significance for color breeding, because they are frequently mutations along the genetic code.

CATTLEYA SILVER SWAN (*C.* Bob Betts × *C.* White Dove) again repeats all the moves that make up Bob Betts and introduces further the albino form of *C. lueddemanniana. C.* Silver Swan represents as well as any other cattleya the points of excellence that might be looked for in premier type flowers.

CATTLEYA WOLTERIANA (*C. aurantiaca* × *C. schroderae*). To get into the more brilliant colors in pure cattleyas it is necessary to use smaller species and this limits to some extent the size of the flowers. Although this hybrid was raised in 1909 it has lost nothing over the years and it is to be regretted that many brilliant hybrids of this period have been phased out in the search for so-called award-type cattleyas like the pure whites.

CATTLEYA HALLIE REGERS (*C. walkerana* × *C. o'brienianum*) is also representative of a hybrid type which in its own form may be classified as 'just another cattleya.' But it is in further cross-pollinations that the good points of crisp shape and lovely clear color could be used to advantage. The labellum shape should be noted. It is probably the archaic type of the original cattleyas and the convoluted and exaggerated front lobes of the labiata types a comparatively recent adornment of, say, the last few thousand years.

LAELIA ANCEPS (Lindley) as a garden plant, growing on a casuarina or she-oak, as it is sometimes called. This is one of the hardiest of the cattleya-type Mexican orchids and although it flowers in almost midwinter, the blooms are larger and more colorful when grown like this. Starting with four small pseudo-bulbs, in five years it built up to a plant of forty-eight pseudo-bulbs growing in southern Victoria in my garden.

LAELIA ANCEPS var. *chamberlainiana* is usually considered the best of this species, although several other fine varieties are known. Originally purchased as an imported plant of considerable size in the late years of the nineteenth century, it has been propagated into divisions which may be found in almost every orchid-growing community in temperate zones.

LAELIA ANCEPS var. *williamsiana* is the white form of this orchid, for which apparently there is no albino form. Like all the clones of *L. anceps*, the stem and sheaths enclosing the buds and even the buds themselves are coated with a sticky resin or sap and this spoils an otherwise beautiful white flower for decorative purposes.

LAELIA GOULDIANA (Reichenbach f.) is a cool-growing Mexican orchid, just as much at home in outdoor conditions as *L. anceps*, but flowering a little better in a glass-house, where the spike has a better development and the flowers become less weather marked.

LAELIA AUTUMNALIS (Lindley), a Mexican species similarly at home as an outdoor plant or garden orchid planted on a casuarina tree, flowers in midwinter. Most glass-house-grown specimens are fortunate if they have seven or eight flowers on a spike, but outdoors they may have up to twelve or thirteen flowers.

LAELIA FURFURACEA (Lindley), also a Mexican species, grows at fairly high altitudes but will not tolerate outdoor conditions in other than sub-tropical climates and even there may not be easy to grow. It is among the most beautiful of the laelias, but like other orchids, seems at home in its habitat and difficult to acclimatise in artificial conditions. Its origin has aroused speculation and taxonomists and botanists have theories about its result from natural hybridism.

LAELIA SPECIOSA (Humboldt, Bonpland and Kunth), with the synonym *L. majalis*, is another Mexican orchid from fairly high altitudes. Although it will grow outdoors on suitable host trees in cool to moderate climates, it is hard to flower outdoors. The small, egg-shaped pseudo-bulbs are almost the first to show new growth in the spring and mature fairly early in the summer season. Neither it nor *L. furfuracea* has had much use in hybridising and one can see no good reason for this other than perhaps incompatibility with the other laelias. Considering the long lists of contacts which the Brazilian laelias have had, the Mexican laelias are almost nonentities so far as *Sanders' List of Orchid Hybrids* is concerned.

LAELIA RUBESCENS (Lindley), with the common synonym *L. acuminata*, is a fairly common orchid in some of the Central American states and consequently is warm growing. It has sprays of up to twelve and more flowers varying from pale lilac pink to deep rose and with the occasional white variety. It is a good subject for semi-tropical climates as a garden plant provided the humidity is not too high in its growing period. More laelia and cattleya growths are lost from this cause than from any other and good air circulation is essential to protect the plants. Probably in natural habitats wind and rain go together and this creates a set of conditions to which the plants are accustomed over many thousands of years.

74

LAELIA CRISPATA (Thunberg) (syn. *L. rupestris*), from Minas Geraes province, Brazil, grows almost entirely on rock surfaces, which in the usual habitat meaning would indicate a rather hard-growing type of orchid. It belongs to a group which has miniature flowers, the significance of which is covered more in the text on laelias.

LAELIA LUNDII (Reichenbach f.), also from Minas Geraes, Brazil. Perhaps insignificant as to plant and flower, it was not well known before about 1910. It grows only about 15 centimetres high, the leaves almost terete, indicating an exposed habitat and with strong light. Some of these small laelias have never been found growing as epiphytes. The flowers of this laelia are about 3 centimetres across.

LAELIA MILLERI (Blume) escaped collection until about 1955. Its fate was sealed soon after its habitat became known and collectors almost cleaned out the area. If it were not for cultivated specimens and considerable seed raising it would now be almost extinct. *L. milleri* is remarkable because it is so adaptable, growing and flowering in cold conditions as well as warm. It comes from climate 3 and flowers in midwinter, cross-pollinations with it producing a series of brilliant red hybrids.

75

LAELIA PURPURATA (Lindley and
Paxton), a Brazilian species from
the south of that country. The
outstanding laelia which, conjoined
with cattleyas, produced the
thousands of hybrids adorning the
Sanders list. In 1945 there were
more than 3000 registered
laeliocattleyas. It is variable in color
but consistent in shape. The plant is
a rapid grower but can prove
difficult to flower in glass-houses. It
should grow and flower well as a
garden plant in warmer climates.

LAELIA SINCORANA (syn. L. pumila)
(Hooker) is the species which
contributed more to the shape of
1980 hybrids than L. purpurata. It
has the peculiarity of producing its
flowers quite early in growth
development, so that once the
flowers are gone the plant goes into
the winter still maturing its pseudo-
bulbs. Pure white forms are known,
but rare in cultivation. It is more
commonly known by its synonym,
grows in cold conditions and is a
most durable flower for late summer
and early autumn.

LAELIA CINNABARINA (Bateman) is
a Brazilian orchid with a most
colorful past and future potential for
colors between red and yellow.
Although it is spidery and has
nothing to contribute to flower
shape, a glance at some of the
other orchids in these pages and a
little investigation will soon indicate
its effect on color transference. As
a cultivated orchid it is fairly easy
to grow in moderately warm
conditions. One of its early hybrids,
Laeliocattleya Charlesworthii, has
been used in the 1970-80 decade
with good effect. It also is
illustrated and would add nothing to
the shape wished for in hybrids.

LAELIA COWANII, a species for which it is difficult to find an authority, resembles *L. cinnabarina* and appears to have been introduced to cultivation by the Cowan nursery near Liverpool, England, about 1898. Louis Forget knew of it much earlier. It appears to be a hybrid from *L. cinnabarina* and *L. flava*, but despite its origin in Brazil, Pabst and Dungs do not list it.

LAELIA FLAVA (Lindley), like the previous two laelias, indicates with its yellow flowers and narrow, deeply channelled foliage a habitat not noted for its lushness. If any of the genus could be termed xerophytic these laelias are in the first rank, the climate in the Minas Geraes province of Brazil alternating between daytime temperatures up to 40 degrees, and dry with it, to night-time zero. Extended dry periods occur in this climate at an altitude of 500 to 1000 metres.

LAELIA HARPOPHYLLA (Reichenbach f.) comes from the same general area as *L. flava* but from a totally different climate where it grows as an epiphyte. It is a laelia which proves the exception to the rule that color and morphology dictate the origin. In common with the other yellow to red laelias it has been the source for a great amount of color breeding in its own genus and also inter-generically. The plant has all the characteristics of exposure to strong light and should be grown that way.

LAELIA TENEBROSA (Rolfe) (syn. *L. grandis*), from Brazil, in addition to contributing a share to the colors of laeliocattleyas, was also the clue to correcting so much misinformation about the habitat of *C. labiata* var. *warneri. Laeliocattleya gottoiana* is the natural hybrid result of their cross-pollination and it came from the Espirito Santo region on the eastern 'hump' of South America, not far north of Rio de Janeiro.

The use of liquid fertilisers is simplified with a proportioner such as this. The liquid nutrient is mixed according to specifications and an adjustment made to the gauge on the tank to deliver so much of it to a measured amount of flow through the system. With these proportioners a hose is fitted to the water supply and the whole job is made much easier and done in considerably less time than with a bucket or watering can. Several suppliers of misting and watering equipment are located in most capital cities and they should be approached for information.

LAELIA CRISPA (Lindley) belongs to a laelia-associated group once known as schomburgkias. Most have tall flower spikes, some extraordinarily long. In the period when this lithograph was transcribed the plants were known as cattleyas and because they were scarce they were very much sought by fanciers. This is a photograph of an old lithograph of the period and the painstaking care of the artists of the time would be rare in modern art circles.

LAELIA SUPERBIENS (Lindley), originally imported from Brazil about 1828. At a sale of plants about 1856 a specimen of this orchid some 5 metres (17 feet) in circumference and with more than 220 pseudo-bulbs was sold for about £75 — in 1981 currency equivalent an unthinkable amount. It was nearly twice the annual wages of some employees in the nursery. Like the other 'schomburgkias,' the flowers all grow over the last 30 or 40 centimetres of the stem, which on this species could be up to two metres high.

LAELIA THOMPSONIANA
(Reichenbach f.) is one of the more beautiful of these tall-spiked orchids. This laelia varies considerably and several types from localities in the Caribbean islands are known. The flower spike is shorter than some in this section, seldom reaching a metre high.

LAELIA LATONA (*L. cinnabarina* × *L. purpurata*), raised by Veitch in 1892, remains one of the most beautiful of the straight laelia crosses. The outstanding influence of *cinnabarina* is the most noticeable feature. In the period from its generation to about the 1914-18 years of war many such hybrids were raised, most long since superseded and lost.

LAELIA CORONET (*L. cinnabarina* × *L. harpophylla*), raised by Charlesworths in 1902, is another of the laelia hybrids which has survived and was quite capable of winning prizes in the 1970-80 decade. The foliage is similar to that of *L. cinnabarina*, but the color comes from both parents. *L.* Coronet grows in warm conditions and may be developed into large plants carrying a lot of flower.

DIALAELIA VEITCHII (*Diacrium bicornutum* × *L. cinnabarina*) is also a Veitch 1905 production still with us and illustrates the inquisitive nature of early hybridists. It is one of the few cross-pollinations which stifled the influence of this dominant laelia. Diacriums are now known as caularthrons.

LAELIOCATTLEYA WRIGLEYI (*L. anceps* × *C. bowringiana*) is not typical of the hybrids appearing in the late nineteenth century, but indicates the lines which hybridists followed. Compared with the laeliocattleyas which soon followed, its deficiencies are clearly apparent, particularly relating to *L. anceps* as a parent.

LAELIOCATTLEYA SALLIERI (*L. purpurata* × *C. loddigesii*) is included in these illustrations because it is here growing as a garden plant on a casuarina tree at my home at Somers, southern Victoria. It is a matter of pride. Growing these summer-flowering laeliocattleyas throws a lot on to the plants and they program growth and flowering sometimes to miss each alternate year. It is an 1895 vintage hybrid.

LAELIOCATTLEYA PARYSATIS (*L. pumila* × *C. bowringiana*) is included for the same reason as *Lc.* Sallieri. It also is a vintage laeliocattleya, but indicates what selection based on parent characteristics can do for an orchid grower. Both had only one cold-tolerant parent, but it was dominant. This orchid is also growing attached to a casuarina tree and has been a vigorous grower.

LAELIOCATTLEYA CHARLESWORTHII (*L. cinnabarina* × *C. dowiana*) is a very old orchid, raised and named by Charlesworths in 1900. Both parents have such influence on color breeding that *Lc.* Charlesworthii was resurrected in the 1970-80 decade to pursue a line including *Sophronitis coccinea* among others from the complex, resulting in some very beautiful and unusually colored hybrids.

LAELIOCATTLEYA KINGAROY has both *L. milleri* and *Lc.* Charlesworthii in its immediate background; on the other side, *C. schroderae*, *L. cowanii* and *C. aurantiaca*. It is not to be wondered that it is golden with an overlay of red, measuring about 8 centimetres across.

LAELIOCATTLEYA AUTUMN
SYMPHONY (*Lc.* Medon × *Lc.*
Cardinal) is unusual because the
labellum is a distinct throw-back to
C. bicolor. However, the overall
beautiful coloring may be traced
back through one line to *C.
dowiana, L. tenebrosa* and *C.
hardyana*. The rest of the pedigree
defies the usual rules of inheritance.
But, after all, it is the label which
counts, and *Cat. bicolor*, from
generation 1, has the final
determination of labellum shape in
this flower.

LAELIOCATTLEYA, unnamed. (*Lc.*
Orange Charm × *Lc.* Orange
Sherbet) is an inbred line which
traces right back to the beautiful
early hybrid *Lc.* G. S. Ball, and
through it to *L. cinnabarina* and *C.
schroderae*, from the last named of
which comes the lovely orange
throat of the labellum. It is of
medium size but intense color.

LAELIOCATTLEYA MOLLY TYLER
(*Lc. Mrs W. N. Elkins* × *C. Leda*), an
old but beautiful cluster type
cattleya, owes color and number of
flowers to the species *C.
bowringiana*, from which it is only
two steps away. Most of the
bifoliate cattleyas dropped out of
breeding tables after the first
generation.

82

LAELIOCATTLEYA FEDORA
'Yarrum' (*Lc*. Laguna × *C*. Hardyana)
was raised by Charlesworths in
1931, but was still good enough to
gain an award in the 1960 period.
This orchid is typical of the
cattleyas sought by many growers
who have in view a collection of
high-priced, highly awarded plants,
an aim which does not suit all.

LAELIOCATTLEYA HERTHA
'Wondabah' (*Lc*. Momus × *C*
Monarch) was also raised by
Charlesworths in the same year as
Lc. Fedora. It is obvious that since
that period little has changed in
shaping up the hybrids of the genus
toward the next century. The full
potential of the genus or mixed
genera is not too easy to forecast,
but it could not alter very much
from this standard.

LAELIOCATTLEYA CHIT CHAT
'Lorna' (*C. aurantiaca* × *L*. Coronet)
is almost a primary hybrid. A superb
grower, it makes up easily into a
specimen plant. When compared
with laeliocattleyas bred from the
labiata strain these small hybrids
must have something to
compensate and the masses of
bright flowers they produce make
them sought after additions to
collections. It was common in much
earlier times to use small cattleyas
and laelias to breed such
ornaments.

83

LAELIOCATTLEYAS bred from certain varieties of *C. mossiae* run to such white flowers with colored labellums as this cross-pollination of *Lc.* Mygdon × *C.* Mrs Fred Knollys. The species used to produce this hybrid was probably *C. mossiae* var. *reineckiana*, a beautiful white with a rich purple front lobe of the labellum. The larger proportion of white cattleyas are those bred from the albino forms and hybrids such this are not common in collections.

BRASSAVOLA DIGBYANA (Lindley) or *RHYNCOLAELIA DIGBYANA* of Schlechter. The title is immaterial when compared with the influence of this orchid on the flowers produced from association with cattleyas and laelias. As a cultivated orchid its delicacy of labellum and tendency to discoloration do not make it a very satisfactory species. No other orchid, however, has quite the same extraordinary feature exhibited by *R. digbyana* and it is difficult to imagine what the hybridists expected to gain from using it. Were they surprised? History does not tell us very much at all.

RHYNCOLAELIA GLAUCA (Lindley) Schlechter. This minor relative of *R. digbyana* has been compelled to live in the shadow of its exhibitionist associate. It grows well in cattleya conditions and the flowers last well, though they also tend to discolor a little. Some clones are pure white, others creamy white, the flowers long lasting. Its potential as hybridists' material does not seem to have been fully exploited.

BRASSOCATTLEYA MADAME HYE (*B. digbyana* × *C. loddigesii*), 1905, is one of the very early hybrids between these two genera. Neither flower had the petals or sepals to expect much in that part of the hybrid, but the beautiful labellum of *B. digbyana* was modified and translated into a different form. This invariably happened and nearly all the fimbriation was lost in every instance.

BRASSOCATTLEYA MOUNT HOOD (*Bc.* Deesse × *C.* Claris). This 'cattleya' is unusual because it has the white or albino forms of *C. gaskelliana, mossiae, lueddemanniana, warneri* and *labiata* in its make-up from the *C.* Claris side of the pedigree. On the other side it goes back to *C. warscewiczii, trianae* and *dowiana.* There is little else which could have entered this pedigree other than *B. digbyana* and a laelia. In all those species the preponderance of the white cattleyas was overwhelming and although there is the faintest tinge of color in the petals and sepals, it is to most outward aspects a white 'cattleya.'

BRASSOCATTLEYA MOUNT ANDERSON (*Bc.* Deesse × *C.* Bow Bells) has what *B. digbyana* gave to most of its progeny, the delicate shadings of mauve in the sepals and petals. From such parents it could have been expected that most of the seedlings would have been white. The exaggerated frilling of the labellum is the main feature of the flower, which is some 18 centimetres across. The labellums of many of the brassocattleyas and even the flowers with laelia included are so convoluted that there is little chance for them to open out properly and display their true area.

85

BRASSOLAELIOCATTLEYA
MEMORIA CRISPIN ROSALES (*Lc.*
Bonanza × *BLc.* Normans Bay). It is
not easy sometimes to pick the
difference between the flowers with
two genera and those with three.
The labellum of this hybrid is peak
development for the combination
and the cleft in its front lobe, unlike
that of *Bc.* Mount Anderson, is
effectively masked. Although it is a
disfigurement, this cleft is a natural
attribute of the flower and should
not be thought of as a deformity.
Such a view is, however, common
and mistaken. (See pedigree chart
on page 57.)

BRASSOLAELIOCATTLEYA
DESTINY (*Blc.* Xanthette × *Blc.*
Primate). The logical follow-on from
the simple inter-generic hybrid such
as a laeliocattleya was something
entailing three genera. This orchid
from that combination was bred
along yellow-gold lines already
outlined in the laeliocattleyas, but
the shape is obviously a throwback
to *B. digbyana.*

How to turn gold to green in one
simple cross-pollination is the
theme of this beautiful cattleya, the
parents of which are *Blc.* Destiny
and *Blc.* Helen Morita. The cross-
pollination was unnamed at the time
this was printed. The green came
from two sources, but there is little
doubt that *B. digbyana* contributed,
as reference to the picture of *Bc.*
Madama Hye will show. Green
cattleyas are not unusual, but none
of the species was green. It is a
cross-pollination involving recessive
characteristics and clever breeding
selection.

BRASSOLAELIOCATTLEYA
MALWORTH 'Orchidglade' is a
direct descendant from *L.*
Charlesworthii, illustrated on
another page, and *Blc.* Malvern. The
color comes again from *L.*
cinnabarina and *C. dowiana* var.
aurea. The number of quality clones
to be expected from such a cross-
pollination would be problematical
and it is not a pollination many
hybridists would make. *Blc* Malvern
is a super-'A' line cross with
reference to the breeding graph.
(See page 56.)

BRASSOLAELIOCATTLEYA
DINSMORE 'PERFECTION.' This
flower embodies all the good points
of each genus involved, the color
possibly inherited from laelia as
well as *Brassavola* (Rhyncolaelia)
digbyana (Lindley). The petals owe
their development to selective
breeding and this type of flower
would need careful cultivating and
shading.

BRASSOLAELIOCATTLEYA
HARLEQUIN (*Lc.* Memoria Albert
Heinecke × *Blc.* Nugget). It would
have been difficult to foresee the
elaborate extension of the labellum
pattern of *Rhyncolaelia digbyana*
exhibited in this hybrid, one of the
most beautiful flowers in a complex
breeding line, and a logical breeding
clone for the shape of its sepals. It
would be comparatively easy to
tame the labellum and the petals
into orthodox prize-winning material,
provided, of course, that it is not
sterile, as so many of these
complex hybrids are.

BRASSOLAELIOCATTLEYA SYLVIA FRY (*Blc.* Nacouchee × *C.* Bow Bells). It is not surprising that some cattleya fanciers dislike this flower, although it is a fairly good grower and flowers regularly. It is the accentuated rounded shape, which came as much from the albino bloodline of the Edithiae complex as from any other source, which the non-prize seekers find unsuitable. To most, however, it is the ultimate in mixed genera breeding. Go back again and look at some of the species cattleya labellums.

SOPHRONITIS COCCINEA (Lindley). This beautiful small orchid is sometimes called *S. grandiflora* and is related closely to cattleyas and laelias. It was introduced as the fourth member of intricate hybridising that resulted in potinaras. Colors of this species range from pale creamy-yellow through to blood red, but it is the latter which are most used. This flower is about 7 centimetres across. Most plants of *S. coccinea* produce only single flowers on each immature new growth.

SOPHRONITIS COCCINEA grows rapidly in conditions which suit and it is only a matter of a few years until a plant builds up into a specimen such as this. The influence of *S. coccinea* in hybridising is a little overwhelming for color, but is tempered in a lot of cross-pollinations by the gold to orange of *L. cinnabarina* and *C. dowiana.*

SOPHRONITIS CERNUA (Lindley) is a dwarf plant similar to *S. coccinea*, which grows to about 7 or 8 centimetres high. *S. cernua* is free with its flowers, spikes of seven and more being common. Its habitat is widespread in southern Brazil and an area where it grew profusely is described in the cattleya section in reference to *C. intermedia*, where masses of the orchid covered the trunks of trees.

SOPHRONITIS ROSEA. Its correct name is probably *S. wittigiana* when reference is made to the water-colors of *Orchidaceae Brasilienses*, by Pabst and Dungs. It has been known for so many years as *S. rosea* that the name has become permanent. Collectors, nurseries, packing houses and distributors alike have to lot to answer for in the misnaming of the orchids we grow and as the sophronitis are so similar morphologically it is not until they flower that there is a reasonable chance of naming them.

SOPHRONITELLA VIOLACEA (Lindley) was in early cultivation known as a sophronitis, but Schlechter's name for the single-member genus was given to it many years later. It is also a cool-growing Brazilian orchid like the sophronitis and when correctly cultivated soon multiplies and grows into a large clump. It is only some 8 to 10 centimetres high and seldom has more than a single flower to the almost mature growths, which make up in early autumn.

SOPHROLAELIOCATTLEYA
FALCON was an early experiment in tri-generic hybrids. It was raised by H. G. Alexander at Westonbirt between 1910 and 1917, when it was named. He used *Lc* Aureole, which led directly back to *L. tenebrosa* and *C. dowiana* var. *aurea*. It is obvious how dominant *S. coccinea* proved to be in the face of such competition. Westonbirt was the home of Lieut.-Colonel Sir George Holford and H. G. Alexander raised many famous hybrids for the owner in the years he was in charge of his orchid collection. In those days the name given to this tri-generic cross-pollination was sophrocatlaelia.

SOPHROLAELIOCATTLEYA ANZAC (*Slc.* Marathon × *Lc.* Dominiana) was raised by Charlesworths and named in 1921. It has remained the hallmark of excellence ever since and has formed the basis of many other cross-pollinations, none of which surpassed it although many equalled its brilliance.

SOPHROLAELIOCATTLEYA JEWEL BOX 'Dark Waters' is one of the *Slc.* Anzac tributes. Although a little smaller than *Slc.* Anzac, there are many fine clones of this cross-pollination between *Slc.* Anzac and *C. aurantiaca*, some cool growing and all very floriferous and fast growing, with heads of up to four flowers.

SOPHROLAELIOCATTLEYA
PAPRIKA 'Black Magic' (*Lc.* Orange
Gem × *Slc.* Anzac) is another lovely
example of the influence of this
great colored parent. It was raised
by Stewarts, American hybridists
noted for fine orchids of all genera.
Both *Slc.* Jewel Box and *Slc.*
Paprika were bred as small flowers.

SOPHROLAELIOCATTLEYA
HONOLULU 'Encino' was a cross-
pollination using large type
laeliocattleya stock and so
developed almost normal sized
flowers, still with the dominant
color inheritance from the
diminutive sophronitis.

SOPHROLAELIOCATTLEYA
CANZAC (*Slc.* Anzac × *Lc.*
Canberra), a lovely flower, the virtual
battleground between the color
influence of *S. coccinea* and that of
C. dowiana var. *aurea.* It was a
shaded win, because overlaying the
gold of Canzac is a patina of red
veining, partly from *S. coccinea* and
partly from *C. dowiana*, which in
some varieties had a most beautiful
overlay of purple-red. Unlike most of
the sophrolaeliocattleyas, this was
an unusually large flower some 12
centimetres across.

91

SOPHROLAELIA JINN (L. milleri × *S. coccinea).* This brilliant little orchid is a plant similar to its laelia parent and there is little to distinguish its flower from that of *L. milleri.* Both were red and if reference is made to the photograph of *L. milleri* its dominance is easily seen. Most clones of sophronitis are rounded in outline.

SOPHROLAELIA SOJOURN (*Sl.* Jinn × *S.* coccinea) has all the brilliance of *L. milleri* with two infusions of sophronitis. It is a miniature hybrid which surprisingly produces large flowers like this one, which is about 8 centimetres long, much larger than any of its antecedents. Based on *Orchidaceae Brasilienses,* the parent in one of the pollinations was probably *S. brevipedunculata* and not *S. coccinea.*

POTINARA GORDON SIU (*Slc.* Radians × *Bc.* Hartland) is the ultimate combination of the four genera — cattleyas, brassavola, laelias and sophronitis. It is equal in brilliance with *Slc.* Anzac and many other red cattleyas. The word cattleya is generally used to cover most of these flowers, hybrids or not. *Potinara* Gordon Siu also suffers the indignity of a misspelled name, frequently appearing as 'Sui' in some of the most authoritative books and publications. Regardless of the name, all the combined brilliance of the cattleyas and sophronitis is beautifully conveyed into this orchid.

92

LEPTOTES BICOLOR (Lindley), closely related to the laelias and cattleyas, is native to the warm areas of Brazil, growing in no fewer than eight regions and spilling over into neighboring Paraguay. The plant habit is small, with almost terete leaves and short clustering stems. It has been a popular orchid since its first flowering in the collection of Mrs Harrison, of Liverpool, to whom relatives in Brazil sent many famous orchids in the 1830-50 period. The seed pod or fruit is aromatic and was used at times as flavoring in those years. There are several species in the genus, which was once known as tetramicra and in the total family group it is probably one of the most ancient forms in the laelieae.

Epidendrums grown as balcony plants in an eastern suburb of Melbourne. Provided the outlook is to the east or north they do nearly as well as in the more favored parts of Australia. This is the hybrid *Epi. Obrienianum*, which is one of the best for cooler climates and flowers more easily than *Epi. radicans*. (Right)

EPIDENDRUM IBAGUENSE (Humboldt, Bonpland and Kunth) is a species on which it is impossible to get much definition. This spike of flowers is from a plant so named, but it may be a close relative, because it is most frequently called by a synonym, *Epi. radicans*. It is typical of the so-called reed-stemmed members of the genus.

Epidendrums of the reed-stemmed group are easily grown in sub-tropical and tropical regions such as the northern part of eastern Australia, where the rainfall pattern is heavy in the hotter months of the year. As a genus they are hardy, growing in open sunlight or very sparse shade throughout the year.

93

EPIDENDRUM SAGITTARIUS. Through selective breeding the size of hybrids has been increased, although the numbers of flowers on the stem are mostly fewer and their life shorter. Inversion of the flowers is common in many types of epidendrums.

EPIDENDRUM SUNRAY. Climate has a lot to do with the number of flowers and the durability of the elongating spike. It is possible for spikes to last in flower for up to six or eight months and they may be grown just as easily in glass-houses in southern Australia as in the northern states. To do so they must have plenty of light and particularly in the winter months under clear glass.

EPIDENDRUM LILAC QUEEN. Colors of the reed-stemmed epidendrums range through all those familiar in cattleyas, from white to deep red and purple, but the genus almost completely lacks blue factors. *Epi.* Lilac Queen almost looks as though it could be the road to a tint of blue, but that tint may be just as elusive as it is in the cattleyas.

EPIDENDRUM PARKINSONIANUM
(Hooker) is an unusual orchid,
growing completely pendulous, with
only the rhizome from which the
long, deeply channelled leaves grow
each year. The flowers appear in the
axil of the leaf and the growth shoot
from the rhizome immediately above
them. This orchid will grow in
conditions down to 6 degrees
Celsius without too much trouble,
but frost will kill it.

EPIDENDRUM CILIARE (Linnaeus)
belongs to the group which has
pseudo-bulbs and cattleya-like
leaves. While some of the orchids of
this type, particularly the Mexican
species, have been renamed
encyclias, many are still known as
epidendrums and a great amount of
confusion is thus caused.

ENCYCLIA CHACAOENSIS
(Reichenbach f.) (syn. *Epi.
ionophlebium*). This is an orchid
from a distinctive Mexican section
which produces a cluster of flowers
backing on to each other and also
upside down. The plant grows about
30 centimetres tall, has a nice close-
set habit and is fairly easy to grow
and flower. The blooms are
delightfully and strongly perfumed
on a sunny day.

ENCYCLIA LINKIANA (Klotsch). A Mexican orchid which grows at about 1000 to 2000 metres. It has a creeping rhizome system similar to that of *Coelogyne cristata* and so different from the reed-stemmed epidendrums. The flowers are sparsely produced.

ENCYCLIA COCHLEATA (Linnaeus). One of the most beautiful of the Mexican encyclias with its shell-like labellum and dark coloring. The plant is not unlike a brassia, but this species is fairly easy to grow and flower in a moderately warm glass-house in southern Australia.

ENCYCLIA VITELLINA (Lindley) is one of the oldest cultivated orchids. It was featured in lithographs and colored drawings in the period 1820-40, but no artist managed to capture the beautiful color. It is one of the easiest of the encyclias to grow for a start, but proves most difficult to keep going. Growing naturally at 1500 to 2500 metres, it is comparatively cold-growing and a little outdoor treatment in the summer may suit it better. Like most the encyclias and epidendrums its flowering period is most variable in cultivation, which indicates more than anything else the need for study to get everything right.

ENCYCLIA MARIAE (Ames). Most cattleya-like of all the epidendrums, it remained undiscovered until about 1930, and still remained a secret for a few years more. The color is variable from year to year and it is possible to flower such a yellow-petalled form as this a bright green, which, with the white and green labellum, makes it a most attractive orchid, the size of the flowers a surprise for such a small plant. *Encyclia mariae* grows at about 1000 metres and higher in a cool, rather dry climate.

ENCYCLIA CORDIGERA (Humboldt, Bonpland and Kunth) (syn. *Epi. atropurpureum*). This encyclia is most variable in color, ranging from the palest of shades to dense brown-purple in the petals and sepals. Considered by many growers to be the best of the Mexican encyclias and much easier to cultivate in moderate warmth than some of the others. During its history it has had many names, generated by its color variations as much as for any other reasons, although different 'discoverers' also confused things a bit.

ENCYCLIA CITRINA (Llave and Lexarza) forms a complete two-member section of the encyclias with *E. mariae*. Once known as *Cattleya citrina*, this orchid has always proved a difficult one to cultivate and keep virile. Few growers keep it going for long and there must also be some little facet like a spell outdoors which may prolong and even invigorate the plant. During its history it has had no fewer than five different names (Left).

EPIDENDRUM PATENS (Swartz). Similar to the reed-stemmed types, but the growths much shorter. It prefers warm conditions, as it grows in a number of Central and South American areas, including the Caribbean islands. The usual source for plants is Brazil. Most green flowered orchids attract attention, but *E. patens* must be given the right conditions and light to have the best color.

97

EPIDENDRUM PSEUDEPIDENDRUM
(Reichenbach f.) is a startling
contrast in color, but the flowers are
sparsely produced. A warm climate
orchid not frequently noted in
collections. The flowers are up to
about 4 centimetres across.

ENCYCLIA POLYBULBON (Swartz)
grows over a wide area of Mexico,
Central America and adjacent
islands. It is attractive because it
grows freely, a small piece soon
propagating into a large plant
because of the number of new
growths which may be had from a
single pseudo-bulb. It is a good
subject for slab culture in a
moderately warm glass-house or
even in the open in frost-free
conditions.

EPICATTLEYA PREVIEW (*C.
bowringiana* × *Epi. brevifolium*).
The hybrids from *C. bowringiana*
usually take after it and this one is
no exception. *Epicat.* Preview was a
Hawaiian inspiration from W. W. G.
Moir, an outstanding hybridiser and
experimental cross-pollinator. The
orchid-breeding community is
indebted to him as much as to any
other individual in the craft.

EPICATTLEYA NEBO (*C.* Claesiana × *Epi.* Obrienianum). Few genera escaped the craze for experimental hybridising and *Epicat.* Nebo was a very early attempt. Although there seems sufficient scope within the genera to occupy the attention of hybridists, no one seems to learn from the past mistakes of pollinators. This orchid appeared to be sterile, but apparently it needed only the right combination to set it off again. The labellum inversion was too strong even for the cattleyas, although on this spike they are pointing in all directions.

EPIPHRONITIS VEITCHII (*S. coccinea* × *Epi. radicans*) was raised in the Veitch nursery in 1890. The habit of the plant is miniature reed-stem and the flowers brilliant. But they are not produced as freely as the epidendrums and the only influence of the sophronitis was color — the rest is all epidendrum.

EPIDENDRUM ELFIN (*Encyclia cochleata* × *Epi. prismatocarpum*). The combination name for this hybrid will possibly be epicyclia or something similar, but in the mixed taxonomy of the genus at present there is still a lot of sorting out to be done. This bright little orchid has a great deal to recommend it for further cross-pollination.

ODONTOGLOSSUM CRISPUM (Lindley), the white form of the so-called Pacho type, this specimen being given the varietal name *premier*. The crispums ranged from white to pink and blotched forms, the Pacho type beautifully formed and carrying up to ten or twelve large flowers on a strong spike. This is a spike on a plant I grew in the 1950-60 period.

ODONTOGLOSSUM TRIUMPHANS (Reichenbach f.), another of the many Colombian species. This orchid formed the background to many of the beautifully marked hybrids generated in the golden years of the genus from 1900 onward, and is noted in another illustration. This is a Joan Skilbeck pastel drawing.

ODONTOGLOSSUM PESCATOREI (Linden) was later renamed *Odonto nobile* (Reichenbach f.). This illustration is of a lithograph in *The Orchid Album*. This species had a much wider labellum than *Odonto. crispum* and most of the hybrids developed from it had this characteristic. *Odonto. nobile* has largely disappeared from cultivation, but a number of *Odonto crispums* are still grown.

ODONTOGLOSSUM ALVANEUX
(*Odonto*. Alvara × *Odonto*.
Molyneux), raised in 1945 by
Charlesworths, among the first-
ranking breeders of the genus, was
typical of the large white and faintly
tinted and marked flowers
generated by the pacho-type
odontoglossums. In early species
cultivation high premiums were paid
on the slightly blotched and pure
white varieties.

One of the best indicators of the
health of a glass-house as well as
the general growing system from
the mix to the pot and even the
benching and watering is the growth
of heads of sphagnum moss on the
surface of the mix. Of all orchids
the odontoglossums seem to like
this humidity about the base of the
plant. It indicates by its appearance
when the mix is going dry, also
when the plant is getting too much
water. If moss will not grow the
whole system should be overhauled,
starting with the ventilation and
finishing with the type of pot in
which the plants are growing.

ODONTOGLOSSUM SUNFLY
'Glenda Raymond' (*Odonto*.
Brimstone Butterfly × *Odonto*.
Sunglow) is one of the most
beautiful clear yellow
odontoglossums ever bred. Its
background is largely unknown, but
it goes back to *Odonto. luteo-
purpureum* (Lindley) and both
Odonto. crispum and *Odonto.
pescatorei*, through all of which it
could get the buttercup yellow tint
that makes it so outstanding.

101

ODONTOGLOSSUM CRISPATRIUM
(*Odonto. crispum* × *Odonto.*
Natrium) shows how direct the
influence of *Odonto. triumphans*
can be on its hybrids. It was raised
by Charlesworths, of England, in
1946, the seedlings apparently
surviving the terrible years for that
country from 1939 onward to 1945,
during which many priceless orchids
of all sorts were lost.

ODONTOGLOSSUM HALTON
(*Odonto. crispum* × *Odonto.*
Lartium) is the developed progeny of
the original blotched *Odonto.*
crispum. The markings on all these
species and hybrids were
inconsistent from flower to flower
and, as some of the best cultivators
of all time found out, from year to
year. Sometimes they paid very high
prices for well-blotched forms, only
to find that the following year they
exhibited very little blotching. The
labellum should be noted — it is the
true *crispum* type without the
influence of *Odonto. pescatorei*
(*Odonto. nobile*). *Odonto.* Halton is
10 centimetres across, a very large
flower for the genus.

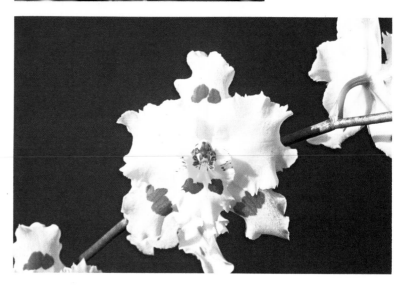

COCHLIODA NOEZLIANA
(Reichenbach f.), the small Peruvian
orchid which brought dramatic
changes to the odontoglossums.
The inquisitive hybridists who first
tried to use it had their problems.
The odontoglossums already had
color in the various species, but the
cochlioda gave them brilliance
where they had only pink and
shades of pale rose.

ODONTIODA VUYLSTEKEAE
(*Cochlioda noezliana* × *Odonto.*
Clytie). This is a propagation from
one of the original clones, the plant
imported into Australia in the
1920-30 period. There is a tendency
for the small size of the cochlioda
species to be imparted to the
complex and they are never quite as
large as true odontoglossums.

ODONTIODA CHARLESWORTHII
(*Cochlioda noezliana* x *Odonto.*
Harryanum), which so quickly
followed *Oda.* Vuylstekeae, was a
totally different type of flower. The
photographs of both these
odontiodas were of plants which I
grew in the 1950-60 decade. Both
were strong growers and flowered
readily, after the fashion of so many
primary hybrids, even in inter-
generic cross-pollinations.

ODONTIODA VALERIE (*Oda.* Evelyn × *Odonto.* Alvara) is a direct throwback in a cross-pollination. The dominance of color and size of the cochlioda is quite apparent. The clear red of the cochlioda is very unusual in the mixed genera hybrids, but it could be expected even in larger inter-generic hybrids if the recessive factors are correctly chosen.

ODONTIODA BRUTUS (*Oda.* Ithaque × *Odonto.* Petit Ami). Not all the cochlioda hybrids run to the red shades and the beautiful sunburnt color of this cross-pollination is a hand-me-down from the species *Odonto. nobile* (syn. *pescatorei*), the influence of which, similar to that of *L. cinnabarina* in cattleyas, is never lost. There is also a touch in it of Odonto. *triumphans*.

ODONTIODA ACTRIX (*Oda.* Actia × *Oda.* Lautrix) has the type of labellum and color, but not quite the shape of the best of the odontiodas. Number of flowers is also a problem with some of the odontiodas, because the species *Cochlioda noezliana* does not have many more than six to nine flowers in the best efforts. Some varieties are known with more, but they are rare and must be well grown.

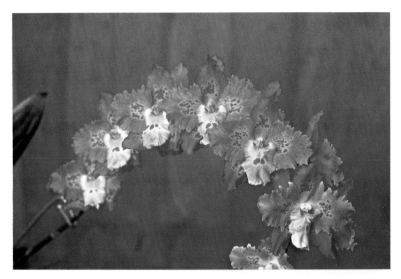

ODONTIODA FLORENCE STIRLING 'The Duchess' (*Oda.* Astoria × *Oda. Melina*) is close to the ultimate aim of the hybridist in shape as well as color, not all of which came from the cochlioda side. If particular note is taken of the petal and sepal markings the great difference in the areas and shapes of the blotches will be apparent.

ONCIDIODA CHARLESWORTHII (*Cochlioda noezliana* × *Oncidium incurvum*) was one of the first steps in a chain of inter-generic cross-pollinations that is still open to innovation. It was named by Charlesworths in 1910 and considering later developments the firm must at times have wished they were not so free in bestowing their name on the early ones. It is still an attractive free flowering and noted plant in orchid collections seventy years later.

ODONTOCIDIUM JACOBERT (*Odontocidium* Tiger Butter × *Odm.* Toralis) is the beginning of another affiliation, although not the first odontocidium in the hybrid list. Like most of the odontoglossum complex, the odontocidiums follow an odontoglossum style of flower and most traces of the original *Oncidium tigrinum* have been lost.

105

ODONTOCIDIUM JOE JACOBS was bred on one side from *Oncidium concolor* and its labellum is obvious in the hybrid. The color also comes largely from the oncidium, petals and all, which have been narrowed by the same influence.

ODONTONIA LULLI (*Miltonia Babiole* × *Odonto. Nabab*). This orchid, like so many of the odontonias, has inherited the odontoglossum shape but includes some of the miltonia labellum. These orchids are not all so much inclined toward the miltonia lip, but the influence of the original species miltonias has carried through to make it a most attractive hybrid line.

VUYLSTEKEARA ESTELLA JEWELL (*Vuyl. Aspasia* × *Miltonia* William Pitt). The vuylstekearas include the genera miltonias, odontoglossums and cochliodas. In all the inter-generic hybridising the basic shape of the flower remained largely unchanged and the morphology, although reflecting some differences from odontoglossums, has also remained similar. *M. William Pitt* had a background almost wholly derived from the species *M. vexillaria* and *M. roezlii*. On the other side the line went back to *Oda* Charlesworthii and the same miltonias.

WILSONARA SALGRIN (*Oncidium tigrinum* × *Oda* Salway). These inter-generic hybrids were first tried some time in the 1910-20 period and faded out with the dereliction of odontoglossums in the cymbidium age, which ranged from 1930 into the 1980 period. First-generation wilsonaras included some specimens with flower spikes well over a metre long and with gaps of 10 to 15 centimetres between the flowers. Selective breeding reduced length and spacing and use of different oncidiums also had an effect. The American breeder R. B. Dugger and the German hybridiser Wichman brought the wilsonaras back into favor with some rather startling hybrids. (See pedigree chart on page 57.)

CUITLAUZINA PENDULA (La Llave and Lexarza) Halbinger (syn. *Odont. citrosmum*), a beautiful Mexican species rarely noted in collections. The collector Roezl, quoted from 1883, wrote: 'Great was my surprise to see the trees clothed with a profusion of orchids which proved to be *Odontoglossum citrosmum*, whose pendulous spikes, a yard long [little less than a metre], were adorned with innumerable white and lilac flowers . . . During several days' march we noticed that all the oak trees were clothed in this way by the same orchid, which flowers more freely when it is exposed to the direct rays of the sun.'

LEMBOGLOSSUM ROSSII (Lindley) is one of the hardiest of the family, its history more thoroughly covered in the text. It is one of the few orchids introduced into the odontoglossum complex which has a dominant influence, casting its image in no uncertain way on most hybrids, particularly in the shape and number of flowers.

107

*ODONTOGLOSSUM
STAMFORDIENSE (Odonto.
bictoniense × Odonto. uro-skinneri)*
was raised in 1909, using two of the
smaller species, with the beautiful
characteristic of long spikes of
flower 60 centimetres and more
high. The flowers reflect perhaps
more of *Odonto. uro-skinneri* than
the other parent. The flower spikes
of both grow erect, each bloom
about 3 to 4 centimetres across.

*ODONTOGLOSSUM LOIS JOY
(Odontoglossum rossii ×
Odontoglossum Moselle).* The
species *Odm. rossii* almost totally
dominates. It may take another
generation to break that influence and
bring out its true potential in colors of
an unusual kind. The generic title
odontoglossum is retained because
this is the way it appears in Sander's
List of Orchid Hybrids.

ROSSIOGLOSSUM GRANDE
(Lindley), one of the most
flamboyant of all orchids. A native
of Guatemala, it has been featured
in text, lithographs, drawings,
paintings, and finally in color
photography. The color photographs
capture its brassy, glossy, unusual
coloring best of all. *Rossioglossum
grande* would not cross-pollinate
with odontoglossums and seemed
to have no affiliations whatsoever,
but a breakthrough finally came
with an odontonia, before which
Odonto. (Rossioglossum) grande
accepted the pollen of *Miltonia
regnellii*. However, there is still no
breakthrough to the main
odontoglossum stream.

OSMOGLOSSUM PULCHELLUM is better known as *Odontoglossum pulchellum* (Bateman). Rudolf Schlechter's name has been adopted for the genus, which is among the easier orchids to grow. As it flowers in winter, its bright spikes of bloom make it a most attractive cool-climate orchid. The labellum is inverted like that of the reed-stemmed epidendrums and some of the encyclias, and this aspect of many orchid flowers still intrigues botanists.

MILTONIA VEXILLARIA (Reichenbach f.) is the dominant species in a group of orchids which caused the discard of other species in the collections of England and Europe. As the odontoglossums were ruthlessly collected and exported, so too were the miltonias once their habitat became known. *M. vexillaria* carries up to five or six flowers, which are much smaller than the hybrids developed from it. A Joan Skilbeck pastel drawing.

MILTONIA VEXILLARIA var. *superbum*, the flower noted in the text, as related by John Day. This is not his drawing of the flower, but is a lithograph from the hand of J. Nugent Fitch, reproduced from *The Orchid Album*, and known in that period as *Odonto. vexillaria*. (See page 197.)

MILTONIA ROEZLII (Reichenbach f.) became the partner of *M. vexillaria* in producing *M.* Bleuana about 1885 and subsequently back-crossed to produce variations responsible for many of the miltoniopsis of the 1970-80 decade. The adoption of the name miltoniopsis is not general, but serves to distinguish these orchids from the totally different Brazilian orchids.

109

MILTONIA VICTORY (*M.* Armanda × *M.* Princess Margaret) has taken the pink coloring of *M. vexillaria* through several generations. On well-grown plants many of the hybrids in the fifth and further generations still carry five or six flowers, all of them larger than the original species.

MILTONIA (*M.* Gascogne × *M.* Alderwood) with the white from either of the two original progenitors, as *M. vexillaria* ranged from rose-pink through to white. The labellum is a combination of both, and modern breeding seeks to make the petals and sepals broader than the originals. Neither this nor the other *M.* Gascogne hybrid were named when the book was printed.

MILTONIA (*M.* Gascogne × *M.* Woodlands). Both parents here were colored and the white factors from *M. roezlii* did not have much chance to show through. This photograph shows just how dominant the labellum is, particularly the mask just underneath the column. The cleft in the lower edge of the labellum is a disfigurement which may be bred to a minimum to produce a near-perfect flower.

MILTONIA (Bellingham × Yarrow Bay) like the other unnamed seedlings in these illustrations, is a comparatively recent hybrid of the 1970-80 period. The source of the yellow coloring is uncertain because the parent *M.* Yarrow Bay apparently also was not registered at the time this was printed. *M.* Bellingham goes back into a shadowy unrecorded past in *M.* Princess Margaret. There are very few yellow miltonias and the original coloring may have come from *M. warscewiczii.*

MILTONIA CELLE 'Wasserfal' has petals, sepals and labellum all fully developed and it is this type of flower which hybridists produced to gain recognition in award and show judging. The raisers were the German hybridists Wichman. There is not a great amount of variation in the pansy-type miltonias except for color.

In summer, when so many orchid growers are lamenting that they have few if any flowers, the miltonia grower may have a show such as this, with color and size variations almost unlimited. However, some care must be taken to keep the plants going through the winter and into summer without too great a variation in temperature. Some other orchids will not tolerate this.

MILTONIA CLOWESII. A reproduction from an old lithograph. As noted in the text, it has been renamed and is now transferred to the oncidiums. For most purposes it will remain a miltonia because of hybrid affiliations. It was named by Lindley.

MILTONIA REGNELLII (Reichenbach f.). This Brazilian miltonia has been involved in a considerable amount of hybridising by two or three specialists. It is a moderately small flower but has some appeal in the work owing to its labellum.

MILTONIA SPECTABILIS (Lindley). The most beautiful of the Brazilian miltonias. With *M. clowesii* it was the parent of *M. bluntii*, a natural hybrid, recognised by Reichenbach in 1879. The material on which he based his surmise came from England, hinted at by a nurseryman named Richard Bullen, who had a consignment of plants from Brazil which contained the stranger.

MILTONIA BLUNTII (Reichenbach f.). Many of the early collectors who saw species orchids in flower noted strange members in the plants they gathered and if they were careful enough to tag and record their finds the botanists to whom they were referred had little trouble identifying them as combinations of species.

MILTONIA FLAVESCENS (Lindley) brings the sober reflection that not all the flowers in a genus can be big, bright and beautiful. This Brazilian and Paraguayan species has a habit like some of the oncidiums with its steeply climbing rhizome and rather long spikes of some twelve to fifteen flowers spaced out over their length. It is a good talking point in a collection or exhibition.

MILTASSIA ESTRELITA (*M. regnellii* × *Brassia maculata*) was raised by the Hawaiian hybridiser Kirsch in the 1950 period. Of all the miltonia inter-generic cross-pollinations this ranks one of the best. Despite the opinions of some of the hybridists that *M. regnellii* does not discolor, *Miltassia* Estrelita inherited this failing from some source and unfortunately the flowers do not retain their original freshness as some orchids do. Probably cultural, the problem may be solved by treatment of the plant and flowers after opening in the same way as other flowers are treated relative to temperature and air freshness.

ONCIDIUM VARICOSUM (Lindley). A considerable amount of work done with oncidiums is based on this orchid. Until 1945 no one paid much attention to it, but after that time a flood of hybrids appeared, nearly all of which bore its indelible stamp — the broad yellow labellum. The other flower parts are insignificant. Well-authenticated records show that O. varicosum var. rogersii had been flowered with a labellum 7 centimetres across about 1890.

ONCIDIUM CRISPUM (Loddiges). A cool-growing Brazilian species which flowers in autumn from the new pseudo-bulbs. The branched spike may carry up to fifty or sixty flowers. This plant is growing naturally on a tree in southern Victoria, but oncidiums generally need a warmer climate to grow and flower well.

ONCIDIUM CRISPUM flowers are glossy and long lasting. The pseudo-bulbs are larger than those of O. varicosum and the leaves broader and stouter.

ONCIDIUM LANCEANUM (Lindley), with its tough, leathery leaves and little or no pseudo-bulb storage capacity, soon shows signs of poor growing conditions. An ideal subject for warmer areas, it should do as well in garden culture as any of the cattleyas. The flowers are among the most colorful of all oncidiums.

ONCIDIUM MACULATUM (Lindley), native of Mexico and Guatemala, has more balance to the flower, the petals and sepals much more prominent than in some of the Brazilian oncidiums. Unfortunately, the labellum usually discolors after the flower has been out for some days and for some reason the hybridists have done little with what appears to be a promising subject. It has been used more in inter-generic hybrids than within its own genus.

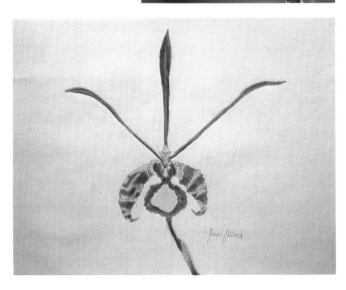

ONCIDIUM PAPILIO (Lindley). A Joan Skilbeck pastel drawing of this beautiful and graceful orchid. The plant which produces it is unimpressive, the pseudo-bulbs usually small, flattened, shrivelled and an unhealthy brown-yellow, aged appearance giving the impression of something on its last legs, which unfortunately is too often the truth. It is seldom suited to artificial culture and fortunate indeed the grower who chances on a happy home for it.

115

ONCIDIUM HAEMATOCHILUM
(Lindley), a natural hybrid between
O. lanceanum and *O. luridum*. The
flowers are scented and last well on
the plant, which has the same
appearance of leaves with nothing
to back them up, after the style of
its parent *O. lanceanum*. It is a
native of Colombia.

ONCIDIUM KUQUAT (*O. splendidum*
× *O. haematochilum*), a hybrid
raised by the American Karl Kugust
in the 1960 period. *O. splendidum* (A.
Richard), although having deeply
channelled thick leaves, has a little
more pseudo-bulb than similar
orchids and the flower with a bright
yellow-gold labellum, the stem
capable of growing to a metre long,
with complementary flower
numbers.

ONCIDIUM HASTATUM (Bateman) is
remarked on in the text, but Veitch,
rather than remark on its odor, said
that 'its long, loose panicles over
which its star-like flowers are not
very thickly scattered are made
attractive by the surprising variety
of colors ...' Owing to the spread
of the flowers on a spike it is a
photographer's nightmare.

Many oncidiums prefer to go almost dry for some months during their dormancy and pots like these slotted examples are very suitable because even if they get an occasional watering they soon aerate and dry and the root systems do not suffer. Mostly such pots and wire racks are more suitable for small seedling plants, and once they start to grow and show their climbing habits they should be treated as such and mounted on slabs or fern sticks to suit.

ONCIDIUM SARCODES (Lindley). This Brazilian orchid has been in cultivation for almost 150 years — some say longer. Originally coming from Rio de Janeiro, the source of the plants was kept secret for some time and it was rare in collections. Unlike some of the other species used to produce the hybrid oncidiums, *O. sarcodes* has good petal and sepal development. From an old lithograph.

ONCIDIUM MICHAEL JUPP (O. Splinter × O. sarcodes). This is an Australian-raised hybrid, free flowering but small, on long branching spikes. There is little doubt where the petals and sepals came from. *O.* Splinter was the cross-pollination of *O. sphacelatum* and *O. leucochilum,* one of Moir's beautiful productions.

117

ONCIDIUM SAVANNA SUNSET — small is beautiful just as big is beautiful. These flowers are less than 3 centimetres long and originated in the species *O. triquetrum* and *O. pulchellum*, two species occurring in the islands of the Caribbean area of the Central American region. The plants have no pseudo-bulbs, thick and deeply channelled leaves and the whole plant somewhat reminiscent of the aerides of the Asian area. The spikes are long and wiry and the flowers usually sparse. It is developed from warm-growing oncidiums and this section, being so different morphologically from other oncidiums, has been suggested as a separation from that genus.

An unnamed oncidium. Developed from *O. Palmyre* and *O. Sultamyre*, both of which are descendants from *O. varicosum* and the section to which it belongs. The inclusions are *O. forbesii*, *O. gardneri* and *O. tigrinum*. *O. gardneri* is a natural hybrid between *O. dastyle* and *O. forbesii* and was discovered by Gardner in the Organ mountains in Brazil. The bright, flat labellum is the focal point of all these flowers bred in the complex since then, with little improvement or elaboration of the petals until hybridists worked on that section. (Left)

ONCIDIUM HAMILTON GOLD (*O. Phyllis Wells × O. varicosum*) perhaps best illustrates the futility of some cross-pollinations, where the petals and sepals are no larger or prominent than in the species. Although it is a beautiful flower it is to some degree a replica of the results of so many previous cross-pollinations.

ONCIDIUM, unnamed. (*O. Kuron × O. crispum-O. Sultamyre*.) Again the hybridist has outstripped the registration process. But by going back to the species *O. crispum* a definite enlargement of the petals and sepals has been achieved, although perhaps outweighed by the magnificent labellum. Few hybrids surpass this example — it is large as well as beautiful. Typically, the number of flowers has been reduced with the increase in size, but this is quite tolerable.

Probably this hybrid came from the species *O. flexuosum* (Sims), but is the victim of carelessness with labels. It has no name. There is a number of such plants about and the common name for them seems to be *O.* Golden Shower whether they have labels in the pots or not. Most of them have a rhizome system which does not climb too steeply and may be cultivated into fairly large plants without the usual difficulties of a 'climber.'

ASPASIA LUNATA. This genus as well as *A. lunata* were named by Lindley. They are related to the oncidiums and indefinitely to the odontoglossums and all similar genera interbred over the last eighty years. The aspasias are fairly widespread over South America and some of the Caribbean and Atlantic islands, only recently coming to the knowledge of most growers because of hybridising. *A. lunata* is a Brazilian orchid from a number of provinces in the south-eastern sector.

ASPASIA EPIDENDROIDES or *ASPASIA PRINCIPISSA* (Reichenbach f.), although mostly single-small or two-flowered, was exploited with the odontoglossum complex in the search for inter-generics with the style of odontoglossums and tolerance to warmer conditions, the ultimate aim incorporation of miltonias in the section through odontonias. This orchid and its variants grow in much of Central America and Colombia.

119

MILPASIA ANCON (*Milpasia* Spectacular × *Miltonia* Anne Warne), which, through *Milpasia* Spectacular combined *A. principissa* with *M. spectabilis* and possibly commenced a line which could be inter-bred with the odontoglossum complex. *Milpasia* Ancon had few flowers, but little else could be expected considering its antecedents. (Left)

MILTONIDIUM LEE HIRSCH (*M. spectabilis* × *O. varicosum*), allowing for some incompatibility, is another avenue of approach toward the odontoglossum complex. There is more possibility for this type of hybridising within the Brazilian miltonia section, but the Colombian miltoniopsis species and hybrids should also be in the reckoning because of their labellum features. The continuation of the oncidium petals and sepals would be a hazard and neither of the two miltonia families has much to recommend it in that section of its flowers.

ADA AURANTIACA (Lindley) was discovered in Colombia by the Belgian collector Schlim about 1850 at some 2500 metres altitude. It is a beautiful, free-growing orchid with a root system similar to many of the masdevallias. Like that genus, it may be grown in cool conditions and should not be allowed to dry out. The foliage discolors and browns at the tips in the same way as masdevallias and this is usually due to poor ventilation and high humidity.

ADA AURANTIACA flower spikes usually arch over with the head pendant, the individual flowers about 3 to 4 centimetres long. As it is more of a tube of petals and sepals, pollinators must be small. Color is the attraction and ada has been cross-pollinated with odontoglossums, brassias and other species, the hybrids retaining some of the color but losing much of the ada identity.

An unnamed brassada (*A. aurantiaca* × *Brassia brachiata*). Some of the ada color tints this hybrid, but it is all brassia in shape and the flower quite large. The number of flowers is sometimes reduced in various hybrids by the influence of *A. aurantiaca* and they have only about six or seven blooms.

BRASSIA VERRUCOSA (Lindley) is possibly the commonest and best known of the genus. An easy orchid to grow, it likes to remain undisturbed for a few years and its habit of 'going to sleep' for some months respected. When the flowers open they last better if removed to slightly cooler conditions and may even be taken into the house and used for effective decoration. As a 'talking point' they would liven up any party, but are hardly suited at times to scent the surroundings.

BRASSIA ANTHEROTES is a Colombian orchid according to some authorities, with others listing it as Central American. It is among the larger brassias and like *B. gireoudiana* well colored. It was found originally by two brothers named Klaboch somewhere about 1879 and little was known about it for many years thereafter.

121

BRASSIA LONGISSIMA or *B. lawrenceana* var. *longissima* has been known to develop petals some 20 to 25 centimetres long. Like most of the genus it flowers in early to midsummer, occasionally surprising in warmer conditions with spikes in other seaons.

MACLELLANARA PAGAN LOVE SONG (*Odontocidium* Tiger Butter × *Brassia verrucosa*). Each year an extension of the various alliances comes to light and it is rather hard to say where it will all stop. In this flower something of the brassia shows out as well as the other genera.

BRASSAVOLA NODOSA (Linnaeus) growing in a slat basket. This type of container has been quoted freely in the text and this example was made from strips of red pine, a very durable wood. Other timbers may be used, but should be selected from two points of view — in addition to lasting qualities it should be inert and not able to affect orchid roots. The stiff, slender, terete-type leaves of *Brassavola nodosa* are a give-away to the amount of light under which it should be grown.

BRASSAVOLA ACAULIS (Lindley and Paxton), from Central America, is an early to late summer flowering species, morphologically similar to most of the other brassavolas and requiring warm conditions. Many of these orchids will tolerate quick-dissolving organic fertilisers like blood and bone in their growing season, with nothing at all in dormancy and little water also in that stage of their life.

BRASSAVOLA CUCCULATA (Linnaeus), sitting like some great tropical spider waiting for its prey. This is a more spectacular member of the genus, remarkable for its long, ribbon-like petals and sepals and the long, slender labellum which broadens out just under the column in the centre of the flower to a beautiful fimbriated adornment.

BRASSOLAELIA RICHARD MUELLER (*B. nodosa* × *L. milleri*). All the color and brilliance of the small laelia has been lost in this bright little hybrid. The brassavolas as a genus are readily cross-pollinated into several other genera by hand, but in natural conditions such associations would be almost impossible.

123

ZYGOPETALUM MACKAYI (Hooker), probably the best known of the genus. It is non-variable, but several different types seem to have been known over the years. The largest of the zygopetalums, it grows spikes sometimes a metre tall and carrying up to ten flowers. Supposed to be a cold-growing species, as indeed it will grow, the results are always a little better, with no leaf blackening, when grown in a warm glass-house through the winter months after it has finished flowering.

ZYGOPETALUM CRINITUM (Loddiges). This photograph of a plant growing and flowering in my garden in southern Victoria, planted in the fork of a casuarina tree, well fed on organic fertilisers such as animal manures and leaf mould. It is also given a spray with liquid nutrients whenever the rest of the collection in similar situations get their periodic dose. The winter temperature frequently falls as low as 6 degrees.

ZYGOPETALUM BLACKII 'Negus' (*Z. crinitum* × *Z.* Perrenoudii), a hybrid of some age (1914) yet still freely cultivated. It is as colorful as any of the hybrids raised since that year — and there were few up to 1980. The hybrid *Z.* Perrenoudii was the result of the cross-pollination *Z. intermedium* × *Z. maxillare*, raised in 1894. Most of the species are not well known or easily recognised from descriptions and some confusion and wrong naming exist, particularly with the species *Z.* (Loddiges). (Left)

ZYGOPETALUM JOHN BANKS (*Z. Blackii* × *Z. crinitum*) is a comparatively modern hybrid, richly colored, but losing some of the intensity of *Z. Blackii*. It was raised and named in 1975, the number of flowers also consistent with the species in the cross-pollination.

124

Frequently exhibited as *Zygopetalum crinitum*, this species is typical of the confusion over names. It is most likely a variety of the Brazilian species *Z. triste*, identifiable in the watercolors of Pabst and Dung's *Orchidaceae Brasilienses.*

PROMENAEA XANTHINA (Lindley). In a period when the aim of all hybridists is to breed larger and larger flowers and growers to own a collection of orchids which will win prizes instead of admiration this little orchid comes as a pleasant relief. The plant itself seldom grows more than 12 centimetres high, with the flowers encircling the base like a coronet. Left undisturbed it will grow quickly into a specimen about 15 centimetres across. Preferably grown in shallow pots, it should be accommodated in a light cymbidium mix.

PROMENAEA STAPELIOIDES (Lindley). Never bearing as many flowers at once as its bright relative, this pretty little orchid is similar, but the leaves tend to stay lower and the flower stems a little shorter. The silvery-green leaves always look as though suffering an attack of red spider, which could be the real thing unless watched.

RODRIGUEZIA SECUNDA
(Humboldt, Bonpland, Kunth). The
genus was named by Kuntze in
honor of Barbosa-Rodrigues, a
noted Brazilian botanist and
authority on orchids. *R. secunda*
was introduced from Trinidad about
1818, but its habitat is widespread
over Central and South America. It
became one of the 'toys' of
hybridists over the 1950-80 period in
combinations with the
odontoglossum-oncidium complex.
Its beautiful coloring was the
attraction and this is one of the
best plants possible to see in
cultivation. Some of the genus are
cool-growing.

RODRIGUEZIA VENUSTA (Lindley).
This Brazilian orchid is a contrast to
R. secunda with its purity of color.
When naming it Lindley remarked:
'This beautiful species is
remarkable for the delicious odor
which its flowers exhale.' Epiphytes,
the rodriguezias are remarkable for
the masses of aerial roots they
grow. Potting such plants is useless
and they should be grown on tree-
fern sticks or in slat baskets. Their
host tree in Brazil is the cedrela and
they grow in the topmost branches.
There is a number of species in
the genus and some authorities
quote Emanuel Rodriguez, a
Spanish botanist of the late
eighteenth century as the source of
the name.

SCUTICARIA STEELII (Lindley). This
Brazilian orchid also grows in the
northern states of South America. It
came to cultivation from Guyana
about 1836, and the Schomburgk
brothers later collected it on the
banks of the Demarara River in that
country. One of the orchids grown
best when fixed to a block of cork,
fern or wood, its foliage is pendant
and quite terete, indicating, with the
coloring of the flowers, that it will
do best in bright light. It is
uncommon in orchid collections,
sparse flowering and its origin
indicates warm culture. The genus
was named by Lindley in 1843, with
the known species grouped as
maxillarias before that time, like so
many indefinite genera from the
South American continent.

PLEUROTHALLIS OSPINAE
(Schultes). This diminutive orchid was once known as a restrepia. The pleurothallis, a genus named by R. Brown, are among the largest family groups in the orchid world. *P. ospinae* is a small plant growing about 7 or 8 centimetres high, but in good health growing so rapidly that it soon forms a neat little bunch of leaves that will fill a shallow pot in just a year or so. The plant comprises only a rhizome and the leaves on short stems, the flowers coming from the stem just below the leaf axil, the labellum being about 1 centimetre long. The flower is practically all labellum. This orchid is a moderately cool-growing type, the fronts of the leaves green and the backs liberally spotted with fine red dots and stains.

STELIS PAPAQUERENSIS
(Reichenbach f.). The stelis are rain-forest orchids from some 1000 metres and more. The flowers are diminutive, about 5 to 7 millimetres across, but produced in such profusion that the overall effect is beautiful. *S. papaquerensis* is also known as *S. porschiana*, only one of its twenty-one or more synonyms. As plants they are not unlike masdevallias but need a little more warmth than those orchids. The colors of the species vary from almost white to the rich burgundy purple of *S. papaquerensis*.

SIGMATOSTYLIX GUATEMALENSIS
(Schlechter). Another diminutive flowered orchid, this Central American species belongs to a small family of tropical plants. The flowers themselves are like small gongora or cycnoches flowers, but the genus is allied to the oncidiums. *S. guatemalensis* has the very nice habit of flowering for a few days or sometimes longer, the flowers then fall off and later a new set of buds develop on the stems and the display is on again. How many times this is repeated would depend on seasonal as well as cultural factors, but eventually the process stops and the spikes brown off. The name indicates the origin of this species and the genus was named by Reichenbach. 127

Zygopetalum crinitum
(Loddiges)

Cattleyas and Cattleya hybrids

Dr John Lindley who died in 1865 after devoting most of his life to orchids.

The genus was named by Lindley in 1824 as a tribute to William Cattley, of Barnet, England, who, while not flowering the first cattleya in that country, had the distinction of flowering the first *Cattleya labiata* somewhere about 1818. It was allegedly collected in Brazil, near the city of Rio de Janeiro, by William Swainson. William Cattley was more interested in exotic plants other than orchids.

The cattleyas of Central and South America are among the most beautiful and unusual flowers of the world. Long before the Europeans came to the area the native races knew and used them in various ways in ceremonies and for decorative purposes.

There are several types of cattleyas, but for ease in dealing with them as a genus they may be conveniently divided into two sections — the bifoliates and single-leafed types. Some of each section are cool-growing, particularly in the bifoliates. But as a genus they should be considered warm-growing orchids which should be cultivated in glass-houses even in warmer climates. In tropical climates where there is high humidity as well as high temperatures at some periods of the year they may still be grown if provided with ancillary equipment to create a constant air flow and proper shading.

Most of the so-called cattleya hybrids are really combinations of several genera, principally laelias, brassavolas (rhyncolaelias) and sophronitis. These combinations are called respectively, laeliocattleyas, brassocattleyas, brassolaeliocattleyas, sophrolaeliocattleyas and the combination of all four are potinaras, a name coined to obviate the use of a more unwieldy combination.

In addition these mainline hybrids are joined by numerous inter-generic crosses such as those between epidendrums and cattleyas, which are known as epicattleyas and many others, some of which also have coined names to simplify the system. The only book where they may all be identified is *Sanders' List of Orchid Hybrids*, although extracts are published by various periodicals.

The bifoliates

In the strange fashion of journals supposed to be authentic sources of information regarding the naming of various cattleyas and other orchids, differences occur in ascribing names of species to various botanists and other people. Where confusion is found, reference has been made at times to the list supplied by the Royal Botanic Gardens, Kew, England, particularly with the commoner bifoliate cattleyas such as *Cattleya loddigesii* (Lindley), *Cattleya intermedia* (R. Graham), *Cattleya bowringiana* (Veitch) and *C. skinneri* (Bateman). There are a number of others, but these are probably the most significant.

Cattleya loddigesii was the first cattleya flowered in England, by the Belgian nurseryman Loddiges, to whom it was known as *Epidendrum loddigesii*. *Cattleya loddigesii* originated in the higher parts of the Brazilian area where this type grew, consequently it tolerated moderate temperatures. It was confused with *Cattleya harrisoniae*, although the two are now synonymous. *Cattleya harrisoniae* and *Cattleya harrisoniana*, however, are different to the point that while the first was probably initially thought to be separate from *Cattleya loddigesii, Cattleya harrisoniana* came from a lowland area and flowers later than its highland counterpart. Morphologically this seems to be the only difference, therefore the three are considered synonymous.

However, in *Orchidaceae Brasilienses* Pabst and Dungs not only list the two as separate species, but also allocated the climates 1 and 2 as their zones. Climate 1 is listed as temperate, mostly in foothill country with plentiful rain and high humidity and also with a good clear air flow in all seasons. Most of the world's orchids grow in this type of climate. Climate 2, in which *Cattleya harrisoniana* is found, has higher temperatures, higher humidity, with 35 degrees common for months at a time. The rainfall in this climate is seasonal, therefore at times it is both hot and dry.

Cattleya harrisoniana in cultivation tends to hold its buds in the sheaths longer than *Cattleya loddigesii* and usually flowers up to three months later.

With *Cattleyas brownie, elatior, forbesii, intermedia* and *violacea, Cattleya loddigesii* belongs to the bifoliate *Cattleya intermedia* complex, with habitats in three different climates. With *Cattleya bowringiana*, which is a warmth-loving Central American species, all these orchids need a winter minimum preferably not falling below 10 degrees. *Cattleya bowringiana* is one of the earliest autumn Cattleyas in the southern hemisphere flowering sequence.

Cattleya skinneri, another of the Central American bifoliate types, also needs the same treatment. The size of some of the specimens of early importations of the bifoliate cattleyas is unbelievable in present-day terms. One plant of *Cattleya skinneri* sold in Stevens' auction rooms in 1884 was 2 metres (about 7 feet) across and about 6 metres in circumference.

Among the bifoliate cattleyas there is little doubt that the species *Cattleya bowringiana* (Veitch), a native of the western areas of British Honduras and Guatemala, is most prominent because of its impact on the hybrids of the section.

It was discovered and shipped to England somewhere about 1884 and first flowered by J. C. Bowring. *Cattleya bowringiana* is mostly rupicolous or rock dwelling and in its habitat has the benefit of bright sunlight during the day and very heavy dew at night. The growing season is warm and humid, with the result that the pseudo-bulbs are quickly made and it flowers soon after or near completion of the growths, which are up to 60 centimetres, with six to ten blooms.

The hybrid *Cattleya* Browniae (*Cattleya bowringiana* × *Cattleya harrisoniana*), although raised about 1904, is an excellent example of the breeding potential of *Cattleya bowringiana*, as it has pseudo-bulbs up to 90 centimetres tall (about 3 feet) topped by six to ten beautiful flowers. *Cattleya* Portia in many varieties is another good example.

Cattleya intermedia was known early in the nineteenth century. It flowered in the Glasgow Botanic Gardens in 1826 and Hooker described it as follows: 'We received our specimens ... from Mr Harris, of Rio de Janeiro ... They have been kept in the stove in pots of decayed bark. The specimen now described flowered for the first time in spring, 1826, but met with an accident before it could be figured or described. It bloomed for the second time in April, 1828 and remained in perfection several days. Other specimens subjected to the same kind of treatment have remained without the least alteration in their appearance since they were imported. The subject of the present notice is now pushing its roots freely over the pieces of bark'.

That is the first mention of this type of potting or growing material which has come to my notice. A stove, of course, was nothing more or less than the compartment we know as a 'hot-box', used chiefly for propagating recalcitrant pieces of orchids that seem to be inclined to die rather than live. It is the horticultural counterpart of the intensive care unit, and used as it was in the years quoted above the 'stove' was a failure for growing semi-tropical or temperate zone orchids.

Some of the species, by their nature as well as the closeness of the growths on the rhizome, are somewhat easy to grow into specimen plants. *Cattleya intermedia* is one such bifoliate and each mature pseudo-bulb may give four or more flowers in good cultivation. The sheaths of this cattleya are usually made in the autumn to early winter and go into the early to middle spring months before producing their buds from the sometimes straw-colored sheaths.

The island of Santa Amaro, just off the coast of Brazil in the vicinity of the city of Santos, west-south-west of Rio de Janeiro, was at one time thickly covered with forests of mangroves and featured granite hills about 300 metres high. The average daily temperature is about 30 degrees and the humidity mostly about 90 per cent. On the south to east sides of the island is the home — a correction — was the home of *Cattleya intermedia* and many other orchids. But a quote from J. J. Keevil, of Santos, tells it all:

'*Cattleya intermedia* of several varieties, including *alba*, exists in a variety of positions. I have found them occasionally on beds of sphagnum in marshy depressions of raised sandy beaches under the low shrub, which shows that nature has anticipated man as to this method of cultivation. They will colonise a few square yards on the top of a bare granite boulder, surrounded by the tide, dashed by spray and subjected to scorching sun and every wind. They also exist high on the branches of trees 1000 feet above the sea level. Their special metropolis, however, is a low, narrow wind-swept marshy valley with the ocean at both ends and a steep granite headland and hill at the sides. In the space of an acre there are many thousands. One has to wade to the knees in mud and swampy water. The gnarled, crowded trees are stunted by the wind to a 7 foot growth. Every trunk and branch teems with sturdy intermedias, their roots stretching to the perennial moisture below. In April and May their flowers are resplendent.

'*Cattley guttata* prefers the higher trees, which would take hours to cut down. Their roots descend the trunk 40 feet and more and their pseudo-bulbs attain to 5 feet and corresponding thickness. The perianths of different specimens vary in color from very dark spotted brown to light greenish spotted yellow. Some are quite free from spots and of bright brick red or a delicate yellow with vein-like markings'.

The island is about 29 kilometres by 10 kilometres and every centimetre of it at that time was covered in orchids, including zygopetalums, catasetums, gongoras, *Sophronitis cernua* and many other species and including bromeliads.

Cattleya intermedia grows in several areas in Brazil, mostly in warm locations and in cultivation it is partial to wintering over its dormancy in good cattleya conditions. It merits cultivation, even at the expense of pushing out an awarded hybrid.

Cattleya guttata — possibly the described form was one of the many varieties common to Brazil — is an orchid which takes a special type of grower to appreciate its flowers and beautiful scent. Not everyone likes spotty flowers, even scented.

The labiata cattleyas

Several of the Colombian, Venezuelan and Brazilian cattleyas were once commonly grouped under the title *labiata*, which originally was supposed to have been collected not far from the city of Rio de Janeiro, Brazil. All these species are invariably single leafed.

The main members of this labiata group are *Cattleya trianae* (Linden and Reichenbach f.), which some people prefer to spell '*trainaei*'; *Cattleya mossiae* (Parker) *Cattleya mendelii* (Reichenbach f.), *Cattleya gaskelliana* (Sander), *Cattleya warscewiczii* (Lindley and Andre), also known as *Cattleya gigas*; *Cattleya dowiana* (Bateman) and the variety *aurea* (Williams and Moore), *Cattleya warneri* (S. Moore) and *Cattleya lueddemanniana* (Reichenbach f.), which flower at various times during the year.

In addition to these species there is a large number of other cattleyas which do not feature so much in cultivation or hybridising. They are endemic to the same areas of Central and South America, varied in their morphology, but mostly climatically suited for glass-houses with winter minimum temperatures of 10 degrees or slightly higher. Unless grown in semi-tropical climates they are scarcely suitable for natural cultivation as tree- or rock-grown plants and the nature of their flowers suggests protection.

Before noting the various dates and the circumstances under which they were brought into cultivation it may be as well to analyse the information about them. The original list of the species belonging to the group comprised: *Cattleyas vera* (possibly the true *labiata*, original but also unidentifiable at the time this book was written), *dowiana*, *gaskelliana*, *lueddemanniana*, *mendelii*, *mossiae*, *percivalliana*, *schroderae* (considered by some authorities as a variety of *Cattleya trianae* but having distinguishing characteristics), *trianae*, *warneri* and *warscewiczii*.

The first cattleya was sent to William Cattley, of Barnet, Suffolk, England, by a man named Swainson, allegedly from near Rio de Janeiro, about 1817. Cattley stated: 'The most splendid perhaps of all the orchidaceous plants, which blossomed for the first time in the stove of my garden in Suffolk during 1818, the plant having been sent to me by William Swainson during his visit to Brazil.' The quote does not say that the plant originated in Brazil, only that it was sent from that country.

The rest of the story is plain, Lindley having named the new genus cattleya in tribute to the grower. The author and collector George Gardner, in his book *Travels in the Interior of Brazil*, states firmly that he found *Cattleya labiata* near Rio de Janeiro in two situations in 1836. Returning the following year, he found that the habitats in which he found the plants had been destroyed by charcoal burners and timber fellers. Gardner is also said to have found plants of *Cattleya labiata* northwest of Rio de Janeiro, on the border of that state and Minas Geraes.

It should be noted also that William Cattley was not very interested in orchids, but more in other exotic plants from tropical areas. Swainson was said to have sent the cattleya more as packing material than as a cultivable specimen. Additional circumstantial evidence that *Cattleya labiata* was unlikely to occur in the region of Rio de Janeiro can be deduced from the types of orchids growing in that region, such as the cold-growing sophronitis and similar temperate-zone plants. It has also been suggested that Swainson's plant was what could be termed an inheritance, because he took over the collection of another man who died during his travels as a commercial orchid seeker, and there is no record of the origin of these plants.

As for Gardner, the following extracts, while they still prove nothing, do at least throw some light on the whole matter of the habitat of the original plants.

Some idea of the confusion caused by collectors and their misinformation may be appreciated by this extract from the records of Louis Forget, a brief note of whose influence on orchid collecting is given in the first section of the book:

'Louis Forget remarks that it is fair to suppose that Swainson explored the provinces of the north of Brazil, because this plant (*Cattleya labiata*) was never indigenous in the province of Rio de Janeiro and still less of the Organ Mountains, which have been quite wrongly indicated as its habitat. As to the plant which Gardner found on the Gavea, near Rio, in 1836, he says that it is much more probable that Gardner mistook for *Cattleya labiata* — which alone was known and described at this period — the *Laelia lobata*, which still exists in this locality in numerous examples.' — (From R. A. Rolfe's summary of the evidence.)

This is in direct conflict with information that *Cattleya labiata* did indeed occur in the region of Rio de Janeiro. The statements go on:

'Gardner's specimens, fortunately, still exist, though the flowers are not well preserved. On soaking one out and examining it in detail I find that Forget's suggestion is right, for the segments, though not perfect, match those of the laelia and not of the cattleya. The pollinia are not present. This gets rid of the whole of the argument based on Gardner's record and specimens so far as this particular locality is concerned.'

Further to that excerpt from R. A. Rolfe's summary about *Cattleya labiata*, the following interesting information concerning its habitat is most clear, but which member of the group then designated *Cattleya labiata* is still most unclear:

'Concerning the range of *Cattleya labiata*, Louis Forget remarks that it grows spontaneously in the mountains of the interior, in the state of Pernambuco and in the neighboring provinces to the north of Parahyba and to the south of Alagoas. It is difficult to realise the conditions under which it grows. During the rainy season, which is of three months' duration, the vegetation grows with incredible rapidity, after which, owing to the torrid heat, the leaves fall from the trees, giving the aspect of winter in Europe. The stranger would never dream that *Cattleya labiata* or its allies could exist there. But towards the summits of the mountains one discovers here and there ravines and gorges where the virgin forest still persists. It is here that the plant is found, growing on the large trees, whose trunks are garnished with aroids, begonias, ferns, etc. The cattleya grows chiefly on the lateral branches of the trees in company with other orchids, bromeliads, and lichens, its roots enveloping the branches to a length of nearly six feet, with their tips intact and finding in the air the ingredients necessary for their existence. Here, in the shade of the evergreen foliage and in the breezy mountain air the cattleya luxuriates. It never grows on dead trees, because the bark quickly perishes and falls off.

'In these localities the plant flowers from January to March, more or less regularly, according to the epoch of the passing of the trovoadas — storms which blow up from November to January and seem to announce the approach of the rains and the revival of the vegetation. It is under this influence that *Cattleya labiata* develops and expands its flowers. During the rainy season, from April to June, under the action of this constantly humid but healthy atmosphere, because of the altitude and the constantly moving air, the new growths and roots are produced. After growth is completed the plant then rests until the epoch of the storms again arrives. Thus we see that its peculiar habit of resting after growth has a quite natural reason.'

Unfortunately, it is impossible to produce such dramatic changes in our glass-houses to suit all the plants we grow and they must accustom themselves to a set of averages which does little to promote regular growth and flowering. Occasionally a grower flukes a set of conditions to suit a genus and he produces fine growths and flowers on that particular genus but few other plants in the collection are completely happy. Nevertheless, that portion of the extract referring to the constantly moving air is applicable to the limits of glass-house cultivation and should be incorporated as part of the growing system.

Since those extracts were published considerable information about *Cattleya labiata* has appeared. In *Orchidaceae Brasilienses* (Pabst and Dungs) its habitat had been proved widespread and the states of Ceara, Paraiba, Pernambuco, Alagoas, Espirito Santo and Guanabara, in addition to the original site were known origins. A fairly large map is needed to note all these areas.

As far as this species is concerned, it seems to make as little sense to consolidate all the South American species like *Cattleya labiata* under the one heading as it does to consolidate the Indo-Asian cymbidiums of similar morphology and call them varieties of *Cymbidium lowianum*. While the basic likeness is there, it is a long time indeed since there was any real contact between, say, the true *Cattleya labiata* and its distant relative *Cattleya mossiae* in Venezuela or any of the related species in the other South American countries.

Most of the states quoted above are on the eastern hump of South America in the general area of the coastal city of Recife and it needs a special insight into the ways orchid species spread to have any idea of the time involved in a species arriving in a certain area and becoming established in the numbers said to have grown there.

Regardless of all the evidence brought forward to discredit Gardner's original story, he found it in more than one location, as this quote indicates:

'We made an excursion to a mountain called the Pedra Bonita, immediately opposite the Gavea ... Near the summit of the Pedra Bonita there is a small fazenda or farm, the proprietor of which was then clearing away the forest that covers it, converting the trees into charcoal ... On the edge of the precipice on the eastern side we found, covered with its large rose-colored flowers, the splendid *Cattleya labiata*, which a few days before we had seen on the Gavea'.

He not only obtained plants, but also flowers, which were preserved and later sent to various herbariums. A year later when he returned from another part of Brazil the whole mountain top had been cleared and with the destruction of the general ecology naturally the cattleya could hardly be expected to survive. So far as most records go, *Cattleya labiata* did originate in the vicinity of Rio de Janeiro, Brazil, for whatever importance may be placed on the information.

An interesting point to note in his brief description of the habitat of the orchid is the orientation of the place where they were growing toward the east. If this is reflected in our glass-house culture of orchids, regardless of the genus, there is always an added factor in it that will produce better plants and flowers.

It is difficult to convey any impression of the enormous numbers of these species cattleyas which were collected from the interior of Colombia and neighboring countries and shipped to England and the continent of Europe during the years referred to as the 'orchidomania' period. A short quote from a book written during the later stages of this era is interesting because it relates to many other genera as well as specimen plants and collections of plants other than orchids:

From a book written by Albert Millican somewhere about 1890, after a collecting expedition to Colombia: 'I had been informed that *Cattleya mendelii* was still to be found in quantities on the eastern ranges of the Andes, so after leaving the precipices of Subi I turned off in the direction of a small village called Curiti, at the foot of the range of mountains so celebrated for orchids ... The vegetation is somewhat sub-tropical, lovely ferns and selaginellas being very luxuriant, as well as feathery bamboos, but with an absence of the fine rich timber trees and towering palms of the lower grounds ... I had not far to go before I was rewarded with the object of my search in the myriads of bromeliaceae and orchids which literally covered the short, stunted trees and the bare points of rock, where scarcely an inch of soil is to be found. The most magnificent sight for even the most stoical observer is the immense clumps of *Cattleya mendelii*, each new bulb bearing four or five of its gorgeous rose-colored flowers, many of them growing in the full sun or with very little shade ... Some of these plants, considering their size and the slowness of growth, must have taken years to develop, for I have taken plants from the trees with five hundred bulbs and as many as one hundred spikes of flower.'

Cattleya mendelii was first introduced to England by Messrs Hugh Low and Co. It was named after S. Mendel, of Manchester, England. In the following years many thousands of plants of this cattleya and others were imported into England by various distributors from their collectors in Colombia and other South American countries. The original plant of *Cattleya mendelii* was sold in April 1873, for 34 guineas.

It is easy to understand the awe and admiration of recipients of these plants when they flowered in their glass-houses. The varietal distinctions were untold, particularly in what was known at that time as the labiata group. Even after the lapse of over 100 years several of these varieties are as well known and grown as in the period of their introduction. But against that must be set the depredations of the collectors and the unfortunate loss of the plants before they reached their destinations, as well as the discard of the clones which did not have the type of flowers looked for at that time. Hundreds of thousands of plants were lost and destroyed.

Practically all of Central and South America was at one time the happy hunting ground of collectors, and the intensely rich flora of the various countries was also destroyed when the forests were razed and coffee production taken up.

It should be remembered also that the poorer types of the species which were discarded in cultivation represented an important part of all genera and this unrestricted collection and deliberate destruction of some of these species altered the pool of genes in a way which was never intended by nature.

A British consul in Pernambuco, Brazil, about 1910, named George Chamberlain left an interesting report on the exports from that area in which cattleyas had special mention:

'The state of Pernambuco produces a large variety of orchids, principal among which are *Cattleyas labiata, leopoldii, guttata* and *granulosa* ... Of *Cattleya labiata* Pernambuco exported about 15,000 plants of eight leaves and upwards during the season ending with April, 1909. The plants are gathered at three central points — Caruaru, Garnahuna and Timbauba. The method is simple. Buyers representing foreign firms or a firm on the coast take up their residence at these points and announce that they are ready to receive plants. The news soon spreads and on every market day the plants come in, sometimes brought in by poor peasants in little bunches along with a goatskin or two and corn for the general market, sometimes brought in by regular collectors in large cargoes ... The labiatas having less than eight or sometimes seven leaves are discarded, as they are too small for profitable shipment. Their collection is discouraged, as should it be long continued the plant would absolutely disappear from the regions worked ... Plants of eight leaves are received in great quantities and are paid for at about 9 cents apiece; plants of 15 leaves or over bring 18 cents, 20 to 30 leaves 32 cents, 30 to 40 leaves 45 cents and above 40 leaves a special bargain is made for each plant.

'During the present season an extraordinary plant was brought in numbering 260 leaves. This plant was bought for about 5 dollars (one pound sterling) and is worth in the United States about 150 dollars. In full bloom it should bear 500 flowers. Like the grape cluster of Eschol, it was carried into market strung on a pole and borne by two men, who said they had brought it 40 miles. *Cattleya labiata alba* is also occasionally found in this district. Its exquisite bloom is snow white. It is exceedingly rare, one collector having gathered 8000 labiatas without securing an alba. A good example will sell for as much as 300 dollars.'

'In spite of such rare finds as these, the returns from the orchid trade are not great, as there is competition with heavy expenses. The preparation, transportation and shipment of plants in the Pernambuco district is not expensive. Correctly packed, the plants will stand 30 to 40 days' confinement and remain in good condition. Freight and expenses to New York per average case of 80 plants amounts to about 15 dollars. An export duty of about 64 cents per 100 plants is charged and they pay in the United States 25 per cent ad valorum.'

The extraordinary number of plants shipped from South America as a whole is beyond imagination and the country when the plants were in flower in the various districts must have resembled a vast garden. While they did not grow in masses extending for kilometres over the country, the gullies and ravines and cliffs where they grew must have been most colorful, a scene possibly never to return. George Chamberlain did not express any concern, but it must have been an intensely dull brain which could not see the end of it all in the decimation which took place, as an analysis of the figures he quotes amply reveals.

It is almost impossible to say which of the species is most important. *Cattleya trianae* (the correct spelling is used), of which there are several notable varieties, would be first choice for many. It was named after the eminent Colombian botanist Jose Jeronimo Triana.

One of the 'orchidomanians' named Rucker, of Wandsworth, first flowered *Cattleya trianae* in England on a single plant sent by one of his correspondents in Colombia. It is one of the spring-flowering cattleyas and among its varieties are several which have gained awards. But it was probably in the glass-houses of American growers that its greatest numbers were found in the early collecting days, as some of these growers had hundreds of fine varieties. It tends to flower in odd seasons in cultivation.

It was Rucker's submission of a flower to Lindley in 1849, however, which caused such admiration. Lindley named it *Cattleya quadricolor* because of the four colors, white, yellow, lilac and purple, which so beautifully blended to give it brilliance. Before Lindley's name was given catalogue in 1864, Reichenbach had named it *Cattleya trianaei**. At that time it was a widespread part of the flora of Colombia, and the collector Weir shipped many plants to the Horticultural Society of London in 1863.

The collector Roezl found immense quantities of the plant near Buga, Colombia, which was a centre for coffee growing, about 1869 and he also shipped out large numbers of plants.

*This was nomenclaturally incorrect — see *Growing Orchids* Book 3.

F. C. Lehmann, perhaps noted more for his love of masdevallias and mentioned in that regard in Book 3, wrote to the *Gardeners' Chronicle*, England, in 1883:

'Many years' observation in indisputably one of the richest fields of epiphytal orchids on the globe have shown me that orchids, growing in different localities and under varying orographical and climatical conditions, are capable of great abnormal developments. I have, indeed, seen so much variation in orchids that I have given up all talk about new varieties. To give an example, I may mention that during my last travels in the Magdalena basin — devoted exclusively to the study of the country — a locality was visited in which *Cattleya trianae* grew very abundantly. Of the many hundreds of plants which were seen in bloom I was unable to select two that had flowers of equal size and color, so great was the variation. I think every English amateur of orchids might have two special varieties from that spot without exhausting the number of them. Now supposing all these varieties of cattleyas were described and named, what a catalogue! I think such plants might receive a local name — say, Mr Gosling's dark-colored variety or Mr Pfeifenhauer's extremely large-lipped plant — as this is of considerable importance to the horticulturists; but as far as the botanist is concerned these varieties can only be simply recorded with the remark that such-and-such a species is capable of great varying development.'

Cattleya trianae also produced pure white varieties like most other *labiata* associates, but there were few real albinos among them. This cattleya, unlike the *labiata* section described by Louis Forget, has a much more even rainfall in its habitat — or perhaps we may amend that to say that where it once grew the rainfall was more equally spread over the year.

Cattleya mossiae was first collected in Venezuela in 1836 and flowered in the collection of Mrs Moss, Liverpool, one of a number of women interested in the cult in the early days of the nineteenth century. It was named in her honor by Sir William Hooker. This orchid is one of the largest of the labiatas and grows at an altitude of about 1000 metres, which is a little over that of the habitats of other labiatas. A nurseryman by the name of Green was the source of Mrs Moss's plant; in view of the altitude at which it grew it is one of the easiest of the species to cultivate, but as it flowers in autumn to winter a little warmth is needed to keep it going in cooler regions.

Returning to the size of some specimens collected from the jungle in the best days of trading, this story from the book *Woodlands Orchids* is interesting:

'Since orchids never die unless by accident and never cease to grow, there is no limit to the bulk they may attain. Mishap alone cuts their lives short — commonly by the fall or burning of the tree to which they cling ... The most striking instance of the sort I myself have observed, if not quite the biggest, was a *Cattleya mossiae* sent home by Mr Arnold. It enclosed two great branches of a tree, rising from the fork below which it was sawn off — a bristling mass four feet thick and five feet high, two feet more if we reckon the leaves. As for the number of flower scapes it bore last season, to count them would have been the work of hours; roughly I estimated a thousand, bearing not less than three blooms, each six inches across. Fancy cannot rise to the conception of that gorgeous display ...'

Even allowing for some exaggeration, it must have been a magnificent specimen plant. A brief history of the collector Arnold appears elsewhere, in *Growing Orchids*, Vol. 3.

Cattleya dowiana has a confused history and background. It was possibly originally found by the Lithuanian collector Josef Warscewicz in Costa Rica. His shipment of plants, however, did not last the voyage and his suggested name died with the consignment. Even the dried specimens he sent to Germany, probably to Reichenbach, also failed to withstand the trip sufficiently well for analysis and naming. It was subsequently brought to European cultivation and a collector named Pfau discovered a most beautiful form which was designated *Cattleya dowiana* var. *rosita*.

Cattleya dowiana var. *aurea* was found in Colombia by Gustav Wallis, who was collecting for Linden at that time, somewhere about the year 1868. It is still a most curious paradox that two similar yet so different cattleyas found so far apart, some 1000 kilometres, should bear the same specific name, although divided into varieties. Compared with *Cattleya dowiana* var. *aurea*, the type form is a pale shadow, although beautiful varieties of this species are known. On this score and the matter of the distance separating their habitats, some botanists and plant specialists would still prefer to have them separated.

While the color of *Cattleya dowiana* var. *aurea* is variously pale yellow to deep nankeen yellow and even with darker overlays of orange, *Cattleya dowiana* is frequently a murky color and a little smaller than the variety *aurea*. In the 1910 to 1920 period the two were cross-pollinated and very beautiful forms were subsequently brought into being. It is probable that since its original appearance it has become confused with the true species and traces of it are hard to sift out from the masses of orchid literature available. In the early period of collection many different varieties of *Cattleya dowiana* var. *aurea* were found.

By 1930 *Cattleya dowiana* var. *aurea* had become so rare in Colombia that it took some months for a collector to locate, collect and ship out 500 plants. It is in 1980 so rare as to be almost non-existent. Fortunately, with modern seed-raising techniques it is possible to rehabilitate with seedlings suitable areas in Colombia, so that this species will regenerate.

Cattleya warscewiczii was discovered about 1848 by the man whose name it bears in the province of Medellin, Colombia, and in some ways was the consolation prize for having missed out in the matter of *Cattleya dowiana*. To many growers it is known as *Cattleya gigas* and it is small wonder that this is so. Whether writing the name in script, typing it on a typewriter or writing it on a plastic label the feeling must be the same — anything but that name! Reichenbach named this cattleya, but who coined the diminutive *gigas* is not known. He should be remembered in some tangible way in orchid history. Linden and Andre are given some of the credit for it, but it was commonly used in Britain.

The name *gigas* is descriptive of the flowers, for they are among the largest of the cattleya family. One purist from about the year 1927 had this to say: 'The name is quite simple, really — it should be pronounced "Varshevich."' But that hardly solves the problem — it is the writing of the name more than the pronunciation that is the hurdle.

After Warscewicz finding the orchid and Reichenbach naming it, this species dropped out of sight and once again it was Wallis who rediscovered it and sent large numbers to Linden in Brussels somewhere about 1873. Roezl also collected *Cattleya warscewiczii* for Linden and it became a very popular orchid in collections in both Europe and America. Some varieties discovered in locations other than the original proved easier to flower in cultivation and frequently buyers were left mourning because they could not flower this magnificent orchid. Some of the varieties were white with beautiful purple labellums and the variety *Cattleya warscewiczii* var. *firmin lambeau* is an albino with all white segments. This orchid received a First Class Certificate and a gold medal at the RHS show in 1912.

The Belgian grower van Imschoot, immortalised in the hybrid list in lycastes, had a large collection of *Cattleya warscewiczii* and usually flowered some hundreds of plants each year in a special glass-house devoted entirely to this species.

Cattleya warneri remained one of the mystery species of the genus for quite a long time. Like other species, southern Brazil was the supposed and alleged habitat, but according to Veitch the real habitat had not been disclosed as late as 1894. Some points were scored for the sleuths when two inter-generic hybrids were flowered in collections. One was recognised as a cross-pollination between *Cattleya warneri* and *Laelia tenebrosa*, the other between the same cattleya and *Laelia grandis*, which is somewhat similar to *Laelia tenebrosa*. Both these laelias were known to have originated in Bahia, Brazil, and a little insight into the workings of the minds of collectors and distributors alike soon revealed the reason for lack of information following introduction of *Cattleya warneri* to Britain.

Cattleya warneri is a member of the *labiata* group and it seemed a common thing to say that they all originated in the vicinity of Rio de Janeiro or southern Brazil. At length this statement was recognised for the laughable joke of the late twentieth century.

To go back to the Louis Forget section, it appears obvious that he was mistaken and the real origin of Swainson's plants is unknown. *Cattleya warneri*, it was possibly correctly surmised, originated in Bahia in the same area as the two laelias with which it cross-pollinated. It flowers in summer to early autumn.

To confuse things further, even some modern authorities say that the two laelias originate in the east central area of Brazil and as far south as Rio de Janeiro. How much of this information is repeated misinformation is hard to gauge, but the real truth is hard to find among all the stories and they must be taken at face value for what they are worth. The *labiatas* were known in England as early as 1818, but there is no way now of identifying those early cattleyas, or more particularly where they came from.

There is little doubt that the whole of the *labiata* group has moved up and down and across South America over a period of some considerable time, perhaps hundreds of thousands of years as the environment and ecology changed. Viewed from the proposed angle of the plant migration routes sponsored by Pabst and Dungs in *Orchidaceae Brasilienses*, it is not surprising that the original botanists and collectors alike were confused. So far as these authors and botanists are concerned *Cattleya warneri* is merely a variant of *Cattleya labiata*, even a synonym for an orchid which grows in seven different states or provinces.

They all have different flowering seasons and habits. *Cattleyas trianae*, *mendelii* or *mossiae* may flower with or without sheaths, while *Cattleya gaskelliana* must produce its buds and flower as the new growth matures or it will not flower from those growths at all. It usually flowers in the summer.

Cattleya warscewiczii was one of the few for which a cultural hint was given, as stated in Veitch's *Manual of Orchidaceous Plants*: 'In all these localities (where this species was found) this cattleya grows chiefly upon trees by the sides of streams and often well exposed to the sun. Plants growing in the shade have their stems much drawn and rarely flower.'

The natural hybrid *Cattleya hardyana* was noted by discerning growers as early as 1885 in the collection of G. Hardy in England. It arrived in a batch of plants of *Cattleya dowiana* and *Cattleya warscewiczii*, which was also known by some as *Cattleya sanderiana*. This batch of plants was imported under that name from Venezuela and the hybrid flowered in 1883, 1884 and 1885, the year in which it was named. Many other examples of *Cattleya hardyana* appeared in batches of plants, particularly those handled by Charlesworths. The first grower to flower the hand-made cross-pollination of this hybrid was Norman Cookson, who set the seed pod in 1887 and bloomed seedlings in 1896.

Cattleya hardyana was a most successful parent and by 1945 more than 250 beautiful hybrids had been raised and named from it. Its influence on secondary hybrids and through to those of the present day is extraordinary. Indeed, by the same year all of the *labiata* series had a total of more than 2000 registered cross-pollinations in *Sanders' List of Orchid Hybrids*, not counting the secondary hybrids bred from them.

Cattleya lueddemanniana is the last of the *labiata* division included in this survey of an elaborate and beautiful group of species cattleyas. Like many of its counterparts, it is usually rose-purple to paler colors, and like some of its relatives, the labellum is more tubular than wanted in the 1980 hybrids.

It first appeared in France about 1850 and was named after the German gardener-orchid grower employed by Monsieur Pescatore, who is noted in other contexts that deal with orchids.

Cattleya lueddemanniana was known originally in England as *Cattleya speciosissima* and was handled by the Veitch nursery in the early 1860 period. Warner included it in his book *Selected Orchidaceous Plants* as *Cattleya dawsonii* and Rucker also flowered it about this time.

The origin of *Cattleya lueddemanniana* was unknown until Low and Co. imported a consignment from Venezuela. It is somewhat similar to *Cattleya mossiae* but grows at a lower altitude, consequently needs slightly warmer conditions, and flowers in late summer to autumn from the new growths made in that season. Like *Cattleya gaskelliana*, if the buds do not follow through in a constant surge it fails to flower in that season and this could be taken with any cattleya, species or hybrid, to indicate incorrect culture.

All sections of *Cattleya labiata* have white varieties, some with slight tinges of color, others which are true albinos and indicate this by carrying a light or darker yellow splash in the interior of the labellum as the only added color.

These albinos had a tremendous influence on cattleya breeding in the 1945 to 1960 period, when several outstanding white hybrids were bred, with superlative shape and great substance in the flowers.

No real scale may be put to the importance of one of the white species over the others, but at least *Cattleya mossiae* var. *wageneri* had a place in nearly all of the white hybrids. This cattleya was known from as early as 1854, after it was found in 1851 in or near Caracas, Venezuela, at about 1000 metres (4000 feet) and the plant was sent to a German grower named Decker. It was noted at the time that its beauty was enhanced by the yellow throat of the labellum. Another fine albino was flowered in a batch of plants consigned to J. Backhouse and Sons in New York and it was also noted at the Royal Botanic Society Show when exhibited by a grower named Jackson in 1857.

Cattleya trianae var. *alba*, also a true albino and not one of the more common white types with colored labellums, was first recorded in 1882 by James Veitch and Sons. Linden was also said to have flowered an albino *Cattleya trianae* in 1867. An albino *Cattleya mendelii* was flowered about the same time.

The first albino *Cattleya gaskelliana* appeared in the collection of R. H. Measures in 1888 and this was an added bonus plant because of its summer flowering period. *Cattleya lueddemanniana* produced an albino form in the collection of F. Finet in France from a batch of plants imported by Godefroy Lebeuf about 1882.

The real puzzle albino was *Cattleya labiata*, which flowered in the collection of Warocque in Belgium in 1891. *Cattleya labiata* does not signify very much to the growers of the twentieth century and one could well be forgiven for asking: 'Which *labiata*?'

The hybridists became used to the production of hundreds or thousands of pure white flowers from cross-pollinations of these albino cattleyas and soon found that they bred true. It was perhaps the chance find of plants with unusual chromosome numbers in their cells that changed things so dramatically in the 1945-60 period.

The manual hybridising of cattleyas began somewhere about 1850 and so far as most records go the parents were *Cattleya guttata* and *Cattleya loddigesii*. This cross-pollination confirmed the existence of a suspected natural hybrid and it was registered later as *Cattleya* Hybrida. It appears in *Sanders' List of Orchid Hybrids* under that name as a natural hybrid.

Further hybrids were rather slow in coming, but by the late years of that century a veritable flood of cross-pollinations came to seedling stage. It may seem strange to refer to it as a flood, but considering the seed-raising methods and the general lack of knowledge in treating these tiny plantlets, it was at least the beginning of the flood.

It should not be imagined that all the progress in breeding for shape, size and color was made in the later years of the following century, because reference to some of the older publications soon indicates that what has followed is more a perversion of the originals to stubby petals and rounded outlines. It was impossible from the inception of cross-pollinating to do much about the color except to add smaller genera such as laelias and sophronitis to change it to tones unavailable in the cattleyas.

A few cattleyas had pre-eminent effect on later generations and the hybrid *Cattleya* Edithiae (*Cattleya trianae* var. *alba* × *Cattleya* Suzanne Hye) would be one of the them. *Cattleya* Suzanne Hye was the result of the cross-pollination of *Cattleya gaskelliana* var. *alba* and *Cattleya mossiae* var. *wageneri*. Although the albino cattleyas had such a great part in these cross-pollinations, when bred into the colored strains they lost their character and produced magnificent colors and shapes allied to size. It was not only in the 1950 era that their influence was made plain.

Cattleya Suzanne Hye (1906) was raised by the Belgian Jules Hye de Crom and *Cattleya* Edithiae (1914) by Theodore Pauwels, of Ghent, Belgium. So it was two Europeans, both Belgians, who started such a great line of hybrids. So far as introductions of the laelias and brassavolas are concerned, it is best that they be left to the sections on those orchids other than listing them as participants as they occur in this summary.

Cattleya breeding at the time this book was written had reached the stage of endless recombinations of a few outstanding early hybrids until getting down to the level of novelties which included bloodliness from the smaller and perhaps more colorful species. These novelties mostly included strains of sophronitis and seldom the smaller laelias.

It is tedious to go into all the ramifications of the inter-generic breeding lines, but a brief examination of two is sufficient to indicate the lines followed by the breeders of the 1950-80 era. First, a look at the pedigree of *Brassolaeliocattleya* Sylvia Fry, which produced clones both fast growing and slow, strong and weak, good flowers and bad from the point of view of award winning characteristics, but at least embodying in the various fine clones what was most sought, namely, good symmetry overall, good color and an attractive, balancing labellum.

The pedigree discloses an astounding use of the albino *Cattleya mossiae* var. *wageneri*, which appeared nine times; *Cattleya trianae* var. *alba* twice, *Cattleya gaskelliana* var. *alba* twice, *Cattleya warneri* var. *alba* once, with the color over-rider *Cattleya hardyana (Cattleya dowiana x Cattleya warscewiczii)* once. As remarked previously, introduction of a colored flower inhibits the albino factors. *Brassavola digbyana* appeared only once and *Laelia purpurata* once. This combination produced *Brassolaeliocattleya* Nacouchee, one of the parents of *Brassolaeliocattleya* Sylvia Fry.

A brief note on the inter-generic hybrids may help beginners to understand the system. A cattleya cross-pollinated with another cattleya remains a cattleya, when a laelia is introduced to a cattleya it becomes a laeliocattleya (Lc) and when a brassovola is introduced to the line it becomes a brassolaeliocattleya (Blc). Once it reaches that stage, any further cattleya or laelia introduction does not alter its hybrid line. But once another genus is introduced the name changes again to a predetermined combination such as when sophronitis is introduced and it becomes a potinara. This is dealt with more fully later in the series.

The other side of *Blc* Sylvia Fry is *Cattleya* Bow Bells, which was *Cattleya* Edithiae x *Cattleya* Suzanne Hye, a most intelligent cross-pollination, but one which had to wait from the early part of the century until midway through before its possibilities were appreciated.

Even with the overwhelming use of the albino species, the simple introduction of *Cattleya hardyana* and the laelia and brassovola or rhyncolaelia overcame all the albino possibilities and the *Blc* Sylvia Frys are most beautifully rose-pink with a gold, yellow and purple labellum, as the illustration shows.

It is not necessary to extend into a large number of generations to get most of the features integrated into one flower. In the instance of *Brassocattleya* Deesse (pronounced day-ess) it took only four moves from the species *Cattleyas dowiana, gaskelliana, trianae* and *warscewiczii*, with an added *labiata* strain which was not identified, to get to an outstanding brassocattleya, again using *Cattleyas trianae* var. *alba* and *gaskelliana* var. *alba*. It is not understood why these albino cattleyas are usually better shaped than the normal varieties, but it does appear that at times they are tetraploids. If an explanation of this term is needed it is best to refer to the book on cymbidiums and Slippers.

In cattleya breeding — and the term cattleya is applied loosely to all combinations which include this genus — by far the greatest number of cross-pollinations and subsequent registration of hybrids was in the laeliocattleyas in the early years of the craft. Up to the year 1945 almost 3000 registrations were made. This takes on greater significance when it is realised that other introduced genera offered possibilities of variation which the laelias did not possess, such as the labellum of *Brassavola digbyana* or the color of *Sophronitis coccinea*.

As the so-called *labiata* group have different annual flowering periods, the hybrids raised from them are prone to follow a random pattern, although they should all have a warm season or summer growing habit. However, it will be found that the flowering seasons of the various combinations will vary considerably, with plants in different stages of growth or dormancy or flowering during an annual cycle.

Some in which the habit of *Cattleya mendelii* comes to the fore will make the sheath on completed growths and then hold in a partial dormancy for some months before developing the flowers. Others may form sheaths like *Cattleya warscewiczii* and must follow straight through into flowering or the buds will not develop at all and the flowering is lost for that year. Sometimes also these *gigas* hybrids will not flower for years and in this instance exposure to much stronger light in the growing stages may bring the plants into flower.

Occasionally cattleya hybrids will follow a pattern of never producing sheaths, but simply extruding the buds from the apex of the growth and so on into continuous activity to the opening of the flowers. This indicates clearly that it is necessary to work out a pattern for almost all the plants, particularly in the award-winning category and study them in relation to the facility in which they are grown. There can be a difference of some weeks between the growing and flowering behavior of one clone when it is propagated and several people are cultivating it.

Cultivation hints for Cattleyas and similar orchids

Cattleyas are more easily understood and managed in numbers than when grown as isolated plants in orchid collections. The growing conditons should be based on a minimum temperature of 13 degrees and any lapses beyond this should be only occasional and not too far down the scale. Naturally, growing as epiphytes in their habitat they must go through periods of cold weather, but interior cultivation is a quite different environment.

Upper limits should be quite safe even to 30 degrees in the growing stage provided the humidity is lowered slightly and some type of air circulation and introduction is provided, accompanied by sufficient shade to protect the plants. In ordinary growing conditions shade-cloth or other shading should be selected to suit the area where they are grown and any recommendation of the percentage of shade in a mesh used could be misleading. The plants will stand bright light and should not be grown sappy in dull conditions.

Root systems of these epiphytes should be easy to understand, as a percentage of the system is certain to be surface and aerial. When repotting, never bury or enclose such open or aerial root systems if it can be avoided, as these roots will almost certainly die.

Watering is also aligned with the conditions under which the plants are grown, but should be such that the plants get less when they are dormant and no harm can come to cattleyas if the potting material becomes completely dehydrated. After such a condition, however, water should be given only sparingly for at least three weeks to cushion the shock to the plant and allow the root system to re-establish gradually. The root system in good growing conditions is seldom dormant for long and should be studied.

The correct time to repot the plants is when the new roots are emerging from the base of new growths, regardless of the fact that flowers may have to be sacrificed to get it done. Never sever the plants into less than three growths, but at times allowing a new unmatured growth to represent a bulb in the count. It will be noted at times that certain clones never reach their best flowering until the leading or flowering growth is over the side of the pot and occasionally this means a difficult decision about repotting.

Potting material for cattleyas usually is bark chips, the size dependent on the sizes of the pots used for various plants. A normal flowering sized cattleya should be put into a pot somewhere about 15 centimetres across, preference being given to shallow pots usually dubbed fern pots rather than those of standard depth. The size bark used with such a pot should not be fine, but a blend of two parts of No. 3 size to one part of No. 2, referred to in the picture section, would make up a good sized medium for the roots expected on a cattleya in such a pot. One part of charcoal may also be used if that material is suitable, preferably graded through the same sieves and made up of equal parts of No. 2 and No. 3.

Other additives could be considered, always allowing for their effects on frequency of watering and the climate of the glass-house. The additives could be small quantities of leaf mould and twiggy material from oak trees, tree-fern or bracken fern frond or peat-moss. The amount of these additives should be considered carefully, but none of them will do anything other than add a little to the plant food, if any, contained in the charcoal and bark. Drainage is important and should be planned rather than just being a happening following potting.

While some growers may prefer open bench, slat-type accommodation, there is a lot to be said for the closed bench, particularly for dormant or non-growing or flowering plants. Some growers prefer to suspend their plants in hangers and this has much to recommend it from the point of view of air flow if there is room for such a system. One of the best groups of cattleyas grown in Australia was housed in a lean-to type glass-house based on a north-facing brick wall, some 2.5 metres high and there were no benches at all. The plants were all hung in slat baskets from a series of pipes running the length of the house and independently supported. Although it was like climbing into a jungle of plants when one on the inside rows was wanted, the view from the path when they were in flower was superb. The floor, other than the path which ran along the front, was covered in vigorously growing ferns.

Closed benches allow the bed on which the pots stand to be soaked at any time without affecting the plants other than increasing the humidity. Provided there is a good air flow about the glass-house there is little harm in this other than for the flowering plants, which should be a little cooler and dryer than those in growth or dormancy.

Fertilisers for cattleyas cannot very well be based on a general application every week or so because of the restrictions outlined in the previous paragraphs, but the use of pellet type nutrient sources is not recommended. This is also because of these restrictions, where a plant, having flowered and entered a dormant period, should not have left-over pellets on the surface of the potting material. All this, of course, is pointed at getting the utmost out of the collection, but busy growers who have no ambitions other than for a few special plants may care to overlook the possible bad effects of the pellets and find them easier to use than liquid fertilisers. The better idea is to keep shifting the plants about to various parts of the benching to take care of growing, flowering and resting. At no time should cattleyas or other glass-house grown orchids be allowed to become so dry that they shrivel beyond what common sense dictates, so that probably a constant state of moistness directly available from the closed bench is the best system to aim at.

There will always be differences of opinion about the need to water plants in flower. The fact should be appreciated that no matter how much water or fertiliser is poured on to a plant coming into flower, no alteration will be made to the quality or size of the flower. All that has been determined in the months preceding appearance of the buds and once they are formed and visible the plant should be kept damp and no more. The best place, again, is on the closed bench until the flowers are opening; after that the move to cooler and more airy conditions should follow. That such developing flowers should be attacked by pests of any sort is a reflection on the general cultivation of the plants and is already dealt with under the heading of pests and diseases.

Although growing naturally in the mountains of Brazil or wherever the species came from the plants usually flowered in a dry weather phase — or near enough to dry, which is obvious from the nature of the flowers — there is no real intention to convey that they should be dried off in their flowering stage in a glass-house. That is a totally different world. In this same natural habitat the amount of plant food they would get, while difficult to estimate, would not be the sort of rich diet some growers seem to imagine they need.

Little, weak and not too frequently would be a good mark to aim for — and whatever you do, mark it off on a calendar so that after a busy week it is no strain trying to remember when a look at the calendar tells all.

Cattleya bowringiana

Laelias

The genus was named by Lindley in 1831, but his choice of name is obscure and no one is quite sure of its correct derivation. Several references could be quoted.

The Brazilian Laelias

Laelias are easy to divide into two groups, with most of the Mexican species capable of growing vigorously at lower temperatures than their South American counterparts, even when growing at the same distance from the equator. In general the Brazilian laelias need about 4 or 5 degrees more warmth overall. Most of the cultivated laelias come from the Mexican species and not, as could be imagined, from those most used in hybridising. They possibly owe this popularity to the fact that they are easier to manage and flower than the South American series as a whole.

One of the features about laelias and cattleyas is that they come from such relatively high altitudes. Most of the Mexican and Guatemalan species grow at about 1500 to 1800 metres and the temperature is between 10 and 20 degrees in the bottom range and between 40 and 50 degrees in the upper limits at the hottest time of the day. At times the night temperatures are well below the average mean of 10 degrees.

In addition to this, there is a marked difference between the wet and dry seasons at these altitudes, with the year almost equally divided between the two extremes. However, this cannot be accepted as a general cultural recommendation for all laelias, as each has its own environmental needs. Nearly all the Mexican and South American regions where laelias grow have a related weather pattern of rain generated over the Atlantic Ocean, most of the moisture settling on the mountains of the eastern regions of these countries, but with Western Mexico still having a fairly heavy population of laelias.

From the aspect of hybridising, the most important of the genus is *Laelia purpurata*, which was discovered in 1846 in Santa Catherina province, southern Brazil, by Francois Devos, who sent plants to Ghent, Belgium. It was first flowered in England by Messrs Backhouse, of York. A strong grower, it needs more than usual good techniques to make it flower regularly. Commonly a large overflowing plant is needed to get flowers and a winter or cooler season minimum temperature of about 12 to 15 degrees. It was named by Lindley and Paxton.

Large imports of the plant were made into England about 1844 and notes from that period indicate that some orchid growers had upward of 500 plants of *Laelia purpurata*. The color variation is from pure white to rose-purple, the flower large but rather open with its narrow, spreading petals and sepals over some 15 to 20 centimetres. A 'grey' variety is mentioned in older literature and if the illustrated flower was closely examined it did indeed have a 'grey' look about the petals and sepals.

Laelia purpurata is the most cattleya-like of the laelias, with stout, tall pseudo-bulbs and a single leaf. The labellum was the characteristic which

147

invited hybridisation and its deep purple color has been transferred to numerous inter-generic hybrids. It was most used of all the laelias, some of the fine primary hybrids stemming from it including *Laeliocattleya* Cattlisto-glossa, *Lc* Canhamiana and *Lc* Sallieri, which as the other parent is *Cattleya loddigesii*, grows and flowers outdoors in moderately cold climates. It is illustrated growing in this way.

A note on a sale of plants in the auction rooms of Messrs Protheroe and Morris in 1885 is interesting: 'An unusually valuable importation of orchids.' *Laelia purpurata* was described as having sepals and petals grey, lip black-purple, the only new form that the collector could find, a grand mass. The description was followed by the statement that Messrs Horsman and Co., in offering these plants for sale, 'beg the gentlemen purchasing them to clearly understand that they are true to name and that the description is not exaggerated'. The color description seems to be correct only in regard to the labellum.

The cultivation of this species should closely follow that of cattleyas, both coming from much the same climate. The color varies considerably from pure white to white veined with purple and some with an even color tint through the petals and sepals.

In many ways *Laelia purpurata* sets the cultivation pattern for our mixed-genera 'cattleyas' because it needs warm conditions in which to grow. A winter minimum of 12 degrees is preferable and the orchid has a quite long winter dormancy. As new roots appear from the last-made pseudo-bulb in late spring, or if action is noted in the older roots, the plant should be brought back into life slowly over three or four weeks, gradually increasing the amount of moisture to the root system. In company with all cattleyas, *Laelia purpurata* is most at home in a pot of bark-based materials.

Laelia pumila has had a more confused history than most of the genus. Part of this was due to its morphological variation and the fact that various collectors took specimens and sent them to England and various centres of Europe. The latest classification, whether acceptable or not, is by Pabst and Dungs in *Orchidaceae Brasilianses*, in which *Laelia pumila* is noted as distinct from the more commonly grown form *Laelia sincorana*.

The original English source is given as the discovery of the species by Gardner on the Organ Mountains in April 1837, which would be about its flowering season. He found it on the small branches of trees and not in quantities.

Contradictory information is given in other sources, which ascribe its discovery to another collector who sent it to a French dealer named Pinel under the name of *Cattleya marginata*. Loddiges' nursery flowered plants of the orchid in their glass-houses and Rollison's nursery also flowered it under the name of *Cattleya pinelii* in 1842.

In 1850 it was described and figured in the magazine *Florist* under the name of *Cattleya spectabilis* and Loddiges remarked: 'With respect to the *Cattleya spectabilis*, we received a small parcel of orchids from Brazil in the spring of 1849 amongst which were some cattleyas having the appearance of *marginata*; many of these flowered as such. This being stronger in growth evidently appeared different and flowered in June, when it was exhibited at Chiswick; it seemed to be an extraordinarily fine variety of *marginata*.'

Reichenbach correctly identified the species as a laelia in 1853 and gave it the name which it now bears, considering all the other forms which had been flowered to be varieties of the same species. He further confused things, however, by naming an obviously related flower *Laelia praestans* and is recorded as having in 1862 named the same plant *Bletia praestans*.

Over the following years many more variations were recorded, some in English collections, others in European. Veitch's *Manual of Orchidaceous Plants* illustrates *Laelia pumila* and describes two other varieties. *The Orchid Album*, published in the 1880 period, has a beautiful lithograph in Volume 3 which correctly shows the flowers fully opened on the new unmatured growths, appearing from the axils of the single leaves without sheaths.

But each gives a different history. Veitch's manual notes that it became first known to horticulture through a John Allcard, who had received a plant from Essequibo, British Guiana (now Guyana) and flowered it in 1838. But they do list the habitat correctly as southern Brazil, where it grows at about 500 to 1500 metres elevation. It was Boxall, collecting for Low and Company, who discovered the variety *dayana*, a dedication to John Day, the noted grower and artist of the 1860-80 period.

While most illustrations of *Laelia pumila* or *sincorana* usually show it as single flowered, it frequently produces them in twos on well developed growths in good conditions. Following flowering, the growth slowly matures through the winter months and then becomes dormant until early summer, when it recommences growth by first showing new root tips on the bases of the new growths and branching new tips from the older roots.

This orchid seems to be more at home on a cork or wooden slab than in conventional potting mixes and it should be grown in an airy, bright part of the glass-house, freely watered when in active growth if mounted on a slab and with a good air flow about the plant. It may also be grown as a garden plant in temperate, frost-free climates, as the illustration shows. It does not like normal cattleya conditions and is prone to decline if unsuited.

It is not intended to sort out the laelias in the order of importance in hybridising, but the precedence does have some meaning. *Laelia tenebrosa*, which was discovered rather late in orchid history about 1890, had as much significance as *Laelia purpurata* because it added the yellow and gold color to the range of hybrids even as far as the potinaras. Originally listed as having come from Baia or Bahia, Brazil, there was some mystery about its origin, a not unusual circumstance in the history of orchid collecting. Each collector sought to throw competitors off the trail. The area of concentration not far from Rio de Janeiro, however, became the source for some of the better colors in the yellow to apricot-gold tones. One of these was the parent of *Laeliocattleya* Luminosa 'Aurea,' which had a great impact on breeding further hybrids.

Laelia tenebrosa has a close-set rhizome pattern, the pseudo-bulbs about 20 to 30 centimetres high and the flowers about 10 centimetres across but rather open in style. The labellum is usually purple and trumpet-like. *Laelia tenebrosa* was named by R. A. Rolfe, who was founder and the first editor of *The Orchid Review*.

Robert Allen Rolfe, Editor of *The Orchid Review*, 1893-1920.

The description of *Laelia tenebrosa* as a cool or intermediate growing species is incorrect and difficulty is experienced by some growers in flowering it.

This orchid was one of the keys which led to the solution of the habitat of *Cattleya warneri*, but on reading all the available literature on the source of both *Laelia tenebrosa* and *Cattleya warneri* one may very well be confused by it.

Laelia tenebrosa grows in normal cattleya conditions of winter minimums preferably not falling below 12 to 13 degrees Celsius and in the same mixes used for potting those orchids. The flowers are borne singly or in pairs on mature growths, the buds of which are sheathed.

There must be significance in the origin of various clones of *Laelia*

tenebrosa and all the other Brazilian orchids, because Baia or Bahia province is just south of the equator and even plants from high altitudes would be inclined toward tropical conditions rather than the usual cattleya and laelia conditions. However, if *Laelia tenebrosa* and *Cattleya labiata* grow in the same areas, climatic conditions must be modified in some way, as few, if any, cattleyas will stand tropical conditions as understood for phalaenopsis and some vandas.

Laelia milleri is a comparatively new orchid, originating in the Minas Geraes province of Brazil and quite localised from an area of rough limestone country at an altitude of about 1000 metres. It was named by Karl Ludwig Blume.

The climate in this area is widely fluctuating between extremes of heat in daytime and coldness at night. This gives *Laelia milleri* a high degree of tolerance and it is possible to grow it as an outdoor plant in fairly good climates. It seems to have a marked intolerance for heated glass-houses and stable temperatures.

It is morphologically variable, indicated by the two types grown by the author, one with pseudo-bulbs 7 to 9 centimetres high topped by a leaf of similar length, the other with 4 to 5 centimetre pseudo-bulbs and similar length single leaves. Both have flowers about the same size, 4 centimetres across and brilliant scarlet, almost blood colored. The slim bulbs, swollen at the base and tapering off to a fine apex, carry an erect spike of two or three flowers on a long stem.

The hybrid *Sophrolaelia* Jinn (*Laelia milleri* x *Sophronitis coccinea*) usually follows the laelia line and produces a flower remarkably similar to it. Like most hybrids, it is morphologically a little stronger than the laelia species. Back-crossed again to *Sophronitis coccinea*, the flowers are improved in size and shape, although the largest of these are quite starry and beautiful, as the pictures show.

Laelia milleri seems to thrive better mounted on a section of a branch or a slab of cork rather than in a pot. If, however, it is bench grown, the pot should be preferably a tubby fern pot, as the root system is neither long nor dense. Potting material should be graded down to mixtures of 3 to 5 millimetre size granules, plenty of coarse similar sized brick or crock pieces and the addition of a little oak leaf and twig before breakdown seems to suit it. The dormant period is fairly long, the flower spike, from the apex of the growth as long again as the growth and leaves, appearing almost as soon as the bulb is maturing. The spike is usually sheathed and of two or three flowers, variable in season, but usually summer to autumn, even as far into the season as early winter, at which time it coincides with the flowering of *Sophronitis coccinea*.

Laelia cinnabarina, named by Bateman ex Lindley, also played a part in creating some of the gold, yellow and orange colored hybrids in the period since its introduction in 1836. It was first flowered by a nurseryman named Young in England, but was known several years earlier.

A native of Minas Geraes, Brazil, which is on the central plateau, somewhere in the vicinity of 500 to 1200 metres above sea level, it is also found in one or two other districts, including Rio de Janeiro. The climate in the Minas Geraes region is one of considerable fluctuation between daytime and night temperatures and one in which dry periods can be lengthy.

The pseudo-bulbs of this orchid are usually dark purple-red, the leaves thick and pale green colored on the upper surface but frequently purple colored on the underside. The rhizome between the bulbs is short, so that the plant habit is compact. Some forms of *Laelia cinnabarina* are short, some up to 30 centimetres tall, depending on the environment from which the plants originate. Most of these orchids are rupicolous, or rock dwellers.

The colors of the flowers, as the name indicates, are bright orange-red to paler colored. The natural inter-breeding between *Laelia cinnabarina* and other Brazilian orchids of similar families is extensive and some of it unknown, even extending to cattleyas. The differences between cattleyas and laelias include the number of pollen plates, which in cattleyas number four and in laelias eight.

The variety figured in Lindley's *Sertum Orchidaceum*, published in London in 1838, is quite different from the photograph in the illustrations. The plant exhibited at the Horticultural Society's meeting in 1837 carried only three or four flowers on a stem, whereas most of the plants grown in the late 1900s had large spikes of up to ten or more flowers. The spikes are rather fine and need support.

Laelia cinnabarina does not take kindly to cold winter conditions and it should be grown in similar conditions to cattleyas. The potting material should be related to the size of the pot or basket in which it is grown, but finer particles should be avoided and the mix kept open so that water is not held in any quantity. The cultural system should be one of thorough watering and then a period when water is withheld for a day or two after the plant is apparently dry, a system which suits many of the laelias. A little ribbiness of the pseudo-bulbs is unimportant, but when the plant is maturing new growth the water should be increased and fertilisers supplied more than at any other time. Dormancy may be long and in this state the plant should be watered sparingly and very seldom until root action is again noted.

Laelias are no different from the general run of cattleyas and the commencement of all root activity is in early summer, usually spotted first emerging from the bases of the last-made growths.

In conjunction with *Laelia cinnabarina*, *Laelia harpophylla* (Reichenbach f.) and *Laelia flava* (Lindley) were the progenitors of a delightful range of laeliocattleyas when combined with *Cattleya dowiana* var. *aurea*. The colors range from orange through yellow to cream, most of the flowers being about half-size when compared with orthodox cattleya hybrids.

Laelia harpophylla is almost xerophytic rather than epiphytic because of its origin in a harsh climate and in habitats which in the golden days of collectors were considered wholly unsuitable for orchids and not worth the trouble of reaching and searching. *Laelia harpophylla* had counterparts which also remained undiscovered for similar reasons. The name 'harpophylla' in literal translation means sword-leaf and it correctly describes the foliage of this species. In cultivation it reacts to fairly hard conditions and bright light, the only time free watering is given being in the maturing stages of growth. Most growers treat it too kindly and so find it a little difficult.

The three laelias are affiliated and also have other associated species in the genus, which is more Brazilian than common to the other states of South America. There are almost fifty species in Brazil and in general they all grow in the same potting mix. A summary of their treatment is given at the end of the section on the Mexican laelias.

To clarify the question of the various conditions under which these Brazilian laelias grow a resume of the three climatic zones is given and a reference list applicable to a number of the species, in the hope that it may aid in selection from them to suit the facilities available in the glass-houses of various growers. The relative zones are numbered 1, 2 and 3 and are as follow:

Zone 1: Temperate climate in lower mountain and foothill country, plentiful rain and high humidity and with a good air flow or wind right through the year.

Zone 2: Higher temperatures in lowland areas, also with high humidity through the year, particularly in coastal regions. Temperatures as high as 35 degrees are common daily for months, sometimes with seasonal rainfall and therefore in the dry periods with low humidity in those regions and without the same air circulation or wind currents.

Zone 3: Altitudes of 500 to 1000 metres, hot dry days, cold nights, with a temperature variation from 35 degrees by day to almost zero by night. Orchids in this climate mostly occur in river valleys, mountain gullies and along the banks of streams. There are also swamp-marsh areas in these regions with orchid populations.

These are some of the laelias and their climatic zones:

Laelia crispa, 1; *Laelia grandis*, 1; *Laelia lobata*, 1; *Laelia perrinii*, 1; *Laelia purpurata*, 2; *Laelia tenebrosa*, 1; *Laelia xanthina*, 1; *Laelia dayana*, 3; *Laelia jongheana*, 3; *Laelia pumila*, 2, 3; *Laelia sincorana*, 1; *Laelia lundii*, 3; *Laelia harpophylla*, 1; *Laelia crispata*, 3; *Laelia crispilabia*, 3; *Laelia liliputana*, 3; *Laelia bahiensis*, 2; *Laelia briegeri*, 3; *Laelia cinnabarina*, 1, 3; *Laelia flava*, 3; *Laelia milleri*, 3; *Laelia bradei*, 3; *Laelia esalqueana*, 3; *Laelia reginae*, 3.

That is by no means all the laelias, but the various other species may be related to these by habit and appearance and a trial given in whatever modifications of climatic requirements are possible. Naturally, duplication of the stated climatic condition is almost impossible in a glass-house, but it does at least indicate their habitat conditions. Another strange feature of zonal origin is that several of these laelias grow in two zones or, to be more accurate, in the borderline zones or overlaps in the system, altering morphologically in the same way as the cattleya described in a previous chapter, going from a robust plant at one altitude to a dwarf which has little chance of flowering from its tenuous grip on life.

Reference to the colored map in another section gives some idea of the areas and situations of these climatic zones and further reference to the maps of occurrence of the species may throw further light on their origins. Naturally, these maps are inaccurate and definitions of climatic boundaries such as delineated in the colored map are only approximate.

The Mexican Laelias

Laelia anceps was first imported into England by Loddiges about 1834. Dr Lindley, when he saw it in flower, remarked: 'When we say that this plant is equal in beauty to any of the cattleyas . . . we shall have said that it is one of the most interesting of the tribe that has yet made its appearance.' It was named by John Lindley.

In the days when first discovered it was collected from the eastern side of the Cordilleras on the Atlantic coast. Most of the white form was collected on the Pacific coast. The best of the species were the dark forms from certain districts, which were called 'morada' type by the Mexicans.

Usually it was found on trees on the fringes of forests, but it is also rupicolous, or lithophytic. The seasons are something of extremes in its habitat, with considerable rain from May to October (northern hemisphere) the plants saturated at night, and sometimes very cold. Mostly the days are quite dry, with bright sunlight. This should be one of the cultural features. The plants in the habitat flower about November, usually in a short dry season followed by rain in February, with damp, humid weather until May, when the rainy season starts again.

About 1885 the Liverpool Horticultural Company imported an enormous consignment of plants and one buyer relates how he purchased a clump 'as large as a goodsized doormat' for about two pounds. The variety *chamberlainiana* came from this importation and at the time, with so many comparisons to be made, it was ranked as the premier variety. Two others came to light at that time, with the variety *thompsoniana* proving to be a piece of the clump of *chamberlainiana* which had broken away and the variety *crawshayana* running a close second. De Barri Crawshay, an orchid grower of the period, was an authority on *Laelia anceps*.

In 1920 some twenty varieties were known and cultivated, with many others listed as sub-species. Revision is going on all the time, but the natural material is now so scarce in Mexico that it is becoming a rare and endangered species.

As *Laelia anceps* usually grows at some 1500 to 2000 metres, and occasionally higher, it is an ideal cool-growing orchid. In Australia it is a southern states orchid, with a growth habit quite unlike its natural one. The variety *chamberlainiana* is still supreme, although one or two other clones are also fine types.

Of all the laelias, it could be expected that the species *anceps* would have had some part to play in producing hybrids of superb shape and color. However, it fell to other species laelias to far outweigh the influence of *anceps* in hybridisation, not for want of trial, as thousands of cross-pollinations were made.

Laelia anceps is one of the awkward plants to grow because it has an ascending rhizome with a gap of 4 or 5 centimetres between the pseudo-bulbs. But it may be pot grown as well as mounted on slabs of cork or tree-fern. With such a distance between the pseudo-bulbs it is seldom grown into large plants and when such cultivation is taken on it must be moved every couple of years into a larger container or the first broken up slightly and inserted into a container some two or three times larger with a filling around the outside of the inner pot. In this way the root system is not damaged nearly as much as if the plant is removed and repotted. It may be done with either clay or plastic pots, but be sure to break up the plastic pot thoroughly if the pieces are not removed.

Flower spikes on *Laelia anceps* are thrust up from the centre of the immature leaf and long before there is much suggestion of a pseudo-bulb. They are quite sticky and this stickiness persists even after the spike is fully developed and the flowers are open. The usual flowering period is the Australian winter, but *Laelia anceps* is very durable as a plant and should not be given 'soft' treatment.

The root system of this orchid is strong and not very dense, with about three or four tips emerging from the base of the new pseudo-bulbs in early summer and also new branching tips from the old root system, which it is important not to damage in winter cultivation by overwatering.

Liquid nutrients in weak forms are the usual fertilisers for all laelias and they should be given only when the new pseudo-bulbs are starting or when the pseudo-bulbs are swelling in the later stages of their growth, which may occur just before flowering or at the same time.

Laelias anceps, furfuracea, albida, autumnalis, gouldiana and *speciosa* all occur in much the same areas in Mexico. *Laelia furfuracea* is about the same size as *Laelia anceps* and was found by a European nobleman named Karwinsky at Oaxaca, on the Tehuantepec isthmus mountains at about 2000 metres.

Although they grow at varying altitudes, *Laelia anceps* did not grow as much in contact as the other members of the group and this alone prevented a probable intense cross-pollination of this species to produce the natural hybrids which followed the association of the others.

Laelia autumnalis was imported into England somewhere about the year 1836 by a grower named Tayleur, of Liverpool, who brought the plants with him on his return from abroad. On flowering, it was named by John Lindley, probably for its flowering season, and letters were soon sent off for a further supply of plants. Most of the early importations were of only a few clumps, usually with consignments of other species which were already known in England and Europe.

The demand grew, with the result that the known areas were soon denuded and many thousands of plants, through ignorance and greed, were lost. The treatment and despatch of plants by sailing ship or any other means was an unknown art in those early days. It was some time before the lessons were learnt and that the slightest trace of moisture in the packing cases meant the almost certain loss of the whole case.

Laelia autumnalis was fairly common in Mexico, mostly found growing on rock faces, but also on small trees and in situations which at that time were considered most unusual perches for orchid plants. Growing at considerable elevation, much higher even than *Laelia anceps*, it is almost frost resistant and very tolerant, growing best in light, airy situations. In glass-house culture it grows best in slightly warm conditions in winter, but at lower temperatures than cattleyas. It is not an orchid for semi-tropical or tropical cultivation.

Laelia gouldiana was named by Reichenbach after the American Jay Gould, a wealthy speculator who dealt in railroads among other things. It flowered first in the nursery of Siebrecht and Wadley in New York, although Sanders also flowered it about the same time.

This laelia excited the attention of taxonomists because of its similarity to known species and several theories were put forward to account for it. One *Laelia gouldiana* plant was found as a chance plant in an enormous clump of *Laelia anceps* imported into England which turned out to be a white variety of *anceps*. When the stranger flowered it was surmised that its parents were undoubtedly *Laelia anceps* and *Laelia autumnalis*. Although check cross-pollinations have been made, there is still some doubt in the minds of various authorities about this derivation. However, it is generally considered that the parentage was as originally thought, *Laelia anceps* and *Laelia autumnalis*.

Laelia gouldiana is brighter than both its parents, rather more square in shape than either and totally lacking the twisting of the petals and sepals so common a feature in many varieties of *Laelia autumnalis*. The number of flowers is less than that of *Laelia autumnalis*, but more than usual on *Laelia anceps*, so that taken all round we have an improvement on both in some respects.

Laelia majalis, or *speciosa*, as it is called, was one of the first orchids known in the western world. A Jesuit priest named Hernandez, in his book *Natural History of New Spain*, published in 1615, first mentioned *Laelia majalis*. Nothing more was heard of it until Humboldt found it again on the west coast of Mexico between Acapulco and Playas de Coynca. Kunth, who worked with Humboldt, named it *Bletia speciosa*. As Veitch's manual states, the native name for it is Flor de Mayo and the specific name *majalis* is a literal Latin equivalent.

This laelia was later found in many other parts of Mexico and several other names were attached to it. Since doubt was cast on all the names, John Lindley's name of *Laelia majalis* was accepted following the flowering of the plants in English collections. The previous contacts were unknown to Lindley, who thought it was new to horticulture. The collectors Hartweg and Ross, working independently, sent plants to England some time about 1834.

The actual environment of *Laelia majalis* varies considerably, but it is most hardy, with frosts occurring frequently. Its host tree is given as an oak, but what form the oak would take in Mexico would be debatable. One thing is certain: it would be a tree with permanent bark and not one which sheds bark in the growing process. In cultivation *Laelia majalis* prefers a slightly warmer climate with a plentiful air flow about the plant day and night. It has a definite rest or dormant period in the cooler months of the year, starting life again in the spring with a show of new root tips and new roots on the pseudo-bulb of the previous growing season.

Laelia albida seems to have always been a difficult laelia to cultivate, although it grows in much the same type of country as the other Mexican species and natural hybrids between it and others of the genus have been collected in the past. It was usually found at about 2000 metres, which is a fairly high altitude for such orchids.

Brought to England about 1839, it was probably included with a consignment of another species, as a nurseryman by the name of Sadler sent it to James Bateman for identification. It was unknown and he later named it in association with John Lindley. All that was known about it was its habitat at high altitude which exposed it to hot days and very cold nights. A cultivation program is not easy to work out when such plants are included with other orchids. Subsequently it was found that the plant had been known in Europe for some years before it was brought to the attention of Bateman. But growers in England had little success with *Laelia albida* and it was never prominent in collections. The same could be said of it in Australia and after persevering with a plant for some twelve years and never flowering it, I wonder if I will ever see it bloom in my collection.

It is unlikely that the potting medium would make any difference to the culture of *Laelia albida* and if it is accepted as a challenge the same bark potting mix as used for cattleyas should be tried. The root system is not quite as coarse as that of most cattleyas, but is similar to that of most laelias and a little finer blending may suit the orchid. At the time this book was printed the plant showed every indication of flowering. Having seen the original from which the propagation was taken, it is expected to be palest of pink on the tips of petals and sepals, but the flower overall a white. Owing to cultural problems the spikes of *Laelia albida* are apt to brown off at the tips and so spoil a plant for exhibition purposes, which would evoke a lot of comment.

Laelia albida is not alone in being a difficult orchid to grow and where some fortunate fanciers for a challenge may chance on a suitable environment for it, the odds are against it ever becoming a general flowering proposition like its other Mexican relatives.

Most of the Mexican laelias grow in much the same conditions as the moderate temperature cattleyas, despite their origins in cool areas. They will scarcely tolerate warmer than temperate zones and are entirely unsuitable for tropical areas in normal unassisted conditions. It is possible that the best results will be obtained by summer outdoor cultivation and a return to a warm glass-house for flowering and the winter. Growing them entirely outdoors is unrewarding because the flowers, while of good substance and durable, are not weatherproof.

Of them all *Laelia anceps* has a more awkward habit with its ascending rhizome, but all are prone to this habit to some degree. A good method of overcoming this disability, while not giving much scope for growth into specimen plants, is the type of cultivation where the plant grows on a section of a limb stabilised with screenings in a broad-base pot, as in the illustrated section. It is possible to grow *Laelia anceps* in a broad shallow dish, but these baked clay seed pans are seldom available and those growers who have them do not like to part with them.

Most of the members of the group have a single leaf, but the rule is not invariable, as even *Laelia anceps* has been known to grow occasionally a second leaf on a pseudo-bulb, or even no leaf at all, with the flower spike ascending from the apex of the bare bulb. *Laelias autumnalis* and *gouldiana* grow as many as three or four leaves at times.

Each of the laelia species has some peculiar set of natural conditions under which it thrives, but as they must all be grouped usually in one glass-house or situation, a standard should be worked out which suits all or most of them. The situation in a glass-house is worth experimenting with, and it will usually be found that the genus does best when it is in an air flow, preferably from the outside but even induced by a fan circulating the air.

Few pests trouble laelias, but grubs eating the soft new growths seem to be the worst. While slugs or snails will attack the buds, the plants do not seem prone to attack by red spider or other glass-house pests. The soft root tips are vulnerable points and woodlice will chew these if given the opportunity. As the rhizome below the pseudo-bulb usually produces only three or four root tips, damage to these means that the progression is lost and root development further back has to support the plant.

Potting materials consist of the usual epiphyte mixes based on bark; charcoal may be added, also other coarse aggregate such as broken brick and crock from fired clay such as tiles or broken flower pots. A little roughage of this type gives the roots something to work on. When plants are potted into unproved material, a watch should be kept on the root tips and if they brown off on contact with it the plant should be removed and the roots started off again in sphagnum moss. The unsuitable material should be replaced and the reject material either treated to render it suitable or discarded as garden top-dressing.

Fertilisers should be applied only when the plants are receptive — that is, when the roots commence to move and become active or when the plants are maturing pseudo-bulbs. At any time other than these two phases water alone is needed to keep the plants in trim and the water should be proved suitable just as for any epiphyte cultivation.

Solid fertilisers such as blood and bone or animal manures should be used sparingly, again at the correct time, and no other nutrient than these slow-release fertilisers used. Inorganic slow-release pellets or fertilisers are unsuitable because of their lasting qualities and the release of stimulants when the plants no longer need them. If they are used, residues should be removed as laelias go into their dormant period following flowering.

Not all laelias go through this phase, as outlined in the instance of *Laelia sincorana*, and treatment should be judged on the relevant species concerned and its various phases.

Within reason pot size has little importance in growing most of the genus because they have wide-ranging root systems like cattleyas and it is possible with bark mixes to start a good propagation off in a 20 to 30 centimetre pot with the idea of growing a specimen plant, encouraging the plant to break double, that is, to produce two shoots from a pseudo-bulb instead of only one and dividing the plant by almost severing the rhizome and forcing the back-cut also to produce new shoots. It is possible that a plant could be challenged as a specimen if the rhizome were completely severed and the grower found himself unjustly accused of having potted more than one piece to start the plant away. *Laelia anceps* in particular is a good subject for specimen culture because of its ease and good multiplication characteristics.

Schomburgkias

This distinct group has mostly been transferred to the laelias, but they are quite different in habit and the type of country in which they are usually found. The genus was named for its discoverer by Lindley. Two German-born brothers named Schomburgk were associated with a commission sent out to determine the border between British Guiana (Guyana in the modern atlas) and Venezuela about 1836, one, who later became Sir Robert Schomburgk, as a negotiator, the other, Richard, as a naturalist and botanist attached to the mission. He also was later knighted and became Director of the Adelaide Botanic Gardens in 1865.

Richard must have had a wonderful time wandering about Guyana for about three years. Although originally German, in some way the two brothers must have become naturalised and little is known of the ultimate life of Robert Schomburgk or the determinations of the border commission.

Heinrich Gustav Reichenbach, the successor to Dr John Lindley.

Laelia crispa was found by Richard Schomburgk growing on the trunks of trees on the banks of the Essequibo River and it was the typical long stalk of the flower stem, with its terminal bunch of flowers which attracted his attention. The spikes of *Laelia crispa* are comparatively short when compared with others. They are about a metre or a little more tall, the flowers about 6 to 8 centimetres across, rather spidery, brownish-yellow with darker streaks of purple-brown and with a pale rose pink to deep rose labellum. In all it is not an attractive orchid, but most spectacular when in flower.

Laelia crispa was named by the younger Reichenbach from material sent from British Guiana and it is reasonable to suppose that it was sent to him by Richard Schomburgk, although it is known that Lindley also had material and attached a name to it about the same time. He shares the naming with Reichenbach, but he called it *Cattleya crispa*. It was one of the first of the type brought to the attention of botanists in England and Europe.

Schomburgkia or *Laelia undulata* was found by Jean Linden about 1841 in Venezuela. He was instrumental in bringing it to Europe and England and it also was named by Lindley. It is also common to Colombia. Linden found it growing at about 700 metres in a very hot section of the country with a weather pattern of about six months of rain and heat and six months of dry weather. *Laelia undulata* grows mostly on rocky outcrops and flowers at the end of the rainy season. Considering its habitat, it would not be an easy orchid to cultivate and growers have found it so.

Laelia tibicinis is common to Honduras and Panama, so it will be apparent that this section of the laelia group has a fairly widespread region. George Ure Skinner found it owing to the tall flower spikes, which grow over 3 metres high. The patch he found was extensive, growing on rocky country and he was badly stung by ants in the collecting process. He sent plants to England about 1835 and Lindley remarked of it: 'This noble plant is the cow's horn orchid of Honduras. Its pseudo-bulbs, between one and two feet long, are quite hollow and as smooth as the chamber of a bamboo; at their base there is always a small hole which leads to the interior and furnishes access to the colonies of ants which are constantly found inhabiting the plant.'

The pseudo-bulbs of the orchid when leafless were collected by village urchins, who knew them as 'trumpet plants' because it is what they used them for. Skinner and others found them most unmusical when so played by the boys, with a coarse low-pitched note. The species gained its name from this use.

Laelia tibicinis flowers in late spring to early summer and in an orchid publication of the 1926 period a photograph appeared of a plant of this species with a spike of flowers well over 4 metres (15 feet) tall, grown by a Trinidad fancier.

Laelia superbiens was also named by Lindley from material sent to him by Skinner from Guatemala about 1839. But it was the collector Hartweg who sent consignments of the plants to England about 1842 to the Horticultural

157

Society of London and from these plants Mrs Wray, another of the women growers of the period, flowered it in 1844.

It was one of the few orchids cultivated by the natives in or near its habitat. Mostly found by the tall spikes reaching up about 3 metres, it is an unpopular cultivated orchid. Again, like most of the genus, it is rupicolous or lithophytic, seldom found in forest country, but nearly always in bright light in open regions.

The morphology of the genus or section is similar right through, with fusiforme or spindle-shaped pseudo-bulbs, most tall and topped with anything up to three or four hard-looking leaves.

Laelia thompsoniana is from the outlying Cayman Islands in the West Indies and is one of the prettiest of the genus. Many of them have undulant petals and sepals — crisped, some writers prefer to say. This orchid illustrates the type. An English grower first flowered it and his name was attached to it. The spikes are about 1.5 metres high and the flowers, as usual, bunched at the top.

The habitat of the species and its resemblance to *Laelia tibicinis* led to some disagreement about its origin, but it was later confirmed by the Director of Public Gardens as the Cayman Islands some 332 kilometres west of Jamaica. It was a late arrival in collections, Sir Trevor Lawrence being one of the first to put it on show about 1886.

These laelias are not popular, as remarked previously, owing to their very tall spikes and the unusual seasonal differences necessary for their cultivation in glass-houses. However, for tropical areas of Australia they would be ideal garden subjects, particularly if grown on a rockery and out in almost open sunlight for some of the year. Naturally, in these situations the flowers soon become tatty, but that goes for most of the garden flowers we grow anyway. They are impossibilities to photograph except the tip of the spike with the flowers, which all appear on about the final 30 centimetres of its length. There is quite a number of species in the group, most unobtainable in Australia, but the few mentioned here and the illustrations give a general picture of the section.

The relative size of orchid flowers is always aligned to the type of habitat in which they grow. Cattleyas usually have large flowers and this can be attributed to their situation of a protected and, if it can be so described, lush set of conditions aiding development of such a flower.

Laelias are frequently rupicolous; that is, they grow mostly on rock surfaces. In this situation it would not be expected to find a flower such as that produced by cattleyas, therefore we have a large number of small-flowered laelias which evolution has decreed must economise. An analogous force of evolution could also be seen in the long stems of what were once known as schomburgkias, now designated laelias, as they seek to get their flowers above the surrounding environment. Nature cannot be defeated for very long and it is first in survival of pollination of flowers with those longer stems and the dying out of the strains with short stems that a beginning of the fight was made. It is also in the survival of small-flowered laelias such as those referred to above that we have whole families and groups of them now able to grow on rock surfaces through a period of famine toward a season when they may again flower and produce seed.

The flowering habits of various laelias and cattleyas have intrigued botanists and growers alike. *Cattleya walkerana* flowers on a very immature growth; *Laelia sincorana* (syn. *Laelia pumila*) does likewise and the pattern is followed by other orchids. The only natural interpretation to be placed on this style of growth pattern is that although the climatic system suits a growing period following initiation of new growth, the plant has conformed to an adverse set of conditions which follow its maturity and so the flowers are produced early in the growth phase to make sure the seed is set and cast at the right time — *it is the seeding period which determines every reaction of the plant to natural forces.*

Laelia autumnalis

Rhyncolaelias
(Brassavolas)

Rudolf Schlechter

The genus was named by Rudolf Schlechter in 1918, the two members mentioned here having been known as brassavolas until their transfer. John Lindley originally named them *Brassavola digbyana* and *Brassavola glauca*. The prefix to the generic name laelia is in reference to the beaked seed capsule.

Rhyncolaelia digbyana is among the orchids which have had name changes over the years since discovery. It was sent to England originally by Mrs McDonald, wife of a governor of British Honduras, a Central American state. It flowered in the orchid collection of Edward Digby, probably a friend of the McDonalds, and was named *Laelia digbyana* by John Lindley in 1846. It also flowered at the Kew Gardens in 1849 and proved to be a star attraction for some time because of its rarity.

The flowers vary considerably in color, but the outstanding labellum is constant. Some of the varieties have the petals and sepals tinted or deeply colored, but the pale form is the plant the hybridists prefer to work with.

When used as a seed parent in early cross-pollinations the unusual 'beak' between the fertilised anther at the head of the column and the actual seed capsule attracted considerable attention; and in 1881 Bentham transferred it to the laelia family from the brassavolas, in which it was included at that time. Later it was given the generic title rhyncolaelia by Schlechter, although it continued to be known as *Brassavola digbyana* because of involvement in *Sanders' List of Orchid Hybrids*.

Name changes are confusing at any time, but as the years go on and the ramifications of the hybrid list become more pronounced and intricate it is best perhaps to leave things as they are and look to synonyms instead of real names.

Rhyncolaelia digbyana is fairly widespread, growing in many parts of Central America, mostly in the very warm lowland areas. It was originally designated a swamp epiphyte accustomed to growing in bright, open conditions.

The first hybrid with a cattleya was with the species *Cattleya mossiae*, raised and named by James Veitch and Sons in 1889 *Brassocattleya* Veitchii, with the synonym *Brassocattleya* Digbyano-mossiae. The seed parent was the cattleya. One of the notable early hybrids, *Brassocattleya* Cliftonii, an admirable orchid raised by Charlesworths in 1908, is still grown.

The effect of the labellum of *Rhyncolaelia digbyana* on hybrids is somewhat lost, having been converted from a beautiful fringe into lacework or lacinations. However, it did add size to the labellums of the hybrids generally and even in the trigeneric brassolaeliocattleyas and potinaras the influence is quite marked.

The use of rhyncolaelias as seed parents provided some unusual problems in hybridising, particularly with small genera like the sophronitis. It was found that pollen development was too short in many instances to reach to the bottom of the seed capsule and seed was formed only in the part nearest the beak, or proboscis. This led for some time to its use as a pollen parent only.

160

Rhyncolaelia digbyana is infrequently seen as a cultivated orchid, but provided it is grown in bright conditions and its dormancy respected it is quite easy to grow and flower. The usual potting mediums for cattleyas suit well and as the rhizome is short between pseudo-bulbs repotting is infrequent.

One of the peculiar characteristics of *Rhyncolaelia digbyana* is the way the labellum never sits square on with the flower, but is always tilted off to one side. And, stranger still, it always seems to favor a one-way tilt year after year. The flower also has a delightful perfume, which it sometimes passes on to the inter-generic hybrids. One of the signals that a flower has matured fully and is ready to cut is development of a perfume in these hybrids.

The only other member of the genus is *Brassavola* or *Rhyncolaelia glauca*, which, although it also has a labellum overbearing the rest of the flower, has had little use as a generator of hybrids.

Both members are somewhat similar morphologically, with grey-green pseudo-bulbs and leaves. Some plants of the species *Rhyncolaelia digbyana* have darker colored pseudo-bulbs, but the leaves of both species are thick and narrow and mostly deeply channelled.

The flowers of *Rhyncolaelia digbyana* are about 10 to 12 centimetres across, with *Rhyncolaelia glauca* about half the size.

One inherent factor early noted in *Brassavola digbyana* hybrids, particularly with the albino cattleyas, were the beautiful mauve tints in the brassocattleya seedlings. This led to development of the tendency and the result was production of some of the most delicately tinted orchid flowers ever seen in all the years of artificial hybridisation. However, there was one drawback to continued use of the line, because the poor petal and sepal development of the brassavola remained a constant feature.

In cultivation rhyncolaelias are treated the same as cattleyas and the warm-growing laelias, but neither are tolerant about cold periods in their annual cycle. If grown too cold they do not flower freely and at times the petals and sepals will go black on the tips or the edges before the flower opens fully. In colder regions winter temperatures should be maintained above 12 degrees to keep the plants going.

Sophronitis

This small genus was named by John Lindley, the name derived from the Greek word *sophron*, meaning small, or modest. The generic name infers a relationship with a small genus named sophronia by Lindley.

Sophronitis coccinea was discovered by the Frenchman Descourtilz at a fairly high altitude in the vicinity of Rio de Janeiro, Brazil about the year 1837 and since its introduction it never lost attraction. In addition to the first area of discovery, it occurs in three other provinces, Espirito Santo, Sao Paulo and Minas Geraes, all in the south central area of Brazil. It was named by Lindley.

Like the other species, *Sophronitis coccinea* is a dwarf, the plants standing some 6 to 8 centimetres tall, the flowers varying in size from 5 to about 10 centimetres on fine varieties. Although the color of *Sophronitis coccinea* is variable from pale golden yellow to orange and red, it is the brilliant carmine red types which are most used in hybridising, also the choice of most fanciers. In cultivation it increases its pseudo-bulbs freely and plants soon build into specimens when suited.

As a genus the sophronitis are epiphytic and at times lithophytic and accustomed to a cool and ever moist climate. The habitat is usually such that small orchids predominate, cool by night but dry and warm during the day and with a definite dormant period, which seems to occur in spring and early summer, when most orchids are starting up.

There are some six members in the genus as listed by Pabst and Dungs in *Orchidaceae Brasilienses*. They are *Sophronitis brevipedunculata* (Cogniaux) *Sophronitis cernua* (Lindley), *Sophronitis coccinea*, sometimes referred to as *Sophronitis grandiflora* (Lindley), *Sophronitis mantiqueirae* (Fowlie), *Sophronitis wittigiana* (Barbosa Rodrigues) and *Sophronitis pterocarpa* (Lindley), which appears a most difficult orchid to grow and flower. Closely allied to these species is *Sophronitella violacea*, also named by Lindley and a beautiful mauve to violet color. It is an easy orchid to grow, preferably on a piece of fern or cork or wood and hung where it gets plenty of light.

It is a somewhat confusing genus, but if identification is taken from Pabst and Dungs' book it presents few problems, as there are water-color illustrations to guide a grower. From these it is fairly obvious that the species known as *Sophronitis rosea* is probably the species *Sophronitis wittigiana*.

The plants seem to do best when mounted on pieces of cork, slabs of suitable wood, fern fibre slabs or grown in shallow pots. The root system is not long, so tall pots should not be used and the miniature size of the plants considered when using any type of pot or dish. It apears that the main cultural idea is to let the plants remain semi-moist to moist all through the year, never wet, and to see that once they start to grow they are kept moving by selective treatment and a little nutrient spray or dipping in very weak nutrient solutions of Aquasol or similar inorganic fertilisers and staining the fluid with Maxicrop or seaweed based fertilisers of the same type.

The impact of this small orchid on the cattleya complex has been tremendous in introducing a color not readily obtainable in any orchids —

clear reds and tints all the way down to orange and up to purple-reds of a density and luminescence found only in masdevallias and few other orchids.

Sophrolaelias, sophrolaeliocattleyas and sophrocattleyas are easier to grow and flower than the combination bringing in the brassavolas. This is perhaps easy to understand and the potinaras, the four genera combined, are sometimes most difficult to keep going in seasonal rhythm.

The word 'potinara' was coined for the complex in 1922, or first used in that year, to attach to the hybrid Juliettae, exhibited at a meeting of the Royal Horticultural Society by Charlesworth and Co. The word is derived from the recommendation of the International Horticultural Conference of 1910 and the dedication to Monsieur Julien Potin, president of the RHS of France and chairman of the Orchid Committee. Messrs Flory and Black exhibited another potinara the following month and so just missed out for the honor of the first registration.

It is not easy, figuratively speaking, to walk away from a section of the orchid world embracing cattleyas and associated genera without considering the enormous amount of work which has been devoted to cultivating them over the slightly more than 100 years of our knowledge of them.

Considering the way the country New Granada, now Colombia, was cleared to take profit from the timber resources as well as the products following the clearing of forests, it is a wonder that any of the species are left at all. It is hopeless to suppose that they will ever return in the way they were found in the first years. As in Australia, one whispered word that 'something' grows at a certain spot leads quickly to the removal of that 'something' so that a profit may be made from it. After seeing the results first hand in Australia, perhaps only one instance will do to convey some sense of the loss people may feel when an act of vandalism is perpetrated. I remember seeing a very large Moreton Bay fig growing some kilometres out of a northern New South Wales town. Covering a patch of the enormous trunk was a plant of *Dendrobium linguiforme* somewhere about a metre in diameter. It was there for two years and then the following year there was only a bare and discolored patch on the tree where it once grew. Who would or could want that much *Dendrobium linguiforme* except a vandal?

The often mentioned hybrid list is to some growers a nebulous thing that they rarely consider, if at all. Yet it is most vital to the cattleyas and their progeny, half-caste though they may be. Almost one-third of the total publication is devoted to this extraordinarily complex group of inter-generic hybrids. To 1975 the list reads:

Cattleya -

× Brassavola	Brassocattleya
× Brassavola × epidendrum	Vaughnara
× Brassavola × epidendrum × laelia	Yamadara
× Brassavola × epidendrum × laelia × sophronitis	Rothara
× Brassavola × laelia	Brassolaeliocattleya
× Brassavola × laelia × schomburgkia	Recchara
× Brassavola × laelia × sophronitis	Potinara
× Brassavola × sophronitis	Rolfeara
× Broughtonia	Cattleytonia
× Broughtonia × diacrium (caularthron)	Brownara
× Broughtonia × laelia	Laeliocatonia
× Diacrium	Diacattleya
× Diacrium × epidendrum × laelia	Allenara
× Epidendrum	Epicattleya
× Epidendrum × laelia	Epilaeliocattleya

× Epidendrum × laelia × schomburgkia	Northenara
× Epidendrum × sophronitis	Stacyara
× Laelia	Laeliocattleya
× Laelia × schomburgkia × sophronitis	Herbertara
× Laelia × sophronitis	Sophrolaeliocattleya
× Schomburgkia	Schombocattleya
× Sophronitis	Sophrocattleya

There is little scope for further innovation and what could be produced from what remains would no doubt be worthless considering the amount of material already seen. The combination of some of the above inter-generic series in further associations will no doubt prove too much for the genera concerned and nature will set up its own barriers. But no doubt the inquisitiveness of the human race will attempt even the impossible simply to gain a new name and perhaps some transitory recognition.

In cultivation all the hybrids which include sophronitis need cattleya conditions to grow at their best, despite the apparent cold resistance of the species itself. In fact, *Sophronitis coccinea* in particular always seems to grow better in moderate conditions than under cold culture.

Epidendrum
Encyclia

Epidendrum

The genus was named by Linnaeus, known as the originator of the system of taxonomy, in 1753. It is derived from the two Greek words *epi* (on) and *dendron* (tree) and was indiscriminately applied to many orchids in the early years of their collection and cultivation.

Encyclia

The separation of orchids from the genus epidendrum continues and the encyclias are a comparatively modern extraction. The name is derived from the Greek word *enkyklein* (to encircle), descriptive of the way the labellum encloses the column. The genus was founded by Hooker in 1828.

The genus epidendrum has always been a very unwieldy one and botanists have so far successfully dodged the issue of separating obviously different plants into other genera. One botanist started to do so, his name Robert Dressler. But for various reasons the work fell by the way and only the Mexican branch of the family has been taken almost the whole way along the taxonomic trail. Robert Dressler and Glenn Pollard produced the book *The Genus Encyclia in Mexico* and it has been used as a guide for the two genera.

It would be some help if the division between the two genera were simple, such as classifying all the reed-stemmed species as epidendrums and all those having pseudo-bulbs as encyclias. This is not possible because of floral differences and the epidendrums of the rest of the American region now wait for reclassification along lines similar to those of the Mexican branch.

The encyclias are more closely related to the cattleyas and laelias and associated genera than the epidendrums, although both hybridise with many of them. If more information is needed about these two genera no better publication could be recommended than *The Genus Encyclia in Mexico*. Considering the size of the epidendrum family it is understandable that taxonomists have some reluctance about taking on the work of reclassifying the genus. As so many of the Mexican branch are duplicated in other American countries it is possible to get along fairly well if curiosity is the driving force.

Only a few of the epidendrums and encyclias are dealt with here, but they form a cultural base which may be applied to other members of both genera.

Reed-stemmed Epidendrums

Two epidendrums are commonly noticed in cultivation; one is red, the other orange, and their colloquial name is 'crucifix orchid'. Mostly that is the only name known by the growers and takes its origin from the inverted labellum which is similar to the stylised cross of the Christian religion.

Epidendrums were among the first orchids imported and cultivated in

Britain and Europe, but they were not the reed-stemmed type now appearing under that heading. They belonged to the encyclias and cattleyas.

The reed-stemmed epidendrums are a common garden plant in warmer regions of Australia and apart from some types sold at nurseries it is almost impossible to name very many of them. The common red form which also grows in cooler parts is *Epidendrum* Obrienianum, one of the first hybrids, a cross-pollination by Seden, one of Veitch's growers, from *Epidendrum evectum* and *Epidendrum radicans*. It is a strong grower, floriferous and almost continuous in warm climates as well as cold.

The commoner orange-colored hybrid is *Epidendrum* Boundii in most instances, the parents being *Epidendrum burtoni* and *Epidendrum radicans* and raised in 1903. It is slightly slower than *Epidendrum* Obrienianum in cooler climates but makes a nice show when grown into a large clump.

The advantage of both these hybrids is the way they throw growths from the bottom of the main stem as well as from upper sections.

In addition to these two commoner forms there is a great number of hybrids raised from various parents. These, although having larger flowers, are in many instances not as fast growing or as floriferous as the commoner forms.

A number of hybrids with various genera have been raised from the reed-stemmed epidendrums, the most notable of which seems to be *Epicattleya* Nebo, illustrated in the color section.

Identification of the group is most difficult, particularly in classifying them as species or hybrids. *Epidendrum radicans* is considered as synonymous with *Epidendrum ibaguense* by some authorities, but not by others, who maintain that they can identify them by the labellum shape and pattern but are not able to say how many generations back the patterns developed.

Epidendrum radicans was discovered in southern Mexico by Pavon about 1830 and it was so named by Lindley, but this find was predated by Humboldt, Bonpland and Kunth many years previously and they named it *Epidendrum ibaguense*. It was first flowered in Britain by Mrs Lawrence on plants found by G. Ure Skinner in Central America. Mrs Lawrence was one of several women who in that period were most successfully cultivating orchids.

These epidendrums are best cultivated in pots and the size of pot is immaterial so long as it is large. The root system is part from the base of the stems or growths, part from the upper areas of the stems, with no indication of where they will come from. The plants could be classified as monopodials because they are single growths which send out plantlets from the main stem. But the flowering habit is different from monopodials like vandas because it is terminal in all instances and once that head of flower is finished a small plantlet develops from its stem or another head of flower may develop instead.

Left to their own devices they will remain erect if they can find an anchorage, but if there is no anchorage and they are not tied erect they will straggle about into a tangled mass. In warmer climates they seem to flower from much shorter stems than in cooler climates, resulting in a far quicker propagation of young offshoots. In all instances they should be grown in open, sunny conditions, which, although fading the flowers rather quickly, will produce continuous flowering. In southern Australia they should be planted against a north-facing wall or in pots facing the east or north if grown as balcony plants as in the illustration.

The mix used for potting reed-stemmed epidendrums should be rich in organic material and the plants given supplements such as pieces of old cow manure or sheep manure or old fowl manure to boost them. They are greedy for humus and provided the material is well drained it is almost impossible to overfeed them. Do not stand the pots in saucers which may hold water, as the habit of the plants is to grow rather dry between copious waterings.

Interest should be shown in the roots where the plants are pot-grown and they should be trained down into the potting material as far as possible. But as their nature is to be epiphytic as well as ground plants, part of the root system will always be aerial. The growths should be staked firmly, and the wiry stem will support a heavy head of flowers without breaking.

Indications that the plants are ill suited are black spotting of the leaves, wet brown patches on the leaves, loss of lower leaf from the main stem and non-development of flower stems from the apex of the growths. If a more suitable spot is not possible it is best not to keep trying to grow them, particularly if they are hybrids. The only one which may do moderately well is the old red *Epidendrum* Obrienianum, which is fairly hardy.

There are many other so-called terete-stem epidendrums, notable among them *Epidendrum pseudepidendrum*, a west Mexican orchid which grows about a metre high. Found by Warscewicz at about 1000 metres in the Chiriqui mountains, it is notable for its brilliant contrasting colors. Reichenbach, the noted German botanist, had this to say of it:

'For 20 years nothing was known of this plant beyond the single very small specimen in my herbarium ... The colored sketch proved to be quite extraordinary, since it presented a nearly frog-green flower with a lip as scarlet as an English soldier's jacket when it is quite new. I had to reproduce it as given by the excellent and gallant collector, who was, however, not very shy in the use of his colors, ever taking the brightest tones ... In June, 1871, I had the good fortune to see a few strong living plants flowering at the Royal Exotic Nursery of Messrs Veitch. It is quite a new thing in the orchid world. I cannot remember so keen an opposition of green and scarlet in orchids, though it is to be seen in some parrots and, as I remember, having seen something similar in ladies' dresses in Vienna ...'

Epidendrum pseudepidendrum is illustrated in the color pictures and although Reichenbach may not have seen it, the colors are almost paralleled in the Malaysian *Dendrobium cruentum*.

As a footnote to the section on reed-stemmed epidendrums, how could a plant of this type of orchid growing up to 3 metres high escape the observation or collection by botanists and plant-hungry collectors alike? A 1971 find in Brazil proved that by no means had all the orchids of that country been discovered or at least catalogued. *Epidendrum warasii*, with green-yellow flowers, was described in *The Orchid Review* of that year. It grew in particularly harsh country as a lithophyte with few accompanying orchids in a region if not totally unexplored at least only hastily covered in order to get back to some greener pastures.

Pseudo-bulbed Epidendrums

Epidendrum ciliare

This orchid is a good example of the impossibility of classifying encyclias on morphological appearance rather than on floral characteristics, because the flowers conform to the epidendrum pattern with the 'column completely united with the labellum and the clinandrium a thin hood enclosing the anther, sometimes denticulate or fringed, rarely several-lobed' and other important characteristics.

However, the laelia-like appearance of *Epidendrum ciliare* may be related to its cultivation. A native of the West Indies and Central America, it was first brought to Britain by a collector named Elcock about 1790 and was grown in the Royal Gardens, Kew, about the same period. It was thus one of the very early exotic orchids introduced into British cultivation. Loddiges had a nursery stock of this orchid also very early in the following century and listed it on their sales sheet.

A grower named Syme at the Botanic Gardens in Jamaica frequently collected plants of *Epidendrum ciliare* and always reported that he found the best plants growing on limestone rock outcrops and in the crevices of the rock. These plants always had up to four leaves instead of the usual two, but they did not produce any more than the usual number of flowers on the species.

Epidendrum ciliare may be grown in exactly the same way as cattleyas and laelias and in the same potting materials. The dormant period of the plants should be respected, as they are dissimilar to the hybrids in the cattleya complex, which may be in growth or flowering phases at all times during the year.

Like most orchids, these epidendrums with pseudo-bulbs naturally select themselves for cultural treatment by their appearance, their root systems and the nature of their habitat if that can be traced.

Encyclias

Encyclia cordigera

Most of the encyclias were classified as epidendrums at some time in their history, but they are now generally recognised by their correct title. They are distinct from the epidendrums, although most flower from the apex of the growths in similar fashion to their relatives. As previously noted, cattleyas were originally known as epidendrums, a term freely allotted to many epiphytes.

Orchid names are peculiar in that so many have been changed in the cultivation history of the various genera. Sometimes it was owing to confusion stemming from the discovery of the same genus by more than one collector and the forwarding of plants, alive or dried, to different herbariums or botanists. One of the South American stelis has twenty-one synonyms, probably a record number for any orchid.

Encyclia cordigera was originally found by Humboldt, Bonpland and Kunth during their travels in Central and South America about 1810 onward. They named it *Cymbidium cordigerum*. In the intervening period to 1964, when Dressler reverted it to its original name, it bore the names *Epidendrum atropurpureum, Epidendrum macrochilum, Epidendrum longipetalum, Encyclia doeringii* and *Encyclia atropurpurea*. The native name for it in Mexico is 'Dragon's Mouth.'

In appearance *Encyclia cordigera* is similar to the laelias and some of the bifoliate cattleyas, but the flower is very different from those orchids. Its habitat is dry scrubby Mexican oak forest and it flowers in spring to early summer in cultivation. The flowers have a light fragrance in sunlight.

It was first described by Karl Wildenow from dried material sent to Germany from Venezuela by Humboldt about 1805. Baron Friedrich von Humboldt lived from 1769 to 1859 and travelled and explored extensively in Central and South America. He is better known for his books on his travels and geology than for his contributions to orchid lore, but nevertheless, in conjunction with the other two, Bonpland and Kunth, added considerably to botanical knowledge.

Encyclia cordigera was first flowered in England about 1836, when Skinner sent the first bulk lots from Guatemala, including the beautiful variety rosea. Hooker described it and named it *Epidendrum macrochilum*.

Quite a number of English orchid growers made trips to the same region during the years 1835 onward. It is easy to imagine their anticipation of collecting their own plants, but for most of them it was a once only excursion, the experience of the heat, poor food, illness, indescribable 'hotels' and the extremes of exertion proving too much for them. However, one enthusiast had this to say:

'One can hardly describe the emotions that possess one when collecting orchids or other plants in a state of nature, compared with their acquisition in the ordinary way; snakes, scorpions, ants and other venomous things are as nothing when on this delightful quest.'

Having experienced the same emotions and similar pests such as ants, ticks and leeches on Australian quests, I can concur — and would willingly face up to them again and again.

Encyclia cordigera is a warm-growing species, and should be treated in the same way as cattleyas or laelias needing a minimum of some 55 degrees over the colder periods to grow and flower well. Some care should be taken when the plants are dormant in the period between completion and commencement of growth. Even in the flowering stage little root activity will be noted and such encyclias should be grown rather dry until fresh root activity is again noticed.

Encyclias citrina and *mariae*

Two of the beautiful encyclias of Mexico are among the difficult subjects to keep going in artificial cultivation. *Encyclia mariae* and *Encyclia citrina* have very different histories, with *Encyclia mariae* remaining undiscovered right through the 'orchidomania' period and being described and brought to the notice of growers only in the 1930 decade. It did so because it grew on the verge of the American area in northern Mexico, almost on the border with Texas. Before that time the whole area was regarded as non-prospective and *Encyclia mariae* grows usually in rather dry scrubby oak forest. Despite the fragile look of the flower, the plant is bordering on the xerophytic like some of the Australian orchids. But it is not an easy orchid to cultivate because of its environmental patterns. It occurs at about 1000 to 1500 metres and is thus to be looked on as a cool-growing species.

Encyclia citrina's history began much earlier, as it was mentioned by a Jesuit priest named Hernandez very early in the seventeenth century. According to Hernandez, to whom we are indebted for a brief and inadequate description and history of Mexican plants and animals, the native name was 'corticoatzontecoxochitl'. Fortunately the name did not carry through to its cultivated history, but botanists have been dissatisfied with its original name of *Cattleya citrina* and it has become the companion of *Encyclia mariae* in a sub-section of the genus.

It was first brought to England about 1824 by the Horticultural Society, which had its own collectors operating in Central and South America. The society had only a single plant and they had just as much difficulty in keeping it alive as most modern growers. The Duke of Bedford's collectors sent him plants about 1838 and these were followed by very large consignments of the species in later years.

Messrs Low and Co. exhibited 100 plants in full flower at a show of the Royal Horticultural Society in 1867, carrying some 1000 flowers and looking, as *The Gardeners' Chronicle* reported at the time, like a sea of daffodils. The simile would be correct, too, because the two have a lot in common on the score of color. These 100 plants were the selection from some 1000-odd plants at the nursery and for plants to carry an average of ten flowers in a show they must have been quite large clumps.

The habitat of *Encyclia citrina* is also harsh, growing as they do at 2000 to 2500 metres on scrubby oak forest. There is little information about the host trees, but they probably had a rough permanent bark something after the fashion of casuarinas.

It was early noted that the plants were pendant and could not be grown in pots like *Encyclia mariae*. Originating at such an elevation, it was thought that the plants would grow and acclimatise well in cool conditions, but they proved difficult to maintain and probably the 1000 plants in Low's nursery, if they were sold out quickly enough, lasted a very short time indeed. The foliage, a strange silvery-green color, is the first to show signs of trouble; it discolors and drops and then the pseudo-bulbs become 'squashy' and the end is in sight. The pseudo-bulbs do not seem to have the fibrous core of most epiphytic orchids.

As one of the triers, I imagined that I had this species going along quite well as a garden plant for two years and then the familiar end-life pattern came in. It is possible that if the right climatic conditions can be chanced on — and it would have to be a chance — a successful cultivator would be able to grow and flower this most beautiful of all orchids. It has been done for a time in southern Australia by at least one dedicated grower, but as a prospect for the usual treatment for encyclias it is a poor one.

Several hybrids from *Encyclia citrina* were produced and named as cattleyas and laeliocattleyas in the period it was known as a cattleya, and it was only in 1961 that it was placed in the encyclias, although Reichenbach had it as an epidendrum.

Would-be growers of *Encyclia citrina* should mount the plant on a slab of tree-fern, cork, or section of a rough-barked medium-size branch from a casuarina or oak tree with the leaves pointing downward. During the non-growing period and until new growths and roots are visible the plant should be kept almost completely dry. If flowering, water sparingly until the flowers are almost fully developed and then cease watering altogether.

Glass-house-grown plants seem to tempt growers to water them, but with this orchid it should be resisted. A winter minimum of about 10 degrees is advisable and in the summer the plant should not be watered over the foliage but soaked at the roots. The pseudo-bulbs are permanently enclosed by soft grey tissue-paper-like bracts and should not be stripped. If pest eradicator sprays are used they should include an anti-fungus component.

Encyclia mariae will grow under slightly warmer conditions than *Encyclia citrina* and apart from the potting should be treated in exactly the same manner. The potting material should be based on cattleya mix, including a small amount of leaf such as dried oak leaf. However, the plant may also be mounted on a section of cork or tree-fern or branch in the same manner as *Encyclia citrina*, with a pad of fibre and moss, just as would be done with that orchid. The leaves of *Encyclia mariae* would be uppermost instead of inverted.

Both these orchids may be fed with weak solutions of nutrients when in growth, the weaker the better, pouring the liquid on to the mount instead of the plant, so inducing the roots to seek it out. Neither orchid is prolific rooted and the more they can be encouraged the better.

Fresh air is an essential component and the plants should not be grown in conditions which are too humid. In their habitat both are found in arid conditions, although at night there is considerable moisture in the air, with wind quickly drying the plants in the morning.

Encyclia cochleata

This orchid has a wide distribution, as it grows from Florida, in the United States, right through Central America, in many different types of country and at sea level to considerable elevations. Naturally, the flowering period of cultivated plants will be dictated by origin.

Encyclia cochleata was introduced very early in orchid-growing history, as a collector named Alexander Anderson brought it to England from the West Indies about 1786. A gardener growing orchids for a fancier named Woodward about this time said of *Encyclia cochleata:* [It is] '...now not uncommon, considering the difficulty attending the culture of plants naturally parasitical.' This was a common view of the period regarding the place occupied by epiphytes, including orchids. *Encyclia cochleata* was also known to Linnaeus, a master of botany in the eighteenth century and one of the founders of orchid taxonomy.

Encyclia cochleata may well have been the first exotic epiphyte to flower in England, as its appearance in 'stoves,' as glass-houses were then known, was in 1787. It was finally named by Lindley with reference to the beautifully colored shell-liked labellum. The Mexican varieties are reputedly easiest to flower, but it is probably a matter of the conditions suiting the orchid.

The pseudo-bulbs of this species are fairly constant, despite its extended habitat, with the thickened base tapering to a slender apex, somewhat flattened, surmounted by one or two rather soft-textured lance-shaped leaves, with a sheath producing a spike from inside these leaves. The spikes grow tall, in some instances up to 60 centimetres, with beautifully inverted flowers as illustrated.

Grown in similar conditions to cattleyas and in the same sort of mix, the dormant period should be respected and less water applied than when in active growth, which occurs in the early to late summer, with the flower spike following sometimes on the still immature pseudo-bulbs.

Fertilisers should be moderately applied, as with most epiphytes. If solid fertilisers like blood and bone are used, liquid nutrients should be discontinued. Blood and bone is frequently mentioned as a fertiliser for epiphytes in this book and, allied to some leaf content such as oak in the potting mix, is a natural fertiliser combining all the necessary elements and trace elements.

171

There is a fairly large group of encyclias similar to cochleata, all of them having the inverted labellum of this orchid. They include *Encyclia fragrans, Encyclia chacaoensis, Encyclia baculus* and *Encyclia abbreviata.* Most of them are creamy colored, but vary through to golden and most also have a very strong perfume on a warm sunny day. The culture of the group is similar to that of *Encyclia cochleata*, but the temperature ranges vary considerably according to the area of origin and the elevation at which they grow. There is little possibility that the name will tell very much and most should be regarded as warm-growing subjects.

Common to the genus as a whole is the dormant or non-active phase through which the plants go after flowering. If the plants do not flower on maturing or nearly maturing growths, they should be rested just the same until they show signs of activity. Their habitats are such that shrivelling to a marked degree does not seem to impair a fresh start in the growing season, but growing areas should be conditioned so that severe shrivelling is not possible in the humidity common to a good atmosphere.

Encyclia vitellina

Encyclia vitellina is a native of Central America and one of the few species with red flowers. It is an orchid which seems to be relatively hard to keep going, a common thing with many species because of the demanding sets of conditions they should be given. Its habitat is from 1500 to 2500 metres growing epiphytically on various host trees, nominated as pine-oak or oak forest, cloud forest, a situation which could be quite cold, and on scrub forest on lava fields.

The Mexican oaks are puzzling because little is known about them. The pine-oak could resemble the Australian casuarinas, but botanical dictionaries give little information. Early dictionaries listed sixteen Mexican oaks, later ones reduced the number to two and modern publications are uninformative. But just as casuarinas are referred to as oaks in Australia, there is little descriptive value in the epithet as applied to the Mexican trees. It would be a hard-barked tree and possibly *Encyclia vitellinum* would be better grown on such a host as cork, tree-fern or a casuarina branch than in a pot.

As a cool-growing orchid it was first collected by Dr Coulter in 1830 in Mexico at about 2000 metres. The collector Hartweg introduced the plants to Britain about 1839 and subsequently better types were collected and exported to that country. Roezl was one of the most voracious of the collectors and he described the conditions under which the plants thrived. During the summer months it rained for the whole period, April to September, tapered off for the next few months and was completely dry from February to the end of April. The maximum temperature during the year was 20 degrees, the minimum 12 degrees by day, but at night there were occasional frosts. That, however, applied to only the habitat from which Roezl collected his large consignment of plants.

Encyclia vitellina, however, should be a cool-growing orchid, with a great amount of respect shown the plant in its various phases, particularly when apparently dormant. The flowering period is most variable in cultivation, again possibly owing to the habitats from which the plants may originate.

The months quoted above by Roezl are not applicable to southern hemisphere seasons, as will be obvious and should be reversed to suit Australia. But as a part cultural guide they may be of some use in solving the problem of unsuccessful cultivation.

Brassavola

Named by Robert Brown to honor Antonia Brassavola, of Venice, a botanist who was also accomplished in other academic fields. In the 1970-80 period a notable plant, *Brassavola digbyana*, was transferred to the genus rhyncolaelia and is so listed in the cattleya section, despite references in the hybrid list.

Brassavolas are not the sort of orchids found in collections generally, but in warm climates they are suited for outdoor cultivation, even as specimens attached to suitable trees. Common orchids in a wide area from Mexico to Brazil and some of the Caribbean islands, they indicate by their terete channelled foliage a light and heat tolerance beyond their related genera. The leaves of some of the genus are more deeply channelled than others.

Most brassavolas are pendulous, but some grow in tangled masses on rock faces, at times in bright, exposed places. None are suitable for growing in temperatures which in winter go below 13 degrees Celsius (55 degrees Fahrenheit).

The two anomalous species *Brassavola digbyana* and *Brassavola glauca* were removed from the genus in the past and catalogued as rhyncolaelias and are dealt with as attachments to the cattleya section. Florally and morphologically they are more similar to those orchids.

Brassavolas were so far down the scale in the late nineteenth century that Veitch's *Manual of Orchidaceous Plants* did not list them in the 1887-94 edition, even the magnificent *Brassavola digbyana*, which was catalogued as a laelia with *Laelia glauca*.

The history of the genus as a whole shows neglect by collectors, nurserymen and growers alike, which could be accounted for by the overshadowing influence of the more elaborate and colorful species popular through the period of expansion.

One of the commonest species grown has always been *Brassavola nodosa*. In its period known to botanists and taxonomists it has borne nine different names. Linnaeus first knew it as *Epidendrum nodosum* in the eighteenth century, but Lindley had the last say with the name it now bears. Although he had no first-hand knowledge of it at the time, in 1839 he described a plant which had been collected in Nicaragua. He was confused by one or two other specimens which were collected and grown in Europe, but they were subsequently noted as varieties of the species, which ranges from southern Mexico to Peru and is also known to have occurred in Jamaica in the zenith years of the collectors.

Brassavola nodosa was once particularly plentiful in Panama, where it was known by the natives as 'Lady of the Night' from its night-time perfume, which almost completely disappears before daylight returns. The flowers appear on old as well as new growths. On pollination and ripening of the pod the structure of the seed capsule is remarkable, as it may be 20 or more centimetres long and with a pronounced 'beak'. This peculiarity is also apparent in some of the inter-generic hybrids from the brassavolas and noted in *Rhyneolaelia digbyana*.

J. C. Harvey, a Mexican resident mentioned elsewhere in these books, cultivated several forms of *Brassavola nodosa* about the turn of the nineteenth century, some of which were much smaller plants than the type form and he also advocated growing this orchid on live trees wherever possible. Harvey found that the plants reacted much better to this method than other forms of culture. His plants of *Brassavola nodosa* were mostly Mexican, but he also grew a large collection of orchids from all parts of the world.

Hybridisers in the early years of inter-generic cross-pollinations were surprised at the ease with which *Brassavola nodosa* and other members of the genus blended into the cattleyas and similar orchids. The results, however, disappointed them. Perhaps they were expecting the same reaction as when *Brassavola digbyana* was introduced.

Brassavola cucullata was introduced to England by Rear-Admiral William Bligh about 1793 and it was the original species on which the genus was founded in the herbariums. It was named by Robert Brown in 1813, when it was transferred from the epidendrums under which it was known in Bligh's time.

Like many orchids, it lived a double life for some years, being identified under other names in the European collections. Wagener, who collected extensively in Colombia, sent specimens to Zurich among other places, where it was known as *Brassavola odoratissima*.

Brassavola perrinii was among the orchids sent to Mrs Harrison of Liverpool, from her relatives in Rio de Janeiro. Her consideration of naming it after her gardener-orchid-grower was no doubt in appreciation of his service to her in acclimatising and flowering most of the orchids she received from Brazil in the 1840 period. A very similar orchid is *Brassavola tuberculata*, which is native to widely separated areas of Brazil and neighboring states to the west. Several intermediate types have prompted the supposition that there are natural hybrids in the genus where more than one species inhabits areas.

One of the outstanding members is *Brassavola martiana*, also from Brazil and the north-eastern states on its borders. Some of the species have short leaves, others somewhat longer, and the stems, which at times could be confused with the rhizomes, also vary considerably in length.

Brassavolas may be grown in any of the ways epiphytic orchids are usually cultivated, but those which indicate a drooping or pendulous habit should be bound to slabs of tree-fern, cork or other bark or put into slat baskets or slotted pots which are suitable for hanging on the tilt, so that the plants may follow their natural inclination. Trying to make these types grow erect frequently affects growth and flowering.

It is not possible to advise on annual cycles because these may vary according to the climates in which they are grown. However, in the southern hemisphere brassavolas should be encouraged to grow in the warmer months of the year and allowed to remain dormant in their own time. They may flower from either new or old growths.

Where the plants are grown in slat baskets a few chunks of tree-fern or staghorn fibre should be included in the mix to act as water reservoirs in otherwise sterile pine bark and charcoal mixes, which are rather quick drying in open suspended containers. In atmospheres which tend to dry out quickly owing to air flow or fast ventilation a top layer of sphagnum moss in the growing season will do a lot for the roots and keep the plants moving, but moss layers should be removed or thinned out for the colder months or when brassavolas are dormant.

In the growing season water should be plentifully applied, not so much frequently as in thoroughly soaking the potting material each time the container is watered. Hanging plants should preferably be soaked for up to ten minutes in a container of water to which nutrients are added. Overdoing the nutrients will quickly be reflected in poor root systems and soured potting mixes. Tapering off watering as the growths appear to mature should be the rule and rather sparing applications given until root activity is again apparent.

Propagation should be by severance of sections of the rhizome, but it should not be by separation into sections with fewer than three growths or leaves. While it may be possible to get a bud from a leafless section of rhizome, it is better to sever sections of the plant and leave the whole plant alone until time to repot. But this time, which may be one or even two growing seasons off, there should be at least two good plants to put into separate containers. The genus resents disturbance by too frequent potting and as the usual potting mixes are long lasting there is little chance of root loss because the contents of the container decay too much.

Odontoglossums

The genus named by Humboldt, Bonpland and Kunth in 1815. The name is the compound of two Greek words — *odous, odonto,* a tooth; *glossa,* a tongue — referring to the tooth-like projections on the callus of the labellum of the first species brought to the attention of botanists. The genus belongs to the oncidieae, has several members and a number of affiliated genera.

'Never shall I forget my delight, on opening the first box of orchids he sent me, all carefully packed and in the best possible condition. Though gathered at random, every plant was new. Masses of *Epidendrum skinneri* (the first to flower, and thence named after him), divers other epidendra, *Oncidium cavendishianum, Oncidium leucochilum* and *Odontoglossum bictoniense,* the first Odontoglot that ever reached England alive.'

The words are those of James Bateman, one of great orchid growers of all time, author of *Orchidaceae of Mexico and Guatemala.* He was a correspondent of George Ure Skinner, who owned a trading business in Guatemala and contributed as an entomologist and orchidist to the wealth and knowledge of the herbariums and museums of England and Europe about the years 1830 onward. Although the first odontoglossum to reach England alive came from Skinner and was not a Colombian orchid, it was the small messenger of such quantities of followers in the genus as to be almost unbelievable even though well authenticated. The South American rather than the Central American group of the genus took collectors by surprise in the vast numbers of plants which grew and flowered there.

The impact of the light green leafed plants on orchid growing was just as tremendous as the introduction of the cattleyas some years earlier and at times the plants realised unbelievable prices. In 1907 the Linden nursery supplied Monsieur Leeman, a European grower, with five plants of *Odontoglossum cirspum* for about 1200 pounds on the basis of colored drawings supplied by the vendors. At 1980 prices, that would be the equivalent of a tremendous sum of money. When flowered they were not as represented and the vendor was taken to court. The verdict was given in favor of the purchaser and the money refunded, together with legal fees and costs after a lengthy trial. It was one of the few recorded instances where orchids featured in legal proceedings.

This period probably represented the zenith of popularity of the genus as cultivated orchids.

Odontoglossum crispum is the most important member of a fairly large group of orchids widespread in Colombia, once known as New Granada. Perhaps it would be better to qualify that sentence with the amendment that it was once a fairly large group when the forested lands were untouched in a wide area of the country about Bogota and other centres.

Climate in the main areas of occurrence of the various species is almost temperate, with daytime temperatures in the vicinity of about 20 degrees and night-time about 10 degrees at altitudes of about 2000 metres, where the first aggregations of odontoglossums were found. The best varieties occurred at about 2400 metres, with 18 degrees in the daytime and 8 degrees at night. The genus occurred at altitudes up to about 3000 metres, where the temperature averaged about 12 degrees in the daytime and as low as freezing at night.

Odontoglossum crispum, or *alexandrae*, as it was then known, grew intermixed with other species. Its color varied from pure white through pink suffusions and red-brown and red-purple blotching into pale to deeper yellow tones.

It was polymorphic, with the flowers varying from open starry shapes to closed form varieties equal to award status applied to hybrids in the 1970-80 era. Fanciers had the delights of flowering species which were pure white or blotched in these good shaped varieties and they were commonly referred to in the late nineteenth century as 'Pacho' type, the name derived from one particular area where the best varieties were supposed to grow. The consensus of opinion in later years was that the term was illusory and that good varieties came from several areas, but usually at the middle altitudes about 2400 metres.

Also found growing mixed with *Odontoglossum crispum* were the natural hybrids *Odonto wilckieanum* (*Odonto crispum* × *Odonto luteo-purpureum*), *Odonto adrianae* (*Odonto crispum* × *Odonto hunnewellianum*), together with *Odonto lindleyanum*, *Odonto odoratum* (syn. *Odonto gloriosum*), *Odonto wallisii* and *Odonto nobile* (syn. *Odonto pescatorei*). The colors of all these species varied between white and shades of pink and rose suffusions to pale and deeper yellow, many with red-brown and red-purple bars and blotches.

Odontoglossum crispum was another species named by Lindley in the early days of its cultivation and it is only by going back to this period that any real idea of the localities and types found in Colombia may be appreciated. There were several zones where the genus flourished, each with its own particular group of species. Another good information source is the booklet printed for the Seventh World Orchid Conference held at Medellin, Colombia, in which Alberto Echavarria, Oscar Robledo and Juan Felipe Posada give an all too short resume of the species and relevant zones.

Odontoglossum crispum far outstripped any of the other species as the source of hybrids. Other species such as *Odonto triumphans*, a golden, red-brown barred type, and *Odonto harryanum* also contributed their share. *Odontoglossum harryanum* was somewhat a stranger compared with the crispum types, but it added a wealth of color and some most unusual flowers.

As a genus they spill over into the countries surrounding Colombia, but that country was at one time the centre or focus of interest because of the wonderful richness of their occurrence. Some of the less spectacular members of the genus occurred well to the north of the isthmus of Panama and surfaced in Mexico and Guatemala. But this section of the book concentrates on the Colombian section, with some of the others dealt with separately.

In retrospect the amount of natural hybridism is almost unknown, as so much of the species material has been destroyed or lost, together with the destruction of the natural environment, where great tracts of forest were felled to convert the country to cropping of sugar, coffee, maize and other products in the early years of colonisation.

The intensity of artificial cultivation of the genus appears to have reached its peak in the years 1890 to 1914, when collections in various English establishments appear to have been anything from fifty or so plants up into figures of the order of thousands. Such collections are freely described in early editions of the *The Orchid Review*.

Some idea of the number of plants of *Odontoglossum crispum* in cultivation about 1880-90 can be gained from Lewis Castle's book, in which he quotes the collection of R. Warner:

'... Writing in 1841, Mr Jas. Bateman said that the collections of orchids were innumerable, and if that was the case then, what would be said now? The plants were then numbered by hundreds, now amateurs possess their thousands, and one, Mr R. Warner, has even had as many as 12,000 plants of one species, *Odontoglossum alexandrae* (*crispum*). In the leading collections a dozen houses or more are devoted to them and coming to the trade stores the numbers are overwhelming. When we talk about plants by the 100,000 we seem to be dealing with bedding pelargoniums or lobelias and not orchids. Yet one firm claims to possess that number of odontoglossums of the choicest species, hybrids and varieties . . .'

Mr W. Swan, of Boystock, England, in the *Gardeners' Chronicle* in 1898 noted that on several occasions some 6000, 8000, 15 000 and other large consignments of *Odontoglossum crispum*, mostly from the Bogota region of Colombia, were sold at the auction rooms of Protheroe and Morris in London, one of several firms then taking part in the distribution of exotic plants, mostly orchids. Too few of their quota survived the next ten to fifteen years.

It surely would not be overestimating the number of plants of odontoglossums only collected and shipped during this period at a figure between perhaps one and two million. Any less a figure would seem to be toying with the proposition when all the evidence is weighed and sifted and an educated guess attempted. In retrospect again, a tragic incident in man's progress.

Florent Claes, a Dutch collector, expressed fears about this destruction and over-collection of *Odontoglossum crispum* from the Pacho area about 1890, adding that he could already at that time see the end of the species. Only about ten per cent of the total exports of Pacho *crispums* from Colombia had the qualities sought. The ultimate fate of the rest must have been an unpalatable thought even for Claes as a collector.

Forgetting for a moment the depredations of the collectors, the clearance of thousands of square kilometres of the country for development had just as much effect in decimating the orchid population. Strangely enough, too, the indigenes thought the reason for collecting the odontoglossums was to distil medicines which were later sold at exorbitant prices — a rather peculiar fixation that was hard to dispel.

One of the first areas from which collections of the species were taken belonged to an Englishman named Bunch and these early consignments occurred somewhere about 1860.

Two botanists — and perhaps incidental collectors — named Funck and Schlim were among the first on the scene and both were also active in pursuit of new genera in other parts of the Americas.

Perhaps it is easy to imagine what the odontoglossums looked like in their flowering season, because in those days they grew so prolifically right through the forest verges and on the rocky outcrops of the lower mountain areas where the conditions suited. Funck and Schlim took only the best varieties from an extraordinary profusion.

Apparently several type species became established in the various herbariums throughout the western world, some with flowers which could well qualify for awards under the most stringent procedures of the late 1970-80 era. The type named *Odontoglossum alexandrae*, later known as *Odontoglossum crispum*, is well recorded in *The Orchid Album* and was polymorphic to a marked degree. Some of the plants collected and later sold at the auction rooms of Protheroe and Morris comprised up to twenty pseudo-bulbs. In later times the best pure white varieties of *Odontoglossum crispum* came to be known as the variety premier and many fine clones are still cultivated. One is illustrated, the plant from my collection about 1960.

The odontoglossum trade became such a competitive and lucrative business that the various collectors became quite secretive and at times completely wrong information has been filed and quoted because of misdirections to put competitors off the trail. This led to much incorrect information about the habitats of the various species and several different versions are likely to be found.

De Barri Crawshay, one of the leading odontoglossum growers of the beginning of the twentieth century, quotes Louis Forget, a French collector, as an authority on the source of the Pacho-type *Odontoglossum crispums*. Monsieur Forget knew of areas where *Odontoglossum crispum* grew freely with other species such as *Odonto hunnewellianum* and from here came some of the most beautiful of the blotched white forms. He stated that this area was to the north of Bogota. Several other species grew at higher and lower levels, resulting in a quite variable and beautiful population.

Many collectors as such never really knew the source of their consignments, because they established themselves in a small native town or village and recruited Indian collectors, who frequently travelled several hundred kilometres in their search for parcels of plants, which they brought into the central depot. The total consignment at times was shipped by unscrupulous collectors as the best type *Odontoglossum crispum* when in reality they were a mixture of many varieties and frequently many species and natural hybrids.

Experience soon taught both the collectors and the final purchasers the difference in appearance between the good and the bad and in this way the poorer consignments frequently were sold out at bargain prices and fell into poor cultivation and final loss.

In the early years of the twentieth century many beautiful garden or horticultural varieties of the species were produced in colors from white through pale pink to rose-purple and yellow and gold. Mostly the yellow forms blotched with red-brown are credited to *Odontoglossum wilckieanum*, but a large amount of the early hybridising material was never satisfactorily tagged for origin.

The seed-raising method itself tended to be careless and by scientific standards primitive. The habit of dipping the seed-carrying pots instead of watering them led to a lot of flotation of seed from pot to pot. But considering all the other things which could be condemned through the *Sanders' List of Orchid Hybrids* it is perhaps best that we do not know all the story.

Of the natural hybrids, *Odontoglossum wilckieanum*, with its sometimes burgundy to violet blotched flowers, was the most beautiful. It came mostly from one small area. Its status as a natural hybrid was recognised from later cross-pollinations, of which a great number was made in the 1890-1914 period.

The first inter-generic hybrid was produced by Monsieur Vuylsteke, a Belgian orchid grower, who cross-pollinated *Odonto pescatorei* with *Cochlioda noezliana* and produced a flowering plant of this red hybrid at a show in London in May 1904. It caused a sensation. A picture of a clone of this hybrid from my collection about 1956 appears in the illustrations.

Among other hybridists, Charlesworths, of England, had parallel inter-generic cross-pollinations on the way, but they were beaten to the first flowers by Vuylsteke by a year or two. Monsieur Vuylsteke was a prominent continental grower who lived at Ghent, Belgium, and was also noted for his cattleya collection.

As a genus odontoglossums and their various hybrids have persisted in popularity since their first introduction. While they may not be as spectacular or as easily grown as cymbidiums, it is perhaps regrettable that they were not more popular and that so much misinformation has been produced about them. As it is, they fall into too low a place in the comparative list of cultivated orchids than they merit. As far as Australia is concerned, many climatic opportunities offer great scope and certainly less problems than, say, phalaenopsis culture.

Becoming rarer in their native country as each year goes by, it is doubtful if very many propagations of the original clones imported into England and Europe now remain in cultivation, particularly of *Odontoglossum crispum*. Most of the best clones used in hybridising are garden or horticultural varieties resulting from successive pollinations designed to produce the rounded, ruffled flower associated with the name *crispum*. Perhaps we are looking at a genus which has become a sign of the times rather than the natural beauty once so eagerly sought.

Cochlioda noezliana was first flowered in Europe by Messrs Linden, of Brussels, Belgium, in 1890 as *Odontoglossum noezliana*. It was discovered by the collector Noetzli in 1888 and sent to them. It was later separated out into a genus of some two or three members by Heinrich Gustav Reichenbach, the German botanist.

Cochlioda has one very significant floral difference from odontoglossums in the construction of the column, otherwise the two flowers are similar. In original cross-pollinations the hybridisers were baffled by the construction of the column and could not get pollen to take on the flowers as it was said by some that they had no stigma. Instead of a normal stigmatic surface like the odontoglossums, it was found that *Cochlioda noezliana* had a stigma on each side of the column near the apex of the tube formed by the union of the labellum with the sides of the column.

The correct name of the orchid is *Cochlioda noetzliana*, but the corruption of the name occurred so long ago to *noezliana* that it is almost impossible to correct it. A native of Peru, it is found in a somewhat warmer climate than the odontoglossums and some growers find it difficult to flower.

Like the cattleyas of Central and South America, the odontoglossums proved to have affiliations with other genera and the hybrids were elaborated into several other combinations. Up to the year 1945 over 3000 hybrids had been registered, the larger proportion of which were listed in the years 1900-30.

French hybridists created the Odontonia with *Miltonia warscewiczii* cross-pollinated with *Odontoglossum* Clytie in 1905; in 1910 the oncidioda emerged from Charlesworth's hybrid *Cochlioda noezliana* × *Oncidium incurvum*; in 1911 the odontocidium was also created by Charlesworths; and in 1916 the combination of *Odontioda* Illustrissimum × *Oncidioda* Charlesworthii had the coined name *wilsonara* allotted to it.

Since then various other combinations had been tried, some of which produced new hybrids, others failing from the barrier which seems to exist against second generation innovations. Most of the hybridism occurring in the 1970 period onward seems to have been reversions to the orthodox line developed between the odontoglossums and cochliodas.

Little innovation has taken place in a minor return of popularity for the genus in the 1970-80 period and reference to the flowers available in the popular period between 1910 and 1930 indicates that neither size, color nor shape has changed in the later period referred to. Further inter-generic work has been done, but the foundation species and hybrids developed in the early part of the century still form the building blocks of 1980. It is to the credit of the English and German nurseries that they still retained pre-eminent odontoglossum and mixed genera material in the face of poor demand for the orchids over a long period of the twentieth century.

Growers such as the Englishman De Barri Crawshay, who specialised in the genus, worked out very efficient cultural techniques. Mostly they consisted of the two features still necessary after many generations of removal from species level — fresh air and moderate temperatures. As with most other growers of the time, he set aside a special glass-house for odontoglossums alone.

The ideal temperatures, year round, for the genus fall between 10 and 20 degrees and this should include most of the inter-generics. Winter and summer both pose problems because fresh air at all times is indispensable. Summer modifications to keep to the limits should be a judicious combination of shade, humidity and fresh air. This almost disqualifies odontoglossums for warmer climates unless some limits are established to temperature rise. In moderate climates they may be grown in open-air shelters provided the humidity and shade are closely watched. The results in flowering are directly related to the conditions under which they are grown, but it does not help to be too dogmatic about where they may be grown. Odontoglossums, like most orchids, are adaptable to a point and I grew them moderately well in a glass-house designed for cymbidiums. In one section the shade was increased, a closed bench made up with 5 centimetres of gravel covering and in this micro-environment they grew quite happily and flowered fairly well with masdevallias and other shade-loving orchids.

Herman von Dratelin, who lived in Mexico, was perhaps one of the world authorties in the culture of odontoglossums in the twentieth century. He recommended that they should always be grown cool, with the temperature never exceeding 26 degrees but the minimum allowed to fall to about 5 degrees, particularly overnight. As von Dratelin remarked, odontoglossums are among a few genera which must have wide variations between day and night temperatures to grow and flower at their best. He recommended some form of air-conditioning to effect this right through the year if the climate is unsuitable for their culture. Considering their habitat and its elevation his advice was soundly based.

While Herman von Dratelin was not the only world authority on the genus, it is obvious on reading his notes that they are not orchids which should be included in mixed collections of species or hybrids. Most failures appear to stem from such inclusions, with contributory factors such as overwatering under the impression that they are 'water plants' that need to be constantly wet instead of damp, or they are given humidity without wetness or dampness. Watering and the ability of the potting material to remain damp are essentials in their culture.

If some notice is taken of the conditions prevailing in their habitat, which apply equally to inter-generic hybrids in cultivation, it is apparent that growing naturally they suffered day to night extremes which they would scarcely tolerate in artificial cultivation. So to start off in the right way they should be given some semblance of these conditions, modified from grower to grower and climate to climate to a consistent level of daytime maximums and night-time minimums.

Probably some form of automation is necessary if absolute time limits and temperature controls are to be kept up. It need not be expensive. If grown as outdoor plants, as they will grow in temperate areas, a clock-based misting system to come into operation at night in the warmer months or in dry periods will certainly mean perhaps the difference between mediocre results and good results.

Naturally, with more air flow about the plants, drying out will be faster and it is in this critical phase that the temptation to overwater should be controlled. Moisture retaining plants such as ferns should be grown in the glass-house or about the growing area to promote humidity and act as a moisture conservation barrier.

While direct sunlight should not be totally avoided, the best condition is diffusion through shade-cloth, the percentage chosen to suit the area and the

181

aspect of the glass-house toward the light source. The amount of light influences the quality as well as the quantity of flower.

Odontoglossums will grow just as well in plastic pots as in clay pots and if a preference had to be indicated it would be toward clay pots. One of the reasons for this preference is that it enables a double-potting system to be used. In most instances the maximum sized pot for odontoglossums would be considered 10 to 13 centimetres. This is a relatively small pot for plants the size odontoglossums can reach and it will dry out fairly rapidly. If placed inside a slightly larger pot it can still breathe as clay pots do and the double layer of clay pots insulates the evaporation to the area between the two pots and a very nice condition is maintained about the roots, which are fairly fine, not dense as in some other genera and usually more vigorous on forward parts of the plant than older portions. They should be accommodated in potting materials which give the roots penetration yet hold the plant firm.

Sphagnum moss has its enthusiasts, but a little thought about using it as a constant potting material for any orchids soon leads to a change of ideas. It grows in damp conditions and this is a prerequisite for odontoglossums. But it will not grow in the depths of a pot and soon decays at that point even if the surface is covered with nice growing heads. The tighter it is packed into pots the faster it decays; and in this condition, although it may support a plant plus a flower spike, the root system must decay with the moss. One thing leading to another means that replacement of the moss could be necessary every few months. As a propagating medium it has no equal, but as a growing medium many alternatives are better.

In common with most orchids, pine or fir bark is suitable for odontoglossums if it is allowed to weather for some months before use. As odontoglossums have a sparse, fine root system the bark used should be sieved to get the coarse part out. Anything which will not go through a 3 to 5 millimetre sieve should be discarded and used for other purposes. After going through this mesh it should be put through a flywire screen to take out all the fine part and the dust. This is also discarded. The drainage additive may be gravel, charcoal or scoria and it should be put through the same sieves. If a preference had to be expressed it would be for coarse sand or gravel, but do not use fine sand.

Sometimes this two-part mix will be found too bony for odontoglossums and a little chopped sphagnum moss or rubbed peat-moss should be used. In addition dried leaf of oak, ash, aspen, birch, beach or fine maple leaves may be rubbed into the mix. All these leaves have been tried and found acceptable to the root systems, but should not be rotted leaf-mould.

The proportions for these mixes is two parts bark to one of drainage material and half a part of sphagnum or peat-moss by measure. The leaf content may be added in the same quantity as moss and need not take the place of it. The potting mixes and variations are numberless, but it is a good idea to give a mix a thorough trial for a full year before discarding it. The test is whether it will grow roots and for the roots to go toward the bottom of the pot and not inhabit only the top layers of the potting material.

If charcoal is used as the drainage portion it should be the same size as the bark used or slightly smaller.

Irrespective of the type of pot used, the potting material should be firmed in without being tightly rammed down. After this has been done a few strands of growing sphagnum moss should be pressed on to the surface. This not only prevents wash-out of the mix when watering, but the moss, if it continues to grow indicates incomparably that the mix suits the genus. It also attracts the roots, unfortunately, and occasionally will prevent them from making their way down through the mix if it is not quite as moist as it should be when the roots are most active.

The general growing conditions for odontoglossums should be as cool as possible in hot weather, accomplished by shading as well as damping down to a maximum of 25 degrees, although these orchids will stand occasional periods above that. They should be cool at night and in warm climates a damping down without necessarily watering the plants will prove beneficial. In summer and winter the potting material should not be allowed to dry out and a form of cultivation which has periods of dehydration and then wetness will not promote growth and flowering. The plants will stagnate. Winter temperatures should not be unduly low, although the genus as a whole has the reputation of cold-growing habits. This is not borne out by cultivators in artificial conditions and the plants will appreciate a constant 10 degrees or over in the winter months.

A sign of poor cultivation is the growth of dark algae on the surface of the mix or the decay of the sphagnum moss. This usually indicates faulty drainage, the potting mix packed too tight, overwetness or two much moss or leaf content in the mix. When made up the mix should be springy when compressed in the hand and should remain so. Color in the leaves usually indicates too bright light and the shading should be increased. The browning of leaf tips may be put down to too high humidity in warm conditions, lack of root growth, disease or conditions too dry both at the roots and in the atmosphere. An analysis of the growing conditions is indicated and a change made. Some combinations of genera seem more prone to this leaf die back than others, but it is a general failing with cultivation of the genus as a whole.

Plants may be purchased in all sizes from seedlings in flasks to propagations of well-known clones. A flask of seedlings needs careful handling, as odontoglossums are among the tenderest orchids to rear. A short section of the procedure is given in another part of the book. It is unwise to buy back-bulbs which have no visible growth, as they are notoriously hard to propagate, yet at times will produce a shoot from the apex of the pseudo-bulb. If separating back-bulbs on growing plants, it should be done when the plant is recommencing its growing phase and not during dormancy. They should preferably be separated away in pairs.

Better propagating techniques are best learned from the plants themselves rather than what appears in books. However, propagation should consist of separating the sections a year before the plant is to be repotted. It is possible to separate away a single bulb with a lead and the propagation seems to be just as strong as when larger pieces are separated. Once divided, the two portions should be tied firmly together and if necessary staked so that they are still firm in the pot. Propagating in this way ensures that both forward and back parts of the plant suffer no root disturbance with its consequent re-establishment problems.

Flower spikes usually show up on mature growths rather than on those maturing and seldom on older pseudo-bulbs of the previous season. They usually appear in between the larger of the leaves from the base of the pseudo-bulbs and are brittle and prone to attack by pests.

In general, the odontoglossum complex of hybrids seems to be almost pest-free. They should be grown in conditions which discourage red spider and it would be unusual to have a collection infested with scale. It is better to stop the possible entry of pests by using a light application of a pesticide once a year, preferably a composite with anti-fungicide and insecticide and with systemic quality.

Fertilisers for orchids like odontoglossums, usually regarded as epiphytes, are always a good basis for disagreement among growers. Grown in small pots as they are, odontoglossums do not need a great amount of nutrient at any time in their annual cycles.

While some growers prefer liquid nutrients, others prefer solids. Among the solid fertilisers blood and bone in small quantities is as effective as any other. In the growth stage, when new roots can be seen at the base of the new lead or even on the older roots on the surface, as much blood and bone as will cover a one cent piece is a good additive on the surface of the potting material. The temptation is always there to give the same amount a week or so later. It must be resisted, however, and the next stage only reached if the plant is flowering. In that condition, liquid nutrients based on fertilisers such as Aquasol should also be sparingly fed when the plant is watered, preferably weak enough to drench the plant in its weekly watering or however long the period between each soaking. A little Maxicrop added to the nutrient is also beneficial.

In general slow-release fertilisers should be avoided, as they continue their release long after the plant has need of them. Experience is a good guide and if plants show leaf tip dieback the fertiliser could be as much responsible as any other cause. It is only in the active stage that the plant can absorb and use nutrients. The quality and number of flowers can certainly be influenced with correct fertilising, but once the spike commences opening the plant should be watered most carefully to ensure that the roots are not killed off. It is only in this stage that the merest hint of dryness in the potting material should be allowed. The pseudo-bulbs may shrivel a little, but that is completely natural with the genus.

One notable thing about growing odontoglossums is that the plants are seldom inactive. Almost as soon as one pseudo-bulb is made up they are commencing another unless flowering. Following flowering the plant may remain inactive for about two months and then seems to go into action once again, so that there is no real series of seasonal stages through which the plants go. The flowering also may be found variable because of the mixed influences in the varieties grown.

A large inter-generic family has been bred from the odontoglossums, mostly having the fundamental morphology of these orchids even when allied to oncidiums. At times they have been given coined names ending with the letters 'ara'. These hybrid names are pronounced with the end syllables as 'arah' irrespective of the look of the word. They are as follow:

Odontioda — Odontoglossum × cochlioda.
Odontonia — Odontoglossum × miltonia.
Beallara — Odontoglossum × brassia × cochlioda × miltonia.
Vuylstekeara — Odontoglossum × cochlioda × miltonia.
Wilsonara — Odontoglossum × cochlioda × oncidium.

There are others, but they appear in sections of the book on oncidiums, miltonias and other genera. The above orchids are treated the same as odontoglossums.

The first hybrid odontoglossum raised was *Odontoglossum wilckeanum*, which confirmed the opinion of some of the botanists, collectors and growers that *Odontoglossum crispum* and *Odontoglossum luteo-purpureum* had in fact pre-empted the hybridists naturally in the Colombian highlands. Several other natural hybrids were recognised and it was to be expected considering the intense occupation of the habitats by a wonderful series of orchids.

Lemboglossum rossii and *Osmoglossum pulchellum* (Syn. *Odontoglossums rossii* and *pulchellum*)

Some of the smaller species of various genera which are not used as the basis for hybridism or cross-pollination tend to fall into niches and are forgotten. At times the niche could be described as a crevasse and they are lost for all time so far as inclusion in collections is concerned.

Neither of the two small odontoglossums dealt with here approaches this oblivion, but they are not as freely grown as their attraction merits. *Odontoglossum rossii* came into cultivation in England somewhere about 1839, thus becoming one of the earliest orchids brought from the 'New World'. It was named by Lindley.

From descriptions by early collectors and travellers, it was once almost the commonest orchid in Mexico at high altitudes, particularly in the Orizaba region, on about latitude 20, just on the equatorial side of the tropic of cancer. The altitude at which *Odontoglossum rossii* grew is the clue to its cultivation, as it occurs at anything from 2000 to 2500 metres. It was first collected by an Englishman named Ross and sent to a Birmingham grower named Barker.

Odontoglossum rossii was the subject of terrible cultural mistakes at first, prompted mainly by Dr Lindley, who remarked:

'A charming plant sent to Mr Barker by his collector, Mr Ross, after whom it is named. The bright white lip, lying as it were in the centre of a rich green, yellow and blue star of three points, produces a peculiarly beautiful and unusual appearance ... It requires to be cultivated in a warm, damp stove, where it may either be potted in the usual way or, which is preferable, suspended from the roof upon a block of wood.'

Naturally, *Odontoglossum rossii* did not long stand up to stove treatment, which would be the sort of treatment given to phalaenopsis. It is one of the hardiest orchids in the catalogue, able to withstand very low temperatures and still flower in late winter to early spring. *Odontoglossum rossii* is an ideal orchid for a cool glass-house and I grow it as an outdoor epiphyte in temperatures as low as 5 degrees Celsius. Shade in the summer is essential and it will not stand hot or humid climates.

The color of *Odontoglossum rossii* is variable, some forms having quite a lot of pink in the petals and labellum. In its habitat it is listed as an endangered species and where it was once growing in countless thousands it would be a fortunate search to find one plant.

The root system of *Odontoglossum rossii* is sparse and about the same as that of other odontoglossums. In cultivation small pots are most suitable, either plastic or clay, and as the orchid has a dormant period in its cycle watering should be seasonal and sparse in its rest period.

The same fertilisers used for odontoglossums may be used for *Odontoglossum rossii* and it is best to use other than the slow-release formulas. It flowers in the winter months.

In cool climates *Odontoglossum* or *Osmoglossum pulchellum* should be one of the first orchids on the shopping list of beginners and once in a collection it will probably remain there as an isolated plant or a number of plants for the rest of a grower's life. This orchid is very hardy, may be grown in an unheated glass-house almost down to frost level, but does a little better in slightly warmer temperatures than that in the winter.

There are two forms of this species and considered as osmoglossums they make up a small genus on their own. They come from high altitudes and the difference between the two is unnoticeable to the ordinary grower. Occasionally the pseudo-bulbs in the species may vary from tall, flattened, tapering types to short odontoglossum-like forms.

Again George Ure Skinner was responsible for the introduction of the species to England and the continent of Europe, about the same time as *Odontoglossum rossii* was collected and consigned. The plants flower in early winter to early spring and regardless of cold weather they last for weeks once they open. At times if the humidity is high and the climate cold the flowers

185

tend to spot. But they are crisp and of quite heavy substance. The wiry spikes are inclined to droop with the weight of the eight or so flowers they bear, but once hardened they do not snap easily and may be tied erect before the buds open. The flowers are delightfully perfumed with an aroma similar to that of grape hyacinths.

Growth and flowering go on all the time and it is common to find pseudo-bulbs with a spike in the longest of the sheathing leaves at the base of the bulbs and new growths on the other side of the pseudo-bulbs at the same time. Over summer the growth process slows down and the new bulbs mature in the autumn and produce their spikes freely.

Potting material may be similar to that used for odontoglossums, but as this orchid is quite easy to grow into large plants bearing up to twelve or more spikes of flower, a little more coarse material should be used in the mix to improve its lasting qualities and encourage the root system. Three or four years is normal between repotting, so planning for this period should be reflected in the composition of the mix. Ordinary cymbidium mix is ideal and as fertilisers will be needed through the pot life of the mix it should be made up to stand this treatment. Bateman originally named this species, but the transfer to osmoglossums was made by Schlechter.

Rossioglossum grande (syn. *Odontoglossum grande*)

Although this name is frequently noted on plants which are not correctly labelled, the differences between the sections of the species are so minor as to escape notice. In *The Orchid Review* of December 1978, Wilma Rittershausen described the species; and although some authorities differ from her notes, in general they are correct. The typical *Odontoglossum grande*, however, in cultivation, seldom has more than three or four flowers and those with more than this number belong to other sections.

The correct name for the genus is now rossioglossum, but it is very doubtful if many growers have changed the labels on their plants. In truth, the relationship between *Odontoglossum grande* and *Odontoglossum crispum* and its varieties is much less than for any other species orchids. In the years since the advent of hand cross-pollinations thousands of hybridists have tried in vain to effect a successful cross-pollination. Only one is listed and that is through the miltonias, to which *Odontoglossum grande* may very well have a closer affiliation than to the odontoglossums.

The orchid again was discovered by George Ure Skinner in Guatemala. Of all the people who worked as collectors and botanists in Central America this man has more beautiful orchids to his credit than others. It was described by Lindley in the Botanical Register of 1840 and James Bateman flowered it in his collection at Knypersley in August and October of the same year. In England that was its correct season, early to late autumn. In Australia in the cooler climates it is one of the first of the autumn orchids in late March and April, and is unsuitable for climates other than temperate.

Skinner sent plants to a grower named Harris, including dried specimens and remarks about the climate and the habitat. John Lindley published this information and thus its fate was more assured than that of many other orchids consigned without any remarks on the place where they were found, the height above sea level and the type of country in which they occurred.

Skinner noted that *Odontoglossum grande* grew in a damp, shady situation where the temperature was almost constantly 20 degrees Celsius (about 68 degrees Fahrenheit).

Lindley remarked of the orchid: 'Certainly this is a most extraordinary plant. Its habit is altogether that of odontoglossums, with which the unguiculate lip and peculiar column also correspond; but the tubercles at the base of the lip are those of oncidium.' This identification of a morphological difference remained with the plant until the 1970-80 era, when the name was changed.

The original illustrations of the species in its discovery years and later portrayed the three or four flowers common to typical *Odontoglossum grande* spikes. One discrepancy in the artistry, however, was the sometimes frequent mistake in portraying the flower spikes on mature pseudo-bulbs.

Odontoglossum grande produces the flower spike with the new growth after the fashion of *Odontoglossum citrosmum* and then matures the pseudo-bulb after the flowers have gone. This habit is variable, however, and occasionally by the time the flowers have gone the bulbs are almost mature.

Several beautiful forms of this species were known in early consignments of plants, including one or two pure yellow-gold forms without nearly so much of the colored bars of chestnut to light brown which are such a feature of the normal forms. Unfortunately, most of these fine forms no longer exist and it is doubtful if they will ever be found again. They were a type of albino.

Odontoglossum grande is one of the periodic orchids, with a fairly marked dormant stage following flowering and maturity of the bulbs. A potting material should be designed which will take this period of dormancy without deterioration. Cymbidium mix is ideal and it is not a good idea to use any fertiliser either in the mix or as a slow-release top-dressing. In growth a small amount of blood and bone worked into the top of the potting mix is an efficient fertiliser and additional light waterings of weak liquid nutrients in early growth stages will increase the size of the flowers and keep the growth healthy.

In the dormant period *Odontoglossum grande* may be rested through the months of May to late September or October, when new growth will be noted from the last pseudo-bulb or even from others back from the lead in well-grown plants. Do not rush the watering, but allow the plants to come slowly into full root and leaf growth over a few weeks. Once into the warmer weather and growth it is almost impossible to overwater it.

The first of these odontoglossums to flower is the species *Odontoglossum insleayi*, the flowers of which are smaller than those of *Odontoglossum grande* and numbering up to seven or eight on the spike.

As the flowers of these orchids open they should be kept in a slightly drier atmosphere and never sprayed or wetted while watering or damping down. In high humidity they quickly develop wet-looking patches and decay. Shade should be as dense as for any other orchids or the pale green foliage will quickly burn. The young growths should also be watched carefully to see that water does not lodge in them and destroy the flower buds, which come within the young leaves and bracts at the base of the pseudo-bulbs.

The root system is medium coarse, somewhat like the less stout type on some cymbidiums. In a well-grown plant this system does not fill a pot, but it should be given sufficient scope to build and develop a substantial plant without getting to the stage of overpotting.

Odontoglossum grande and its near relatives do not suffer the depredations of most of the pests which infest orchids, so they may not need a spray to counteract them. But the young shoots and buds are attractive to slugs and snails, which will quickly spoil the young flower buds.

Propagating *Odontoglossum grande* is not always easy because it tends to shed its leaves very quickly if the plant is ill grown. Severing away portions of the plant behind the first two bulbs and a new lead is the ideal propagation and back-bulbs never seem as viable as with other orchids. In this they are typically odontoglossums and the propagating system applied to that genus should be tried, with the proviso that the front bulb on which the new lead is developing should have the flower spike removed if it has one. It is scarcely fair to the plant to leave it on and the risk is there that in weakness the total division may be lost.

The best method is to survey the plant in its dormant stage and decide on a division. This may inhibit flowering and is all to the general good of the plant. In the next dormant period it will be obvious whether the scheme has been successful and following flowering the plant may be repotted as soon as possible. Do not leave the flowers on plants too long once they are fully open, as this is the correct time to repot if it is not done in the summer. Naturally, with winter only a month or two away, a good deal of care should be taken over the process, with a return to sphagnum moss culture if the root system proves chancy.

Rossioglossum grande

Oncidiums

The genus was named by Swartz in 1800, the name derived from the Greek diminutive of the word indicating a tumor or swelling, applied in this instance to the calluses on the labellum of all the species.

Oncidiums were among the early orchids cultivated in England and Europe and are morphologically diverse. As a matter of fact, W. W. G. Moir, of Hawaii, and other authorities consider that some members should be relegated to other genera or separated into new genera. The unwieldy nature of the genus as presently constituted, as well as the great differences in the present catalogue from country to country in the South American region prompt the proposals.

Oncidiums also have remarkable affiliations with other genera of the same region and the end result of this has been the production of many inter-generic hybrids with up to six members. However, this also has its problems for the hybridist and infertility and paucity of good seed have followed much of the cross-pollinations undertaken by interested growers in the attenuated bloodlines.

Again quoting W. W. G. Moir, interwined throughout most of the cross-pollination is a great amount of sex-linkage, where certain species will act only as seed or pollen parents, seldom combining both functions.

Dr John Lindley, the English botanist and taxonomist, knew over 200 of the species in the early years of the nineteenth century and was responsible for naming many of them. He ruefully admitted, although not without some sense of the humor of the situation, that many European botanists and taxonomists were convinced he invented some of the species he described and named. Lindley's book *Sertum Orchidaceum* of 1838 listed a large number. Considering his work in retrospect from the 1970-80 period, one cannot be less than amazed that this man, partially blind and poorly educated even for his period, accomplished so much.

Oncidiums were cultivated in England quite early in the nineteenth century, usually for only brief periods, as they were quickly killed off. In those and the following years they gained the reputation, which stayed with them until, almost the middle years of the following century, of 'flowering themselves to death'.

The reality was far removed from this, because many of the early species imported came from altitudes of up to 2000 metres, their habitat ill understood and practically unknown and their artificial life span brief. They followed the habitual phase of all threatened life forms and threw flower spikes in an effort to procreate themselves. It was not until they were grown in a more congenial atmosphere than the humid heat of the 'stove' houses of the time that they really prospered and flowered naturally. Lack of understanding frequently still causes the oncidiums to show such signs of poor culture.

One of the growers who early came to terms with oncidiums was Forbes, who worked in the glass-houses of Woburn, where the collection of the Duke of Bedford was housed in the early years of the nineteenth century. *Oncidium forbesii* was named for him in tribute to his skill. This orchid has been part of the primary group with which the 1980 hybridists are still toying, bringing into cultivation all those beautiful oncidiums patterned after the fashion of *Oncidium varicosum* but with much improved petal and sepal shape. *Oncidium forbesii* was discovered in Brazil about 1835.

Most of the genus presents two types of growth — those with what could be termed an ascending rhizome habit, such as *Oncidium varicosum*, and those with a general progressive habit which easily follows the horizontal surface of potting material without attempting to climb up very far out of it. *Oncidium luridum* is one such.

Some, such as *Oncidium lanceanum* and *Oncidium luridum*, have a system of rhizome and large, thick leaves virtually without pseudo-bulbs. Others, such as *Oncidium triquetrum*, are almost monopodial like small vandaceous orchids. Most recognisable are those such as *Oncidium varicosum*, with terminal leaves and enclosing basal sheaths which are soon cast, or *Oncidium sphacelatum*, which has terminal and enclosing sheath-like leaves. The flower spikes of all these emanate from the base of the pseudo-bulb. All these varied features give credence to the opinions of those who would subdivide the genus further than the sub-sections or sub-species into which they presently fall.

It is not possible to grow all oncidiums in similar conditions and they must be selected to suit the various orchids comprising the general collections into which growers wish to introduce them. It is impossible to be dogmatic about the conditions under which they will grow, although there are temperature minimums which should be aimed at, despite the fact that many come from high altitudes. If cultivated in glass-houses the prevailing conditions are far different from those of their habitats.

While many species are still cultivated, it is the hybrids derived from *Oncidium varicosum, Oncidium crispum* and one or two other similar species which are most common. Generally these are hybrids with labellums similar to *Oncidium varicosum*, with long, branched racemes of flower and very showy when well grown. They are usually also what could be termed the ascending rhizome type and should be grown attached to a piece of tree-fern, cork, a section of a small branch of a tree or similar compatible material, after the fashion of some of the illustrations.

Based in a pot, either filled with heavy pebble or bluestone aggregate, with a little basic potting material added, plants so mounted soon send roots downward as well as aerially after the fashion of the original species in their habitat. The general conditions of the glass-house or growing area, if outdoors, seem to dictate the total root structure.

Possibly the most outstanding characteristic of the genus as a whole is the aridity of their dormant or resting period, some of the species growing in areas where there is little rainfall for up to six months of the year. Despite severe shrivelling of the pseudo-bulbs, the plants fatten out again completely when the new pseudo-bulbs of the growing season feed back and the root system seeks moisture.

As a genus some of them are prone to develop considerable root systems, like most epiphytes from such climates, and this is usually transient in cultivation. Commonly the roots also lose vitality on any section of the plant which loses its leaves, but the leafless pseudo-bulbs may still fulfil an important function. They may be severed in twos or threes, preferably never singles.

While the thick, 'donkey-eared' leaves of *Oncidium lanceanum* are fairly long lasting, serving the plant or rhizome as pseudo-bulbs for some years in good conditions, those of oncidiums such as *Oncidium crispum* or *Oncidium varicosum* usually last for only two or three years.

As with all orchids, the surest sign of plant health is the gloss of the leaves and a tendency to multiply the growths from the lead bulb in twos or to recommence growth on parts of the plant well back from the lead.

Glass-house cultivation of all orchids should bring out differences of plant habit compared with that of their areas of origin and perhaps *Oncidium lanceanum* is a good example of this. In the habitat it is found with the large, thick leaves anything from horizontal to completely pendant, whereas in glass-house culture it is quite happy growing vertically on the surface of the medium.

Oncidium lanceanum, of course, was one of the early victims of 'development' in the orchid trade. Lance, the discoverer of the orchid, sent only two or three plants to England and the demand for them was intense. A collector named Colley found a tree in Guyana (British Guiana) near the Demarara River covered from top to bottom with *Oncidium lanceanum*. He took the lot and packed and sent them to England; 'cleaning up,' as they say in modern slang.

Since their original discovery oncidiums have had a tangled history, with species removed from the ranks as well as added. Even as this book was being written two miltonias became oncidiums. They were *Miltonia clowesii*, discovered near Rio de Janeiro by the collector Gardner, and *Miltonia candida*, about the introduction of which little is known except that it came from Brazil and flowered in Loddiges' orchid collection about 1838. The habitat was later found to be almost the same as that of *Miltonia clowesii*.

As a genus oncidiums occur from sea level to great altitudes, with the Peruvian species *Oncidium nubigenum* growing at some 4000 metres (about 13 000 feet), which is well above the elevation at which most epiphytic orchids grow.

Oncidiums have, like most of the orchidaceae, been the subject of speculation, financially and as to habitats. In the instance of *Oncidium haematochilum* its habitat was obscure as late as the years 1890-1900, yet it had been imported and cultivated in Britain as early as 1847. A Trinidad enthusiast named Potter suggested that it was probably a hybrid between *Oncidium lanceanum* and *Oncidium luridum* because he had found it growing in the same general area as these two species.

Oncidium macranthum was the subject of a dispute because it was so known in England and as *Oncidium hastiferum* in Europe. Many notable personalities entered the fray, with the disagreement continuing for about 50-odd years from 1850 onward. It was originally collected on the lower slopes of Mount Chimborazo, in the Ecuadorean Andes mountains.

The number of travellers and collectors in the South American continent beggars the imagination. It depended on which herbarium or botanist received their specimens and catalogued them that the names became fixed. In Brazil alone about 150 early collectors and botanists operated and of the 2300 species of that country about half have synonyms, the real name decided by the date priority of discovery and submission and publication of relevant data.

Oncidium varicosum was named by Dr John Lindley in 1837 from a herbarium specimen collected in Brazil by Prince Maxmilian, a scion of European royalty for whom the Americas were combed to find him a kingdom. It ended in disaster. However, to get back to *Oncidium varicosum*, it was not flowered in England until about 1849, in the garden of the Horticultural Society of London, itself also an avid collector and sponsor of collectors.

The variety *Oncidium varicosum* var. *rogersii* appeared about 1868 in the collection of Dr Rogers. William Bolton, a noted grower of the period, gained a First Class Certificate for his flowering of it in 1898, the labellum being 4 centimetres across.

Oncidium varicosum var. *rogersii* is not the only fine type recorded, as

191

Charlesworths also gained an FCC for a distinct variety in 1902, the labellum of which measured over 6 centimetres across. In the old inch measurement that was some 2½ inches, which is rather magnificent. Several other varieties were given recognition, notably *Oncidium varicosum* var. *moortebeek* and the variety *insigne*, which had a considerable area of red-brown about the crest in the central portion of the labellum. A clear yellow form was known and given varietal recognition with the epithet citrinum. In fact, it was what is commonly and mistakenly referred to as an albino, which signifies a white type.

Messrs Stuart Low had a plant of this type in cultivation for about sixteen years, which at that time was considered exceptional for a plant of *Oncidium varicosum*. There were several fine varieties in cultivation in Australia when this book was written.

An unusual species in cultivation is *Oncidium papilio*. It seldom appears on the show or exhibition benches and attracts a lot of attention when it does so. It was this flower which so entranced the Duke of Devonshire in the early years of orchid growing in England that he was persuaded to form what became the most magnificent collection of its time. His growers were also among the first to perceive the significance of fresh air and lower temperatures than those commonly in vogue. The duke was a contemporary of James Bateman and typified the people who indulged in growing exotic plants. Wealth was usually a prime prerequisite.

Charlesworths also had a variety of *Oncidium papilio* which was a clear yellow with the markings on petals, sepals and labellum a gold-orange color. Again, had it been white it would have been termed an albino. The term which really fits these flowers is 'lutino' — an almost clear color yellow flower.

Dr Lindley's explanation of the name bears repeating: 'The name has doubtless been suggested by the brilliant color of the flower, its singular form, which may be easily likened to the wings, body, antennae and tongue of a butterfly, and its fluttering motion when hanging from its stalk, at the extremity of the weak, elastic, jointed scape.' Those words were well put together and possibly could not be bettered as a description. A pastel drawing is featured in the illustrations.

Together with attributes already described, *Oncidium papilio* has the happy way of producing another flower at the end of the slender, long stem as fast as one fades away, with the number possible as yet undetermined. *Oncidium kramerianum* is similar if more elaborately marked and on usually a shorter stem, native to the West Indies, with *Oncidium papilio* native to Ecuador, Peru and other countries.

The first plants sent to England were consigned by the Governor of Trinidad, Sir Ralph Woodward, from that colony and flowered in a nursery owned by Colvill in Chelsea in 1825. What can we imagine of the surprise when that long slender stem developed its bud and opened? In those days as the wonders of the plant world flowered for the first time in their glass-houses the growers and the proud owners had something which can never be repeated again. A Pandora's box full of the most beautiful flowers possible to imagine!

The temperatures under which oncidiums grow in various countries are not really a guide to their glass-house or artificial cultivation. Although *Oncidium longipes* originates in quite a cool area of Brazil, in glass-house cultivation it always thrives better with a guard against chill below about 10 to 12 degrees Celsius (about 50 degrees Fahrenheit).

Oncidium longipes, in company with many other orchids, suffers the indignity of mis-spelling, being referred to as 'longpipes' even in some orchid literature. As far as commercial advertisers are concerned, very many orchids suffer the same fate.

Oncidium longipes was introduced to Europe before other places, the collector's name indefinite. About six years later a plant was sent to Loddiges' nursery from France, where it flowered about 1850. The flowers are red-brown and yellow, a color combination shared by many of the genus, and in good cultivation about 3 to 4 centimetres across. Like *Oncidium varicosum* it flowers fairly readily and its habitat in southern Brazil is also that of *Oncidium varicosum*, although it occurs in many other centres of that country.

The perfume of orchids merits appreciation when it can be so described and it is always refreshing to find people who commonly appear to have been rather 'stuffy' types showing a nice sense of humor. Reichenbach, looked at from the distance of 100-odd years, seems to have been a man of great dignity and little indication of having a relaxed side to his nature. But when Roezl, an orchid plant collector of that time, sent a large number of plants of *Oncidium hastatum* to him, the eminent botanist remarked: 'One variety has a most powerful perfume of a goat in fullest perspiration on a warm summer day.' Fortunately the aroma is not very common in orchids. This species is illustrated in the color section.

One of the easiest of the genus to cultivate is the Brazilian species *Oncidium crispum*. It grows in several districts of that state, mostly in a climate generated by a temperate foothill ecology which thrives in a dry daytime and moist night. It was brought to England about 1832 and, unlike some of the imports of that time, prospered in the glass-houses of Messrs Loddiges. However, it never seems to flower with the verve described in early records of its habitat, where spikes to 1.5 metres long were common. Mostly we are lucky to get thirty to forty flowers. It also is featured in the illustrations, flowering from a plant grown outdoors on a casuarina tree in southern Victoria.

Only a few of the orchid genera have more widespread representation in the American continent than oncidiums. The Mexican section has some very attractive members, among them the species *Oncidium ornithorhyncum*. Although it thrives at about 2000 metres and more (about 5000 feet), it is not usually found thriving in the temperature equivalent of this altitude when cultivated. Mostly it is a warm area orchid which produces short panicles of pink flowers, but in sufficient numbers to make it a most attractive proposition. The hybrid *Oncidium* Kaiulani, which is derived from *Oncidium flexuosum* as the other parent, flowers more freely and is one of the prettiest and daintiest orchids possible in a collection.

Oncidium ornithorhyncum was brought to Europe and England in the early years of the nineteenth century and John Day, noted for his artistry in portraying orchid flowers as well as his skill in growing them, chanced on a pure white variety in the 1870 period. It later came into the collection of B. S. Williams, another noted grower, who sold it for 50 guineas, which roughly translated into our debased dollar currency would represent somewhere about $2750 or more.

Oncidium flexuosum is one of the members which has extravagant spikes of flower, with records of hundreds of blossoms on some specimen plants. Periodically such plants appear and are awarded certificates, but the difficulty in maintaining such plants in any genus is too much for most growers and they soon fade out and must be cut up and restarted. But one of the highest accomplishments for any orchid grower is at least one outstanding specimen plant in his career.

Cultivation in glass-houses or outdoors brings only two features forward that are common to nearly all oncidiums — either they have a climbing habit in which the plant steadily advances upward year by year with an extension of the rhizome, or the upward thrust is only moderate.

In the first instance the plant should be treated in the manner of the

193

illustrations, tied to a piece of tree-fern, a slab of cork, or a section of a tree branch. While the piece of cork may be suspended, the tree-fern section or a branch section should be planted in a pot, either with a filling of loose 5 centimetre aggregate crushed rock or with a coarse bark potting material. Either should be firmly compacted into the pot, which should be of a size that does not tip easily. This is where the heavier clay pots are an advantage.

If the plant is potted in the normal way the material should be fairly coarse and not as dense as cymbidium mixes. It should contain a fair amount of pre-decay leaf such as oak leaf and allowance made for the fact that for some months of the year the plant will not be watered at all. In the dormant period the natural humidity of a glass-house or growing area should be almost sufficient to maintain it. A certain amount of shrivelling is both natural and inevitable and reintroduction of water should be gradual so that the root system has time to become accustomed again to wetness. Hastening this process will possibly cause some root loss and, if a persistent feature of culture, almost total root loss.

The strange part of all this is that naturally grown plants in wholly outside conditions seem to develop a resistance to this cultivation-induced root loss and even in adverse climates there is little root loss other than from parts of the rhizome which have become aged and unproductive.

Repotting or rebuilding plants from mounts is a little more difficult than transferring plants from one pot to another. The first step is to select the right time, when new root is making out from extensions of the rhizome, from the last season's rhizome or from new growths. The plant mount should be thoroughly soaked to take a little of the brittleness out of the roots and the material. If it is cork possibly the whole slab will have to be crumbled away. If tree-fern, it should be shredded away to preserve as much of the root system as possible.

Taking the three latest pseudo-bulbs and their portion of the rhizome, fasten this propagation to a new mount and leave the older portion of the plant intact on the old mount. It will propagate a new plant in its own time and way and this should be ready for rejuvenation in the following season.

Always take note of the attraction or not of the mount used for the roots. If it seems unacceptable discard that type of mount and try another.

If grown in pots or baskets, coarse bark should be used and there is no need to add gravel or other drainage material. Until established the plant should be held firmly so that it does not wobble about. Nothing discourages roots more than friction on the tips breaking them down into a decaying point. It takes some three or four weeks for them to bud out and if they are short stubbs close to the rhizome they may not bud at all. There is a limit to the number of roots which emerge from the new rhizome, varying from genus to genus, but once they are exhausted the only system likely to stimulate rooting is potting plants into sphagnum moss.

The roots of oncidiums are much the same as other epiphytes, with a proportion free and aerial and the remainder acting as anchorage for the plants and as feeders. Aerial roots seldom grow further when inserted into potting material and are most difficult to get into bud even in sphagnum moss.

Frequently genera which come from the same area and almost the same environment will not thrive in artificial cultivation when grown in the same glass-house. Occasionally this may be overcome by moving the plants about in a glass-house, as a series of environments may be found from the floor to the roof and from side to side. The same may be said for average temperatures in which they are grown, particularly the differences between day and night temperatures and the extremes of summer and winter. It is not possible to be too certain and lay down hard-and-fast rules for oncidiums because of their widespread occurrence, with the same species common to several localities and, indeed, several countries.

Oncidium varicosum is considered to be a moderately cool-growing species, but in artificial culture it is most adaptable and rather better in moderate warmth. With good air circulation, bright growing conditions, and a most definite dormant period in which they receive little or no water, oncidiums of many types do not pose real problems. But in poor conditions such as cold winters and overwatering create, they are quick to react, with possibly a season or two after the change to something better before they show response.

If hybrids form part or all the oncidiums in a collection their parentage should be analysed so that the degree of warmth and other features of their cultivation may be understood. Although all glass-house-raised orchids have a tendency to be products of their environment, their natural background may still be effective as a guide to cultivation.

The oncidiums from, say, the *Oncidium varicosum* line nearly all have profuse root systems, some of it transient and lasting no more than a year or two, but the last made section being a virile core from which a fresh start is made after the resting period. If it is killed off by poor wintering the start and maturing of new growth is that much more difficult for the plant. Once the roots go the leaves follow and for the coarse-leafed section such as *Oncidium lanceanum* the job of resuscitation is even more difficult than for the *Oncidium varicosum* or *Oncidium flexuosum* group because there is no pseudo-bulb system for the plants to fall back on. This is also a good example of the use of older pseudo-bulbs, even when leafless, because they may be sacrificed by the plant to feed the forward parts and should not be removed, even if they spoil the look of a plant.

In the flush of the growth cycle, particularly when the new growths are beginning to make up, liquid nutrients in weak form may be applied after the plant has been thoroughly watered. Quarter strength is sufficient and strong nutrient solutions or too frequent applications soon destroy the plants by killing off the roots.

Shading for oncidiums varies from species to species but they are generally bright-light orchids.

Miltonias
Miltoniopsis

Miltonias

The genus named in honor of Viscount Milton (1786-1857), a patron of horticulture and orchid culture, described as 'one of the oldest and most zealous friends of natural science in this country' (England). The naming of plants or genera in honor of personalities has largely fallen into disuse for good reasons.

Miltoniopsis

The genus established in 1889 by Godefroy-Lebeuf to separate two distinct types of the miltonias but given effect or acceptance only in the 1970-80 decade. Geographically these belong to the Andean section and the miltonias to principally the Brazilian section of the closely related orchids. The suffix *opsis* is a Greek derivative indicating relationship to miltonias.

The differences in the two genera, expressed by Dunsterville and Garay,* are as follows:

The genus miltonia, as typified by *M. spectabilis*, is characterised by scandent rhizome, two-leafed pseudo-bulbs, column auriculate, excavate in front and the sides are firmly united with the nectariferous base of the lip.

Miltoniopsis, on the other hand, is characterised by aggregate, one-leafed pseudo-bulbs, exauriculate column which is united with the lip through a central, keel-like ridge without any excavation.

When taxonomists change a genus from one group of orchids to another or create a new genus by separating species from a recognised group they are certain to cause confusion. This has occurred in the miltonias, although not totally accepted, and the hobby or pastime growers will take some time to come to grips with the new names and types. No doubt some of the orchids mentioned in this book will also go through the same process, but the old name will stick to the orchids for quite some time.

In this sense the miltonias and miltoniopsis are almost inseparable in this rundown on their history and cultivation. As little confusion as possible will be the aim, but the species names should be noted in their correct section even if they are referred to simply as miltonias.

These orchids are common to much of Central and South America, with the miltoniopsis now almost unknown as naturally growing plants. They were recognised as native to Colombia and other places. The miltonias, while principally Brazilian orchids, also grew in other countries. The two genera would perhaps be represented best by *Miltonia flavescens*, with its starry, rather spidery shape, a Brazilian, and *Miltoniopsis vexillaria*, with its pansy-like outline, the Colombian orchid.

*The source of this excerpt is *Venezuelan Orchids*, volume 6.

Dr Alberto Echavarria, a Colombian authority on miltoniopsis, recorded in the publication associated with the Seventh World Orchid Conference a good comparative analysis on these orchids.

The 'miltonias' commonly found in orchid collections are the latter, mostly derived from *Miltoniopsis roezlii* and *Miltoniopsis vexillaria*, with additions of *Miltoniopsis warscewiczii* and *Miltoniopsis phalaenopsis*. *Miltoniopsis phalaenopsis* has a similar shape and color pattern to *Miltoniopsis vexillaria*, but *Miltoniopsis warscewiczii*, although well colored in red-brown and waxy in appearance, has entirely reflexed petals and sepals when mature. All are indigenous to Colombia, with a spillover into adjacent countries, first brought to attention of botanists and cultivators by a collector named Bowman. Unfortunately, he died of one of the various illnesses contracted by Europeans and their origin remained obscure until the collector Chesterton sent or brought plants to England about 1872. They were flowered by James Veitch and Sons in their nursery.

The German consul F. C. Lehmann was responsible for recording the locations and conditions in which the miltoniopsis grew. He was fortunate enough to combine work with pleasure in Colombia but was later to die following an excursion after the orchids he so loved, as related in the section on masdevallias in Volume 3. He confirmed the Peruvian highlands as a source for *Miltoniopsis vexillaria* and at least one other species in his time.

His descriptions are most detailed and may be found in *A Manual of Orchidaceous Plants*, produced by James Veitch and Sons in 1887-94.

Miltonia vexillaria was named by Bentham in 1881 and the growers of that period were faced with a predicament similar to that of present growers when taxonomists change things, because it was known, among other epithets, as 'the red odontoglossum from Colombia.'

Many varieties of *Miltonia vexillaria* were known, ranging from pale pink and white through to deep rose-pink. It was widespread through Colombia, growing at from 1000 to 2000 metres (3500 to 6500 feet). Its habitat was humid throughout most of the year, generally in the fringes of forest land but just above the rain-forest zone. In its growing season copious rain fell and this is one of the facets of its cultivation in hybrid form in artificial conditions.

Some idea of the prices paid for fine varieties of the species sold after importation may be gained by the story of a variety named 'superba' which was sold to Sir Trevor Lawrence, a leading fancier of the time, for about £75.

This variety was collected by a man named Schmidten for Frederick Sander, who sold the plant unflowered to another grower. It was painted by John Day, a noted artist at portraying orchid flowers and he quoted its history as follows:

'This unique and splendid variety was sold in bloom at Stevens' this day. The owner of it, Mr Barth, a farmer in Kent, who buys a good many orchids, bought it at Stevens' among some plants just imported two or three years ago and paid only a few shillings for it. It was knocked down, after keen competition between him and Baron Schroder and Mr W. Bull, to Sir Trevor Lawrence, Bart, M.P., for £75 12s. I made a pencil sketch of it on the fly sheet of a letter in my pocket, and showed it to Sir T., who sat next to me when it was sold, and he immediately picked off a flower and gave it to me to finish my drawing by, which was a right regal thing to do, and which I do not think anyone else would have done.'

A reproduction of a lithograph of this variety appears in the illustrations, together with a pastel drawing of the more common type.

Miltonia roezlii was discovered by Roezl in Colombia in 1873 and plants were sent to England and flowered there by the fancier William Bull, who bought the plant together with some other 'novelties', as these unknown and unflowered importations were frequently called. He paid £250 for a large parcel. If related to present-day (1980) Australian currency that would be somewhere near $12500 to $15000.

Following the custom of the times, neither the collector nor the vendor detailed the source of these orchids, so that the habitat became the preserve of one group until perhaps the chance locating of plants by another collector opened up the tract to exploitation. Then, of course, there was a scramble to denude the area.

Miltonia or *Miltoniopsis roezlii*, as it should now be called, was found in several areas of Colombia, growing at about 300 to 1000 metres and in company with odontoglossums, oncidiums and several other genera. A similar species in *Miltoniopsis phalaenopsis* was found at about the same time in northern Colombia at about 1000 to 1500 metres, always in humid, shady conditions and again almost invariably as an epiphyte. It was first sent to Europe by the collector Schlim about 1850 and contributed its broad labellum to the lines of modern hybrids. The overriding colors were pale purple and white. *Miltoniopsis phalaenopsis* was also found later in other locations and at lower altitudes and in a cooler climate.

The importance of ecology was soon appreciated by the early collectors. They realised the type of country in which they were standing at any given moment and the types of orchids which should be found in the area. The orientation of the plant groupings toward the sun and the aspect of the hill and mountain sides were also tricks of the trade to be learned and some of the early discoverers of our orchid species noted these things carefully. Others, less skilful and observant, floundered about and their discoveries were more a matter of chance instead of logical search.

The flowering seasons of the various miltonia species were at first a puzzle to growers, but generally they all flowered in summer to autumn. In developing the hybrid strains a scattering of growth and flowering patterns meant that plants mostly flowered in all seasons except the winter. The first inter-generic cross-pollination was of *Odontoglossum crispum* and *Miltonia warscewiczii* in 1905, created by the Belgian A. de Lairesse and appropriately named *Odontonia* Lairesseae.

Miltonia warscewiczii was found by a German botanist in Peru, but the Lithuanian or Polish collector Warscewicz sent dried specimens to Europe. Linden later sent live plants to Europe and the botanist and taxonomist Reichenbach the younger named it in honor of the Pole. It was also sent to England by the collector Burke, who described its habitat. Mostly the plants were found growing on moss-covered rocks and low trees in a very humid climate at about 1000 metres. It is quite unlike the other miltoniopsis and more like an oncidium.

The hybrid miltoniopsis are mostly derived from *Miltoniopsis vexillaria* and *Miltoniopsis roezlii*, the first of which was *Miltoniopsis* Bleuana, named after the French hybridist Alfred Bleu. It was raised in the 1880 decade and flowered in 1889, as recorded in the *Sanders' List of Orchid Hybrids*. *Miltoniopsis* Bleuana was then back-crossed to both species again, giving *Miltoniopsis* Hyeana and *Miltoniopsis* St. Andre. These were again combined to produce *Miltoniopsis* Nellie Smith and so it goes on, all revolving about the two original species. At one time registrations were suspended while the whole inbred mess was sorted out, but the upshot is that there exists a list with too few species bred into a plethora of names.

Probably the greatest development of the hybrids was in the 1930 period, but it was also along the lines of selective inbreeding and this, combined with a great deal of unrecorded hybridising with consequent unknown parents, has led to the same dead-ends as occur in other genera in the hybrid list. However, with the fine selected varieties used, the spectrum of color in the 1970-80 period works through white and cream and yellow to the pinks and deep velvety reds of such intensity as those illustrated.

These flat, nicely proportioned flowers are no longer miltonias, although the name will remain with them for many years to come. Their flowering season is dictated by the new growths, in which the spikes appear in half-grown form. With incorporation of so many species it is possible to get summer, autumn and spring flowers, with even a few unusual stragglers.

A complicated web of cross-pollinations may be traced through *Sanders' List of Orchid Hybrids*, but it is almost impossible to unravel briefly or describe this inter-generic list to note the first hybrids in the inter-generic crosses. It all began about 1900 and the first odontioda, with the 1910 to 1940 period the development era. The miltonias, Brazilian as well as Colombian, were used indiscriminately as species and through hybrids, although the omission of *Miltoniopsis phalaenopsis* from most of this activity must have had some reason. The same could be said for *Miltonia spectabilis*.

Following the years of popularity the whole inter-generic group, including the odontoglossums, were dropped once cymbidiums commanded so much time and space in orchid collections. Possibly the Brazilian miltonias brought them back into favor with their brilliant and varied alliances with oncidiums, brassias and the whole of the odontoglossum complex. It was to these orchids that innovators turned and there seemed to be no end to the combinations that could be worked out. While some were dead-ends with malformations and incompatibility problems, sufficient material emerged to keep the thing going. At least seven genera seem to be compatible with the Brazilian miltonias, not to mention the miltoniopsis possibilities, although they appeared to have floated off on a line of their own with so much worthwhile hybridism bringing new colors and shapes that breeding them into smaller forms as was done with cymbidiums seemed to have no general appeal.

It is certain that no such combinations were even guessed at by Alfred Bleu or Monsieur Jules Hye, who possibly started the ball rolling with miltoniopsis at least.

The Brazilian miltonias, with the exception of *Miltonia spectabilis*, are quite distinct from the Colombian forms of the closely related genus, some with bizarre color patterns. *Miltonia spectabilis* is the largest of them, several varieties being known and the most colorful illustrated in the picture section. It was, in fact, the species on which the whole genus was based, although the history is shadowy. Known as early as 1835, it was brought to the notice of an English horticultural society by a man named Fry and was flowered by Loddiges some two years later. It was named by Lindley. The type shown in the photographs, *Miltonia spectabilis* var. *moreliana*, was first known and grown and flowered in France by Monsieur Morel. As with most of the orchids found at that time, information about its habitat was minimal, the province unknown to all but the collectors and false 'addresses' given to confuse things further. Ultimately it was found to occur in a wide area of south central Brazil.

It took shippers and packers just as long in the instance of miltonias as all other genera to learn how to dehydrate and pack and ship the plants and there was a dreadful wastage factor in the numbers of plants collected against those which arrived in any shape to face resuscitation.

Miltonia spectabilis was followed by *Miltonia clowesii*, discovered in the Organ Mountains and subsequently in other places, similar to *Miltonia spectabilis*. It flowered in the collection of the Reverend John Clowes in England in 1839. This man was an ardent orchid grower and collector and one must understand the nature of the church and its appointments in England in those times to appreciate how a churchman could be involved in such a wealthy man's pastime. *Miltonia clowesii* has been transferred to the oncidiums and this had its effect in strange ways.

Miltonias spectabilis and *clowesii* were the parents of the natural hybrid *Miltonia bluntii*, which thus became an inter-generic hybrid miltonidium. There are almost as many natural hybrids in the genus in Brazil as there are species, of which there are nine.

Miltonia regnelli was first found by the collector Devos and following its arrival in Belgium flowered somewhere between 1835 and 1840. But it was Dr Regnell who finally had the credit for its discovery in 1846. Veitch considered it the best of the Brazilian miltonias and compared it with the Colombian species for beauty and appeal, and more particularly for its similarity to those orchids, yet it came from the most southerly source of the genus in Brazil.

The relationship between miltonias and milltoniopsis stops short at the cultural requirements, with the miltoniopsis following a pattern already familiar in the odontoglossums and the miltonias following a line similar to the oncidiums.

Beginning with the miltoniopsis, a look at the conditions under which they grew naturally, related by R. A. Rolfe, editor of *The Orchid Review* in its early years, is worth noting:

'The whole region in which *Miltonia vexillaria* grows is well defined and similarly bounded ... almost everywhere about 4750 and 6500 feet above sea level. The average mean temperature of the year between these limits fluctuates between 62 and 67 degrees Fahr., that of the variety albicans from 68 to 70 degrees. The extreme daily range when the mornings are clear and the days bright is from 53 deg. Fahr. minimum and to 77 deg. maximum. Generally speaking, *Miltonia vexillaria* is found isolated in places influenced by local climatic conditions, being most abundant at its medium altitude. It always occurs on the borders of the denser mountain forests which have below them either open, park-like stretches covered with low bushes or coarse savannah grass, and above the extremely humid and almost impenetrable and luxuriant forests that cover the Cordilleras at that altitude.'

Little more need be said about the conditions to be aimed at in cultivating them naturally or under glass. It is obvious that they would be ill suited to both tropical climates and those too cool to promote a good annual cycle of growth and flowering.

The root system of miltoniopsis is fine and very similar to that of odontoglossums, therefore small pots should be used, either plastic or clay. Most miltoniopsis seem to be at various stages of growth throughout the year, so they must be studied and after the plants have flowered and the bulbs mature they should be given less water.

Miltonia plants should be studied to note their growth characteristics. It is obvious in most of the species and hybrids that they have an ascending rhizome structure like oncidiums and should be mounted on slabs of bark or tree-fern to give them free rein, similar to the plants illustrated.

These orchids also have an annual cycle in which pseudo-bulbs are almost matured as the flower spike develops and ends, following which in ordinary suitable glass-house conditions they seem to become dormant for a couple of months and then commence the cycle all over again. In the period when there is no activity they should be kept a little drier but not allowed to dehydrate.

The roots of miltonias, unlike those of multoniopsis, are mostly profuse and habitually aerial. While some may enter a rich potting mix, just as many grow out horizontally from the plant and thrive in natural humidity. Much of the moisture absorption in maturing the plant is taken up by these aerial roots. In the dormant phase they will go white to the tips and the signs that the plant is under way again are greening of the root tips and appearance of new growth in the short enclosing leaf-like bract on the side opposite the flower spike. In good conditions the pseudo-bulbs may shoot on both sides.

Propagation of both genera is along the lines laid down for most orchids. It is best to have three pseudo-bulbs behind a commencing new lead. While the plants may be left until repotting to divide, at times it may be best to sever the rhizome partly as soon as flowering has ended, so that when the repotting season arrives a fresh plant may have started behind the lead. As with most orchids, attempts to propagate too quickly may result in lost sections of the plants.

Overpotting should be avoided, even for plants with ascending rhizomes. In general, a plant of miltoniopsis with anything up to six leafed pseudo-bulbs will thrive in a 10 centimetre pot. Occasionally plants may be seen in shows and at club meetings in 12 and 15 centimetre pots, but the risk with pots of this size is more in the dormant plant stage than the flowering stage, as most growers of miltoniopsis will agree. Some of the miltonias may be grown into quite large specimens in larger pots because of their rooting habits, but even here the risk is just as constant.

Sphagnum moss, despite its mention as a growing medium, is not recommended for either miltonias or miltoniopsis. While it is very suitable for propagating or advancement of young seedlings into the bark mixes, the susceptibility to mistakes in culture leaves no margin whatsoever. Notwithstanding this, it is frequently recommended by commercial nurseries as second to none and perhaps this may be true for this purpose. But for the ordinary grower it is far better to make up a basic mix of 3 to 5 millimetre bark and the next smaller size in equal parts, add very coarse sand or light gravel in volume one-third of a part and thoroughly blend and dampen this mix. It should be put into a plastic bag and thoroughly wetted without any free water in the bottom of the bag, the neck tied and left for two or three days to 'stew'. At the end of this time it will be thoroughly damp and for the life of the potting should be kept that way. Before it is used a half of one part by measure of crushed dry oak leaf added and blended thoroughly into the mix is a good way of giving the roots something to work on, as it holds moisture and in its decay releases quite a lot of nutrients.

The coarser rooting miltonias, if pot grown, should be in a slightly larger bark mix but still using the same proportions and added leaf. These orchids, having a marked dormant period, will need to be left fairly dry during that time.

At one time all the miltoniopsis or miltonia plants imported into Australia came from England, France or Germany and they did not travel very well. Air freight of plants changed that considerably, but a large number is now raised in Australia, obtainable either as flasks of seedlings or as mature plants.

Arthur Yates, founder of the Sydney firm of seed merchants and a name still familiar in horticultural circles, was a noted orchid fancier of the 1910 period onward. He had this to say about importing orchid plants: 'I usually lose from 5 to 10 per cent of the plants shipped. If the loss is greater then in my opinion the sender is at fault. I refer to the hardier genera of orchids such as cattleyas, laelias and their hybrids, dendrobiums, cymbidiums and the like. Miltonias I find most difficult subjects; a few recently imported all died in transit. I know of no more exciting occupation than unpacking a case of newly imported orchids from England'.

A close look at the appearance of miltoniopsis and one cannot be other than convinced that they are a soft type and not among the easier orchids to grow.

To give some idea of the inter-generic hybrids available in the 1980 period, more particularly in miltonias and miltoniopsis, the following combinations are listed; with the two genera listed as miltonias:

Milpasia:	Miltonia × Aspasia
Forgetara:	Miltonia × Aspasia × Brassia
Miltassia:	Miltonia × Brassia
Beallara:	Miltonia × Brassia × Cochlioda × Odontoglossum
Goodaleara:	Miltonia × Brassia × Cochlioda × Odontoglossum × Oncidium
Degarmoara:	Miltonia × Brassia × Odontoglossum
Aliceara:	Miltonia × Oncidium × Brassia
Vuylstekeara:	Miltonia × Cochlioda × Odontoglossum
Burrageara:	Miltonia × Cochlioda × Odontoglossum × Oncidium
Odontonia:	Miltonia × Odontoglossum
Colmanara:	Miltonia × Ondontoglossum × Oncidium
Miltonidium:	Miltonia × Oncidium

These are by no means all the combinations which may be actually available in the future and the only way to understand the treatment needed is by accommodating them in similar conditions to those of miltonias or oncidiums and noting their acclimatisation or not. The plants may be morphologically similar to the general run. That is to say, right through from miltoniopsis to brassias there is a similarity in plant form, regardless of the differences in final assessments of taxonomists, who give them their various generic titles.

Taking one of the combinations, the miltassia, an example appears in the illustrations. It is quite happy in a potting mixture suitable for odontoglossums, but the plant grows larger than an odontoglossum or miltonia and may be grown in a pot of 15 centimetres or more.

In the final analysis, the changes are more marked in cultivating hybrid forms of inter-generic cross-pollinations than in the single-genera hybrids such as cymbidiums, with a consequent need for far more concentration on their culture.

Mixing too many genera and inter-generic hybrids in one collection needs some skill and never more so than in the instance of miltoniopsis or miltonias.

They are not recommended for installations where the temperature falls below 13 degrees Celsius for periods of longer than an occasional night and quickly show root loss by shrivelling of the pseudo-bulbs. This has an effect on plant vitality and continuation of adverse conditions results in gradual plant shrinkage and loss of leaves and flowers. After all, it is better to look at them on the show bench or in another collection than to note the gradual decline.

Brassia

The genus named by Robert Brown, an English botanist of the period 1773-1858. The name is derived from William Brass, a botanical artist of the same period, who collected orchid plants and other specimens in South America and South Africa.

A footnote in Lindley's *Sertum Orchidaceum* to the lithograph of *Brassia macrostachya* reads:

'Thus named by Mr Brown in due commemoration of the late Mr Brass, a skilful botanical traveller and draughtsman, who collected seeds, plants and dried specimens on the Guinea coast for Sir Joseph Banks, Dr Fothergill and Dr Pitcairn and whose sketches, being most liberally lent by Sir Joseph Banks to Dr Afzelius on his visit to Sierra Leone, were maliciously damaged and partly destroyed out of characteristic and wanton brutality by some piratical slave-mongers, under the French flag, during the late war.' — (Smith in Roe's Encyclopaedia).

There are over thirty different species in the genus, but few are seen in orchid collections other than some five or six better known plants. As a genus they are a natural follow-on from miltonias and miltoniopsis, part of the complex of genera which make up many of the hybrids of the late twentieth century.

While perhaps more commonly like the oncidiums, particularly those such as *Oncidium varicosum*, with an ascending rhizome, they are more at home in pots than these orchids.

The root system of most of the brassias is stouter than that of odontoglossums, miltonias and oncidiums, being almost twice the diameter. The system is no less intense, with the same habit of some of their relatives of being partially aerial.

The general appearance of brassias is along the lines of the oncidiums but with much harder foliage and at times pronounced ribbing of the pseudo-bulbs a common feature.

The flowering habits are also similar, with the spike produced from the side of the pseudo-bulbs and enclosed in the longer of the sheathing leaves or bracts at the base, elongating to different lengths on different species and with the flowers borne alternately each side of the stem at the final third of its length.

The color of the spidery flowers varies from pale lemon-green in some of the species to rich golden yellow in others, with a great deal of superimposed colors on this ground.

One of the earliest species described was *Brassia macrostachya*, introduced from Surinam, Dutch Guiana, on the northern coastline of South America, about 1835. It is figured in Lindley's *Sertum Orchidaceum* of 1838 and was so named by him in 1835.

Lindley later confused the nomenclature by renaming it *Brassia lanceana*, after the collector J. H. Lance, who brought or sent plants to England, where it flowered in the collection of the Horticultural Society in London. Since then it has been known variously as *Brassia lanceana* var. *macrostachya* or as

Brassia lanceana, but it has finally been relegated to its original name, with *Brassia lanceana* as a synonym. It seems to depend on which authority is consulted.

It was imported also by Loddiges from Demarara, British Guiana, about the same time. Some idea of the perception of Lindley may be gained from quoting his remarks in *Sertum Orchidaceum*:

'If it were proposed to combine odontoglossums with brassia, it would be difficult to point out any great objection to doing so. Their principal distinction consists in the sepals and petals of odontoglossums being unguiculate and the column winged or bordered by a thin margin. In habit they are very similar and if the genus had not been proposed by M. Kunth it may be doubted whether it would be now distinguished.'

Of course at that time many orchids were termed odontoglossums, but let us give Lindley the credit of being far-sighted enough to visualise what we now look at in the inter-generic hybrids derived from these two genera. *Brassia macrostachya* is common to much of the northern states of South America, although it varies a little from place to place.

While some of the other species grow at low elevations of some 200 or more metres in very warm forest regions, others grow at elevations of 2000 to 3000 metres, which, although in equatorial areas, can still be quite seasonally cold. The species should be selected according to their reputations, although at times they are rather optimistically termed cool-growing. No one has yet been able to describe adequately what the term means and it always means different things from grower to grower and glass-house to glass-house. As orchid growers, we all live in worlds of our own.

Brassia verrucosa, native to Mexico and Guatemala, was introduced to English growers about 1840. Of all the brassias it perhaps could lay claim to the quality of 'cool-growing'. It is one of the daintiest of the species, pale lemon colored, with green speckles on the inner parts of the sepals and petals, the labellum white with dark green warty spots at the base and orange-yellow crests.

Brassia verrucosa

Most growers find that the flowers are inclined to discolor as they age, but this could be attributable to the conditions under which the plants are grown. As the flowers open consecutively along the stem over a period of days, by the time the last are opening the petals and sepals of the early flowers are a deeper color. The younger of the flowers are scented, but again there is a deterioration to an odor as they age.

Brassia brachiata is almost a larger edition of *Brassia verrucosa* and at various times in their history of cultivation they have been classed as a duo, one a variety of the other.

Brassia lawrenceana and *Brassia longissima* (the latter considered a variety by some authorities) came to Britain in the 1830-40 decade and the former first flowered by Mrs Lawrence, one of the few women noted in horticulture in England over the course of that century.

It always seems too much to regard these two as relatives because *Brassia Lawrenceana* is native to Brazil and the variety *longissima* to Costa Rica. As with the origins of so many orchids sent or brought to England in those early years of cultivation, *Brassia Lawrenceana* had a doubtful origin. And again it seems to depend so much on the authority referred to for the history of the species.

Veitch's *Manual of Orchidaceous Plants* is worth a quote:

'*Brassia lawrenceana* is only known to us by the figure and description quoted by Lindley in the Botanical Register and by which we are unable to distinguish it from *Brassia lanceana*. The variety *longissima* is a far more distinct form that cannot be referred with certainty to *Brassia lanceanum* and which may hereafter receive specific rank. Its habitat too is very remote from the supposed origin of Lindley's type or of Knowles and Westcott's *Brassia cochleata*'.

Brassia longissima was exhibited at the Manchester Orchid Society in 1921 and gained a First Class Certificate. The flowers had sepals over 20 centimetres (8 inches) long, the plant carried two spikes on the one bulb for which it was also awarded a cultural certificate.

While the sepals of *Brassia longissima* may be the longest of the species, *Brassia gireoudiana* seems to be the species with the largest flowers. The flowers carry the common lemon-green base color in the petals and sepals, but they are also heavily marked with red-brown.

The collector Warscewicz found it in Costa Rica and the German botanist Reichenbach described and catalogued it. The name came from neither the discoverer nor the proud man who first flowered it. The honor went to his gardener, Gireoud.

Most of the brassias will grow in cattleya conditions in cool to warm climates, but in sub-tropical or tropical conditions there may be some trouble with them unless they are grown in completely outdoor conditions and in moderate shade. As they have a marked period of dormancy during their annual cycle, this may also be a handicap in climates where nothing ever seems to stop growing.

The climate in temperate conditions where they are glass-house grown suits them better provided winter temperatures do not fall below about 12 to 13 degrees Celsius. As they are usually dormant at this time a lapse now and then to a little lower than that mark should do little harm, as the plants may be almost completely dried out once maturity and flowering have finished.

As soon as the plants commence to grow new roots should be seen on the older sections, but watering should be gradually increased and not allowed to kill off the new root tips. In this period the plants are best grown on a closed bench so that there is a lot of natural humidity about them. The best treatment in this position is to thoroughly soak the potting mix and then let it almost dry out again before the next soaking. If grown in plastic pots the treatment should be carefully monitored.

Fertilisers may be incorporated in the potting mix, but additions or fertiliser sprays should not be used until the root system is well under way and then only moderately until the plant is either commencing to flower or making up its bulbs. In this last stage strong applications should be avoided and the plant watered with weak solutions each time it needs more moisture. Fresh air is necessary and the genus does not like 'stuffy' humidity at any time.

Although the foliage of the genus generally is fairly tough, strong sunlight will burn it, particularly the softer new leaves. About 50 per cent shade-cloth in most instances is sufficient, but in places where the sunlight is intense and constant day after day a little heavier texture may be needed.

The potting material may be based on ordinary cymbidium mix, but like most of the epiphytes brassias appreciate a little leaf in the mix. If a special mix is made up it should be based on medium and fine bark, coarse sand or gravel or charcoal, provided it is tested and found suitable. if the mix tends to dry out too fast peanut shells may be added, as they retain a fair amount of moisture after watering.

Brassias seem to flower best when some of the root system is aerial, so there is no need to worry about the roots growing out of the potting material. A sure sign that the material is unsuitable, however, is browning off of root tips and a general non-attractiveness of the mix for them. In this case it is best to get the plants out of such a mix and start all over again, eliminating one thing at a time to find out which is unsuitable. In many instances it will be either the bark or the charcoal if it is used. They are scarcely subjects for slab culture, but a large chunk of tree-fern may prove very suitable if there is room to hang it. On this sort of mount the plant should be backed with a little sphagnum moss or fern fibre such as staghorn or elkhorn.

When grown in pots, the roots should reach the bottom of the pot. If they occupy only the surface layer, the mix is usually of unsuitable quality and should be modified or replaced by a different mix.

Aspasia

The genus was named by Lindley in 1832. Not knowing the intention of this botanist, taxonomists are faced with the choice of two words: the Greek word *aspasios*, meaning glad or delightful; or reference to Aspasia, the wife of Pericles. Although beautiful and clever, Aspasia had other less desirable attributes, or so Plutarch the historian relates.

Aspasias are included principally because of their role in producing hybrids, although *Aspasia lunata* is an attractive orchid in its own right; as the illustration in the color section indicates.

Aspasia lunata is a Brazilian orchid which occurs naturally in a warm climate overlapping into temperate conditions. It was named by Lindley, but little information is available about it. Allied to the oncidiums, it grows in much the same conditions and is not of the ascending rhizome type.

Aspasia variegata is widespread, found in Brazil, Venezuela and other parts of South America and some of the offshore islands. It also was named by Lindley. It grows in hot lowland areas.

Aspasia epidendroides and *Aspasia principissa* are two species which are regarded as singular by some authorities. However, W. W. G. Moir, of Hawaii, who has done as much hybridising with them as anyone else, considers them separate. *Aspasia epidendroides* is the most widespread of the genus, occurring in both Central American and South American states. Most growers are not so much concerned with the niceties of taxonomy that seem to worry the armchair orchidophiles and would prefer instead to see the plants in flower and enjoy them.

Although so well mixed into the odontoglossums and oncidiums, they are seldom seen in cultivation. In allying them with odontoglossums the hybridists hope to create odontoglossum-type orchids which will grow in warmer climates. The aspaglossum will readily grow and flower in warmer areas of Australia, but these hybrids are not numerous and at the 1980 decade no one seems to be going on with further moves. The aspaglossum probably has some way to go both in coloring and flower numbers to a stem, because the aspasias do not usually carry many flowers.

The hybrids between miltonias and aspasias are also few in number, possibly because of sterility or sex-linkage factors in cross-pollinations. There would appear to be some future in the multiple-genera hybrids, but so much has been extracted to the 1980 decade that little purpose could be served in going much further. The growing multiples of the 'ara' orchids are closely bordering the ridiculous, even if they satisfy the innovators.

While they are seldom grown in Australia, aspasias, because of their affiliation with the odontoglossums, deserve a little consideration. Potting mediums do not need to be any different from those for odontoglossums and the conditions in which they are grown should also be similar, although they will tolerate anything up to cattleya temperatures and humidity.

For these single orchids like aspasias, where only one or two plants are grown, the closed bench as illustrated in the black-and-white photographs is ideal. It is not necessary to watch the plants so much for watering, as if the base of shell grit; sand, gravel, scoria or small aggregate stone chips is kept wet to moist the plants are able to absorb so much of their moisture through natural humidity.

Zygopetalum

The genus was named by William Jackson Hooker in 1827, reference being to the thickening at the base of the labellum, which appears to join together all the flower segments. Hooker was an eminent botanist and at one time director of the Kew Gardens in England.

It is most uncommon ever to see such plants as mentioned in reports of early history of orchid cultivation, as in this instance from the report of the Horticultural Society of England in 1841: 'Some beautiful specimens of Orchidaceous plants from Mrs Lawrence; especially a *Zygopetalum Mackaianum* with thirteen spikes of flowers . . .'

At every period of its cultivated history *Zygopetalum mackayi* has been a centre of admiration. In 1827, the opinion of Dr William Hooker: 'It is a plant of great beauty and may be numbered among the most showy of the highly interesting family of Orchidaceous plants. It is so unlike in the structure of its flowers to any described plant that I have no hesitation in constituting of it a new genus.' It is a tribute to the longevity of orchid plants and the interest and professionalism of orchid growers that in 1904 the plants on which Dr Hooker based his observations, imported originally by Mr Mackay, director of the Dublin Botanic Gardens, were still in good health and cultivation. It is quite likely they are still growing.

Some of the species are almost unknown to Australian cultivators. One such is *Zygopetalum brachypetalum*, which is about half the size of *Zygopetalum mackayi*. Lindley knew it well from the first plants imported into Europe and a report of the Horticultural Society stated: 'This species was originally brought into notice by Mr Waterhouse, of Halifax, in the year 1840 and is little known. It is one of the handsomest of the species, having brownish sepals and petals, a little marbled with green, and a deep bluish-violet lip veined with white. The crest of the lip is clearly striped with blue and the column streaked with dull dark purple. Monsieur de Jonghe stated that it had been found by his collector Libon in 1847 on the peak of Itabari, in the province of Minas, in Brazil.' Monsieur de Jonghe received a Certificate of Merit for his plant from the society. It is obvious that a mistake in the date was made and his collector Libon must have found the plant in 1837, because he exhibited the plant in 1844. The beautiful water-colors of the Pabst and Dungs book *Orchidaceae Brasilienses* portray *Zygopetalum brachypetalum* to perfection according to the above description.

Zygopetalum mackayi (Hooker) is the best known of the twelve Brazilian species, but it is by no means the easiest to grow into the sort of plants sometimes seen at meetings and shows. It is a widespread orchid, growing in the provinces of Espirito Santo, Rio de Janeiro, Guanabara, Sao Paulo, Santa Catherina, Rio Grande do Sul and Minas Geraes, which covers much of southeastern Brazil. The climate in which it occurs in all these areas is of fairly high rainfall and a great deal of wind, even if at times only breezes, the type of climate in which most of the sub-tropical orchids thrive.

There is some confusion in the identity of various zygopetalums and it is not always easy to identify them from descriptions in technical publications. As noted *Zygopetalum mackayi* was originally described by Dr William Hooker from material at the Dublin Botanic Gardens in Ireland of that time, now known as Eire, about the year 1827. The history of this orchid is rather shady, but of all the experimental cross-pollination that went on in that century, *Zygopetalum mackayi* had more than its share. Some idea of the crazy projects may be gained from the fact that seedlings between it and such things as odontoglossums and other South American orchids were expected and sometimes did eventuate. None produced any lasting results, but some within the genus did get some lovely flowers which are still admirable about 100 years later.

There are two very similar species which are frequently confused. *Zygopetalum mackayi* is illustrated in the photographic section and it seems to be the only one recognised by the most recent reviewers of the genus, Pabst and Dungs, in *Orchidaceae Brasilienses*. *Zygopetalum intermedium* is its near relative and they do not recognise it. Alex Hawkes, on the other hand, gives the description of both and states that the principal identification lies in the dorsal petal, which on *Zygopetalum mackayi* is slightly longer than the petals, while those of *Zygopetalum intermedium* are all of equal length. There are other minor differences, but over the years the two seem to have become one and any differences blurred into non-recognition. Loddiges originally grew and flowered *Zygopetalum intermedium* and named it.

The two notable things about *Zygopetalum mackayi* are its most unusual coloring and the delightful perfume. The number of flowers on a spike varies according to general culture, but six or seven are usually regarded as normal. It is a late autumn to early winter flower and as such a great plant to have in an orchid collection.

Zygopetalum crinitum (Loddiges) is somewhat similar to *Zygopetalum mackayi* in colors and the shape of the flower, but the spikes are much shorter, the plant not as large and three or four flowers about as many as could be expected. It also is a winter flowering orchid and seems to multiply rapidly in size. It was introduced at much the same period as *Zygopetalum mackayi*, but in the days when size meant a great deal its larger relative took more of the front of the stage. Although hardy, both these zygopetalums grow better in temperatures slightly above those usually considered for cold-growing orchids.

The growth cycle of all the zygopetalums is similar. There is no real dormant stage because of the plants' flowering season. The spikes appear on the new shoots from the previous year's bulbs fairly early in the autumn or even in late summer, they grow quickly and the flowers are mostly gone by May. From then on the pseudo-bulbs and leaves gradually mature until at the beginning of summer they are starting to produce new growth again. *Zygopetalum crinitum* may flower in late winter to spring in some collections.

The root systems of most of the zygopetalums are similar to those of cymbidiums and as dense on well-grown plants left in a pot for up to three years. The pseudo-bulbs, however, grow on a much shorter rhizome than cymbidiums and it is possible to grow a well-potted plant until it is crowded and can produce up to five or six spikes in a 20 centimetre pot. Cymbidium potting mix may be used, but it should be planned a little on the open side so that the interior root ball will not decay before the plant has had a chance to produce its maximum flowering.

If there is a lag in maturity of pseudo-bulbs, zygopetalums will do much the same as cymbidiums and begin a new growth from one of the older pseudo-bulbs until the new growths are fully made up. In this way they miss producing a new leading shoot in one season but will catch up in the next one. The pseudo-bulbs growing so closely, when a plant of zygopetalums of any of the species is divided when repotting, a thin, sharp-bladed knife should be used to divide it. If it is sought to do what is sometimes done with cymbidiums and the plant is twisted or torn apart a great amount of damage may be done to the pseudo-bulbs at the point of division.

In propagating, although single pseudo-bulbs without leaves may produce growth shoots, it is best to leave them in pairs. If singles with no growth shoots left on the base of the pseudo-bulbs are put in a pot of sphagnum moss they may produce new growth shoots from the apex of the bulbs.

The fertilisers used for cymbidiums suit zygopetalums and their culture is in most ways similar. The two genera grow happily in the same conditions, and the same diseases and failings afflict them with the exception of plant virus. Zygopetalums seem to be largely immune to this and the only disfiguration to be guarded against is sunburn, although as plants they are very hardy and will stand bright conditions. In winter, if the conditions are too cold, it is common for the leaves to show first brown wet patches which later break down to necrotic black disfigurations which spoil the look of the plants. The flowers, with the delicate coloring of the labellum, also mark if subjected to cold. Care should also be taken to keep them dry when watering.

In comparative terms only a little hybridising has been done with this genus. An outstanding example is *Zygopetalum* Blackii (*Zygopetalum crinitum* × *Zygopetalum* Perrenoudii), which in turn led to *Zygopetalum* Artur Elle and other secondary hybrids, all of which are intensely colored and very beautiful. Their culture is similar to that of the rest of the genus, but the flowering season is variable and frequently spring instead of autumn to early winter.

Zygopetalum Perrenoudii was one of the first hybrids raised, predated by *Zygopetalum* Sedenii (*Zygopetalum mackayi* × *Zygopetalum maxillare*), one of the Veitch hybrids raised by their noted grower Seden. *Zygopetalum maxillare* contributed a lot of the color of hybrids such as *Zygopetalum* Artur Elle.

In the early days of orchid classification such things as promenaeas and other related orchids were listed under the zygopetalums.

Promenaea

The genus was named by Dr Lindley in 1843. In this instance Greek history has played its part, with the name attributable to Promeneia, a priestess of one of the ancient cults of that country.

Promenaeas make a delightful change from the big and bold orchids. They are neat and do not take up much room and if grown in the right conditions they produce flowers in quantity. *Promenaea citrina* is probably best known of the species but the bizarre and startling *Promenaea stapelioides* takes the eye first.

Promenaea stapelioides was probably the first of the genus collected and sent to decorate the collections of the Europeans. Beyrich gathered the plants near Rio de Janeiro, probably in the Organ Mountains, and the species was named *Promenaea lentiginosa* by Link and Otto in Europe. Lindley named it *Maxillaria lentiginosa*, but subsequently changed this name. Gardner later collected it in the Organ Mountains about 1839 and sent plants to England. Lindley remarked on the similarity of its coloring to that of the stapelias, South African plants, the odor of whose flowers was far from pleasant. He said of it: 'It is now common in collections, where it is at once recognised by its pallid, glaucous, thin leaves, which look as if suffering under the attack of red spider. It is one of the most easy species to cultivate.'

His description could not be bettered. The genus as a whole has these pale leaves and the appearance of the plants suggests ability to stand strong light.

Promenaeas were once classed as relatives of the zygopetalums, but Pabst and Dungs in *Orchidaceae Brasilienses* place them in with the gongoras, which are not frequently cultivated in Australian collections at least.

Promenaea xanthina, also known at times as *Promenaea citrina* followed *Promenaea stapelioides* some years later, but before it was brought to England a similar yellow promenaea flowered in Rollison's nursery in 1837 and was named *Promenaea rollisoni*. It was probably a form of *Promenaea xanthina*.

Although Gardner introduced *Promenaea xanthina* to Britain, the French collector Descourtilz is believed to have found it first, growing on the coastal ranges of Minas Geraes states, Brazil, and named it *Epidendrum jonquille*. His description of the plants in mass flowering is typical of the impression a well flowered plant in a collection has on those seeing it. Lindley believed that the discovery of Descourtilz was the first appearance or knowledge of the orchid, but unfortunately it was unrecorded. It was also known as *Zygopetalum citrina*, but neither name was correct.

Promenaea xanthina is free flowering, the buds appearing on the immature new growths and occasionally on older pseudo-bulbs. As its season is summer, the orchid makes a nice addition to a cool-growing collection with a winter dormant season.

The root system of the promenaeas is fairly fine, much like that of odontoglossums, and not very prolific. The size of the plant indicates a small pot and if it is intended to grow a specimen, which these orchids do very well, a shallow fern pot should be chosen, so that there is never too great a depth of potting material. It would not be unusual for a plant of *Promenaea xanthina* in a 12 centimetre pot to produce anything up to fifty or sixty flowers if it is well grown and in good conditions. It grows much faster than *Promenaea stapelioides.*

There is a tendency for promenaeas to grow closely set pseudo-bulbs, with very short jointing rhizomes between them. Although most orchids resent being divided into too small propagations, *Promenaea xanthina* does not seem to fall away when this is done. The pseudo-bulbs may be a little smaller and the flowers sparse on plants divided into two or three-bulb sections in order to encourage specimen characteristics, but a vigorous growing specimen will soon build up these divisons. A small, fine-bladed knife is the best tool to use in dividing small orchids like promenaeas and it should be sharp. The correct time to subdivide the plant is almost at the end of its flowering, just when the roots become more active and the pseudo-bulbs begin to grow. It is not a good idea to pursue this sort of propagation in consecutive years, but allow the plant to develop.

There is a tendency for small plants like the promenaeas to get lost in orchid collections over their dormant period, but just as much attention should be given to them in the winter months as in the flowering season. They should be watched for pests, as Lindley's supposition of the appearance of the leaves as being due to red spider could quite easily turn to reality.

The potting mixes for promenaeas vary from grower to grower, but they should be fairly open with ability to dry out but not dehydrate to the point where they will not absorb water when the dormant season ends. Peanut shells should be part of bark mixes and the quantities in equal parts of small bark, coarse gravel, peanut shells and a little charcoal. All these materials may be varied to suit and even a little dry oak leaf worked into the mix when it is made up.

Liquid nutrients should be used in the growing and flowering season, but they should not be used when out of flower or growth. A sprinkle of blood and bone after the flowers are gone adds a little more to the plant food.

Promenaeas are not frost resistant and it would be unwise trying to grow them where the temperature falls below about 9 or 10 degrees in winter. Although a plant may survive one year, it would be too much to expect continuity.

Promenaea citrina

213

Endnote

The orchids described in this book are from the Central and South American region, which contain almost two-thirds of the total number of genera in the world. As a glance at the index will show, the number of genera surveyed in this book is a ludicrous tiny section. In Brazil alone there are some 2300 different species and the number could be more than double that for the American zone as a whole. But it will be noted that those orchids which are dealt with are responsible for a major part of the total number of orchids cultivated by people interested in this branch of horticulture. In addition to that, sufficient data is available to work out a cultivation program for the greater part of the whole catalogue. It is doubtful if the average orchid grower has more than twenty to thirty different species, as distinct from hybrids, in his or her collection. There are, of course, exceptions, with growers of, say, paphiopedilums having a larger number than that. However, they are Asian orchids, not American.

In growing species orchids it is not easy to imitate nature and create climates of indefinite numbers in even a group of orchid houses and the best most growers can do is to average out in systems which are borderline. Throughout the history of cultivated plants, not only orchids, the wastage has been a regrettable feature of the process. It should be obvious in a year if a plant is heartened enough by its conditions to grow and flower. At the end of that time good growers will make a decision and keep plants or pass them on to someone else who may be able to do better. It is late in the day so far as nature is concerned and anyone who reads or sees in these modern days of electronics the depredations and destruction of natural environments must realise that every plant of a species which they in their turn destroy or fail to grow is adding to the number gone and lessening the number left — more importantly, each one which goes takes out something which cannot be replaced.

The next book will consist of many Asian species and their history, the hybridism associated with them and the men who originally found them and plundered them. In addition, some of the left-overs from the American section will be included. The history of orchids is never dull to orchid growers, but so little of it is generally available that the motivating thought behind these books has been to educate orchid growers. To answer, perhaps, some of their questions. We can never duplicate nature; and even in hybrid form within each separate genus or into other genera the plants remain the same, with the same dependencies on light, air and water. It is doubtful in all the history of orchid growing if there has been one individual who could say of his orchids that they could not be bettered.

I hope that all who read this book, the one before it and the one to follow, will find something to help them grow their orchids better or perhaps to understand where they came from and how they grew in their natural state.

Bibliography

A Manual of Orchidaceous Plants, James Veitch, original edition, 1887.
Botany: An Introduction to Plant Science, Robbins, Weier and Stocking.
Encyclopaedia of Cultivated Orchids, Alex Hawkes.
Generic Names of Orchids, Schultes and Pease.
Growing Orchids-cymbidiums and slippers, J. N. Rentoul, 1980.
Johnson's Botanical Dictionary, 1917.
Orchids, Lewis Castle.
Orchidaceae Brasilienses, Pabst and Dungs, Vols. 1 and 2.
Paxton's Botanical Dictionary, 1868.
†*Pears Shilling Cyclopaedia*, 1900 edition.
Peruvian Orchids, Volumes 1-4 and supplement, Charles Schweinfurth.
Refugium Botanicum, edited by W. Wilson Saunders.
Sanders' List of Orchid Hybrids, Sanders (St. Albans) Ltd and the RHS.
Sanders' Orchid Guide, 1927 edition, Sanders (St. Albans) Ltd.
Sertum Orchidaceum, John Lindley, 1838 (Johnson Reprint).
The Genus Encyclia in Mexico, Dressler and Pollard.
The Orchidaceae of Mexico and Guatemala, James Bateman, 1837
(Johnson Reprint).
The Orchid World, Vols. 1 to 6, 1910-16, edited by Gurney Wilson.
·*The Orchid Review*, 1893-1980.
The Orchid Stud-book, Rolfe and Hurst, 1909.
Venezuelan Orchids, Dunsterville and Garay.
7th World Orchid Conference Handbook on Colombian Orchid Species.
The Australian Orchid Review, 1939-80.
The Orchid Album, R. Warner and B. S. Williams.
Travels and Adventures of an Orchid Hunter, Albert Millican, 1891.

* *The Orchid Review* (England), recording the history of orchid growing almost in its entirety, is incomparable as a source of information.

†The inclusion of a book such as *Pears Shilling Cyclopaedia* may seem incongruous, but it included an atlas of the period and a large section entitled 'Gazetteer of the World,' which was invaluable for identifying places of the 1900 period which had been renamed or absorbed into other regions.

Index

Figures in italic denote illustrations.

217

218